MADNESS AND GOVERNMENT

American
Psychiatric
Press, Inc.

Washington, D.C.

MADNESS AND GOVERNMENT

Who cares for the mentally ill?

Henry A. Foley, PhD
Steven S. Sharfstein, MD

Library of Congress Cataloging in Publication data

Foley, Henry A.
Madness and Government

Bibliography: p.
Includes indexes.

1. Mental health policy—United States. 2. Mentally ill—
Government policy—United States. 3. Community men-
tal health services—United States. I. Sharfstein, Steven S.
(Steven Samuel), 1942- II. Title. [DNLM: 1. Community
mental health centers—United States. 2. Mental health
services—United States. 3. Government agencies—
United States. 4. Health policy—United States. WM 30
F663m] RA790.6.F64 1983 362.2'0973 83-2824

ISBN 0-88048-001-7

Printed in the U.S.A.

For Frank Foley

HAF

For Margaret, Joshua, Daniel, and Sarah Sharfstein

SSS

Every injury to the health of the individual is, so far as it goes, a public injury. It is an impediment to the general freedom; so much deduction from our power, as members of society, to make the best of ourselves.

Thomas Hill Green
Works of Thomas Hill Green
Vol. III, Miscellanies and Memoir

FOREWORD

In 1946, the National Mental Health Act was signed into law by President Harry S. Truman, and led three years later to the creation of the National Institute of Mental Health. The World Health Organization, also in 1946, defined *health* as a "state of complete physical, mental, and social well-being, and not merely the absence of disease or infirmity." This statement dramatically underscored mental health as a growing *international* concern.

In that same year, Mary Jane Ward's exposé *Snake Pit* appeared, to see even wider exposure a few years later as a successful Hollywood film. In 1948, Albert Deutsch's *The Shame of the States* was published, further focusing public attention on the treatment of the mentally ill.

The Kennedy era, of course, brought the community mental health center movement. As the '60s came to a close, the report, "Crisis of Child Mental Health, Challenge for the 1970s" was issued.

The 1940s, '50s, and '60s, then, saw an unprecedented rise in activities aimed at improving mental health, so long a neglected concern throughout the world. But by the late 1960s and '70s, certain expansionistic tendencies of the mental health movement, while not incorrect per se, may have inadvertently invited political backlash. Many came to feel that the claims of the "tranquilizer revolution" and other therapeutic interventions for rehabilitating the mentally ill had been overstated. Others felt that the strategies put forth for *preventing* mental illness were not yet firmly established. Still others, some for ideological reasons, strongly opposed the (often latent) aspirations of the mental health movement: to reduce international tension and conflict, offset racism and sexism, and deal with other social and political constraints on human fulfillment.

Authors Foley and Sharfstein focus considerable attention on the expansionism in the mental health movement. They also explore the impact of the times in which we live, where, unfortunately, government is being attacked from within, rather than struggling to perfect itself as an instrument for human accomplishment.

The authors obviously favor an appropriate, imaginative and humane role for government. They emphasize the need for government to be involved on behalf of the mentally ill and to assist society's protection of the vulnerable in general. They are, as we all are, concerned with the priorities of government.

In the 1840s, Dorothea Lynde Dix found the mentally ill in the streets, in the jails, in the boarding houses of America. Ironically, over a century later, we find similar conditions. The excesses of good intentions on the part of the mental health movement, coupled with an inadequate commitment of funds, have recreated some of the same distress Dix railed against. It is one thing to favor integrating the mentally ill into the community; it is quite another to guarantee the social and economic support essential to make them welcome there. Rhetoric is not enough.

There is a network of humane and sophisticated policymakers in the private and public sectors who share with the mental health professions a deep-felt concern for those still tragically stigmatized by emotional and mental problems. I sincerely hope these and *all* policymakers—inside and outside government—will read this book. They should remember, too, that as the absolute number and relative proportion of older persons increase, so will the incidence of depression and chronic disease, especially the dementing diseases of old age. This will enlarge the challenge that faces policymakers: to commit appropriate resources to maintain the "physical, mental, and social well-being" of all our citizens *throughout* their lives.

Robert N. Butler, M.D.

CONTENTS

Illustrations

Tables

Members in the noble conspiracy. L to r: Senator Lister Hill,
Dr. Robert Felix, and Dr. James Shannon.

ACKNOWLEDGMENTS

Although we have thought about writing this book for a number of years, we nearly abandoned the project several months ago. Without strong encouragement from Professors Samuel Beer and Rashi Fein of Harvard and from Professor Amitai Etzioni of George Washington University, disappointment at the recent signs of reversal might have prevented our ever committing our views to paper. They reminded us that the pendulum of politics swings as dependably, if not as predictably, as the tide goes in and out.

Many others have offered their support and advice. They include Dr. Gerald Klerman, Dr. Lucy Ozarin, Laurence Lynn and Samuel Buker, who read the manuscript and offered helpful suggestions. They also include Messrs. Lee Dixon, Paul Sirovatka and Ed Goody, and Sylvia Vengrouskie and Dr. Harold Pincus, who provided specific pieces of important information and support. Special credit is due to Henry A. Foley, Sr. and Gina Ryan for their editorial work on the early drafts of the chapters.

We would especially like to acknowledge the critical contribution of Dolly Gattozzi, whose writing and editing made our words more readable and transformed our musings into coherent ideas.

INTRODUCTION

Care for the mentally ill has been radically transformed over the past thirty-five years in America. The current period is one of retrenchment and reevaluation of these changes, with special attention to the proper role of government. What are the responsibilities of the various levels of government—local, state, federal—to treat and sustain our mentally ill and disabled citizens? At stake is the opportunity for a life of dignity and fulfillment for millions of individual Americans over the remainder of this decade.

This book tells the story of the radical transformation. Drawn from first-hand accounts, it is about the personal efforts of citizens, public servants and professionals, the processes of bureaucracies and congressional committees, the power of dedicated presidential families. It describes how individuals and groups interacted to create new public policy that produced profound changes in opportunities for treatment, rehabilitation and support for the mentally ill and disabled. It should be of special interest to mental health professionals and students of governmental process, for it presents a lively case study of public health policy formulation since World War II, detailing the system and service changes of the 1960s and '70s which preceded today's wholly new, potentially perilous circumstance for the mentally ill in America.

The current national administration (1983) is rapidly proceeding to withdraw government from the lives of our people and from the support of our disadvantaged. Yet it is difficult to imagine a turning back to the years of large public asylums for custodial care of the many, and costly, private-office-based treatment for the few. As we look ahead to the tasks of the 1980s, it is important to pause and reflect on how and where we have succeeded, and fallen short, in implementing social policy in the field of mental health care. This account of the recent history of madness and government in America is heartening in several aspects, not least because it tells the story of how individuals can make a difference as they negotiate a humane public policy through the vicissitudes of economic adversity, clashing political ideologies, and bureaucratic obstacles.

A word about our social and political values is appropriate since the story recounted in the pages that follow is clearly our interpretation of selected events in the context of a more objective history. We believe in the positive and creative influence of government in bettering individual lives and society as a whole. Insofar as government in a democracy reflects the public will and consensus, then solutions which emanate from such government should not be oppressive. Rather, government should improve treatment for the ill and enlarge life opportunities for the disabled in ways which individual and marketplace activities are unable to effect.

Indeed, we see government as a critical ingredient in the design of pragmatic approaches to catastrophic events such as mental illness, which not only wreck life opportunities for the individual but also devastate the family and impoverish the community. The provision of service and support to our mentally ill and disabled is too fundamental a public responsibility to be dependent on the vagaries of private charity. Further, our states and communities differ in their perceptions of problems and in their ability and willingness to offer solutions. Only our national government can be mindful of inequities across geopolitical entities and assert the leadership needed to solve national problems.

The national mental health policies which emerged during the years 1945-1980 were forged from a consensus of perceptions by a vigorous leadership, and founded on the belief that the federal government could provide incentives for states and communities to improve the clinical opportunities and the quality of life for our mentally ill and disabled citizens. Clearly, we have outgrown the old consensus and are questioning anew the role of government. This book attempts to bring into focus all of the major issues and their dynamic interactions. Our hope is that, by bringing to bear information, hard-won knowledge and seasoned opinion, the pernicious myths that continue to influence the treatment and care of mental disorder will be exposed and discarded. We hope that objectivity tempered by compassion will guide our future discussion and decision-making.

It may seem that two voices speak from the pages of this book. One voice applauds the advocates who championed legislation to provide quality care for the mentally ill. The other offers a critique of these achievements.

On the one hand, we are impressed with the accomplishments of the groups and individuals who conceived and nurtured a program of great complexity. On the other, we believe it important to become more sophisticated and pragmatic about the products of these victories—that is, learn from our mistakes as we move forward.

In politics, the party that inspires the electorate's imagination may not always be able to translate high-minded ideals into practical programs. Similarly in our story, the architects who laid the foundations may not have been those best suited to raising the edifice. By the time of the passage of the Mental Health Systems Act of 1980, a tangle of often-conflicting mandates, exclusions, rules and regulations had strangled the spirit that originally animated the grand design.

We believe that suppressing criticism of these policies might be sacrificing long-term faith and momentum for a false consensus. We must capture the support of the American people and their government with a vision—that is essential—but this vision must translate to practical programs which do not dilute the quality of care for our more unfortunate citizens.

Henry A. Foley, Ph.D.
Phoenix, Arizona

Steven S. Sharfstein, M.D.
Washington, D.C.

KEY INSTITUTIONAL PLAYERS

Federal Government

Department of Health, Education, and Welfare (HEW) (*later* ... of Health and Human Services)
Public Health Service (PHS)
National Institutes of Health (NIH)
Alcohol, Drug Abuse, and Mental Health Administration
National Institute of Mental Health (NIMH)
National Mental Health Advisory Council
Bureau of the Budget (*later* Office of Management and Budget)
Senate Committee on Labor and Welfare (*later* ... and Human Resources)
House Committee on Interstate and Foreign Commerce
Joint Commission on Mental Illness and Mental Health (1955-1960)
President's Commission on Mental Health (1977-1978)

Special Interest Groups

American Psychiatric Association
American Medical Association (AMA)
AMA Council on Mental Health
American Psychological Association
American Nurses Association
National Association of Social Workers
National Council of Community Mental Health Centers
National Association of State Mental Health Program Directors
Mental Health Law Project
AFL-CIO
American Federation of State, County and Municipal Employees
National Mental Health Association, Inc.
National Committee Against Mental Illness
National Governors Conference
Council of State Governments
U.S. Conference of Mayors
National League of Cities
National Association of Counties

CHRONOLOGY OF EVENTS

1854 President Franklin Pierce vetos the "12,225,000 Acre Bill," which would have built public asylums at federal expense.

1914 The Harrison Narcotics Act authorizes federally funded studies of drug addiction, crime and the emotional consequences of immigration.

1929 Two federal hospitals are constructed for the treatment of drug addiction. The Narcotics Division is established within the U.S. Public Health Service.

1931 The Narcotics Division expands to become the Division of Mental Hygiene within the Public Health Service.

1946 The National Mental Health Act establishes the National Institute of Mental Health; Dr. Robert Felix is appointed as its first director.

1947 Passage of the Hill-Burton Program, which authorizes federal funds for construction of health facilities.

1948 Passage of Formula Grants [section 314(c) of the Public Health Act], which assist in the establishment of community health services.

1955 The National Mental Health Study Act signed by President Dwight D. Eisenhower, which establishes a joint commission on mental illness and health. Dr. Jack Ewalt appointed study director of the joint commission.

1961 Report of the joint commission; publication of *Action for Mental Health*.

1962 President's Interagency Committee on Mental Health is established to recommend future direction of federal role.

1963 *January:* President John Kennedy's special message on mental health and mental retardation submitted to Congress.

February: Community mental health legislation introduced by Senator Lister Hill and Representative Oren Harris.

October: President Kennedy signs the Mental Retardation Facilities and Community Mental Health Center Construction Act of 1963 (public law 88-164).

1964 Dr. Stanley Yolles appointed director of the National Institute of Mental Health.

1965 President Lyndon Johnson signs the Community Mental Health Centers Construction Act Amendments of 1965 (public law 89-105), which authorizes construction and staffing funds for fifty-one months.

1965 Medicaid and Medicare enacted.

1967 Congress amends the community mental health center law, extending the authorization of the program.

1968 The Alcoholic and Narcotic Addict Rehabilitation amendments of 1968 (public law 90-574) establish specialized facilities for treatment of alcoholism and narcotic addiction.

1970 Community mental health center program re-authorized (public law 91-211) with the extension of federal support from fifty-one months to eight years and a new staffing program for children's mental health services. Dr. Bertram Brown appointed director of National Institute of Mental Health.

1972 SSI (supplemental security income) enacted.

1973 President Richard Nixon impounds community mental health center funds.

1975 Community mental health center program amendments (public law 94-63) revise original program, expanding service requirements from five to twelve "essential services." Also added by the amendments: quality assurance evaluation and governance requirements; new programs of financial distress; and grants for consultation and education. Legislation passed over President Gerald Ford's veto.

1977 President's Commission on Mental Health established by President Jimmy Carter's executive order. Community mental health center program re-authorized (public law 95-83).

1978 *April:* Report of the President's Commission on Mental Health calls for a "more responsive services system and a national priority for the chronically mentally ill."

September: Community mental health center program re-authorized (public law 95-622).

1979 *February:* Mrs. Rosalynn Carter testifies to the Senate Subcommittee on Health on the President's Commission on Mental Health.

May: President Jimmy Carter's special mental health message and his submission to Congress of the Mental Health Systems Act, introduced in June by Senator Edward Kennedy and Representative Henry Waxman.

1980 The Mental Health Systems Act (public law 96-398) signed by President Jimmy Carter.

1981 Omnibus Budget Reconciliation Act repeals most of Mental Health Systems Act in favor of block grants to states.

CHAPTER ONE

Who Cares
for the Mentally Ill?

Colonial Times

Dorothea Dix and the Reform Movement

Descent into Custodial Care

The Turn of the Tide

I t will be said by a few, perhaps, that each State should establish and sustain its own institutions; that it is not obligatory upon the general government to legislate for maintenance of State charities . . . . [B]ut may it not be demonstrated as the soundest policy of the federal government to assist in the accomplishment of great moral obligations, by diminishing and arresting wide-spread miseries which mar the face of society, and weaken the strength of communities?

I confide to you the cause and the claims of the destitute and of the desolate . . . who, through the providence of God, are wards of the nation, claimants on the sympathy and care of the public, through the miseries and disqualifications brought upon them by the sorest afflictions with which humanity can be visited.

Dorothea Lynde Dix
Memorial to the U.S. Congress Praying a Grant of Land for the Relief and Support of Indigent Curable and Incurable Insane
Washington, D.C., 1848

I have been compelled . . . to overcome the reluctance with which I dissent from the conclusions of the two Houses of Congress. . . .

[I] f Congress have power to make provision for the indigent insane . . . the whole field of public beneficence is thrown open to the care and culture of the Federal Government. . . .

I readily . . . acknowledge the duty incumbent on us all . . . to provide for those who, in the mysterious order of Providence, are subject to want and to disease of body or mind, but I cannot find any authority in the Constitution that makes the Federal Government the great almoner of public charity throughout the United States. To do so would, in my judgement, be contrary to the letter and spirit of the Constitution . . . [and] be prejudicial rather than beneficial to the noble offices of charity.

President Franklin Pierce
Veto of Indigent Insane Bill
Washington, D.C., 1854

CHAPTER ONE

Who Cares for the Mentally Ill?

The care of the mentally ill poor has always involved a moral choice. In previous generations Americans made that choice on the basis of their understanding of mental health and illness. Each advance in moral awareness and objective understanding has had political ramifications and has led to various public policy decisions.

The process of making a moral choice based on scientifically informed understanding is vigorously active today. Earlier generations asked many of the same questions that now concern us about the efficacy of treatments and the proper disposition of the mentally ill. Indeed, our current discussions hark back to those heard when the insane were first freed from lock and chain in the Enlightenment of the eighteenth century.

But this generation of Americans has something new to consider as well. What is new in the past two decades is the leading role of the federal government in implementing policy decisions. For the first time in history, through direct and catalytic action, the federal government initiated an innovative, comprehensive system of health care services for a wide range of human problems impinging on mental health. Moreover, the federal government also became the prime mover in support of scientific research on mental illness and in the training of mental health professionals.

What follows is a kaleidoscopic overview of how our society has dealt with the problem of caring for the mentally ill from colonial times to the Second World War. The perceptions and values that have shaped the intense political debate of recent decades were expressed

3

in early eras as well. The full story has been told elsewhere with much vividness (Rothman 1971, Caplan 1969, Deutsch 1948, Bockoven 1972, Grob 1973). Common questions and themes emerge.

Financial responsibility has always been the basic question. How shall the cost of the public system of caring for the mentally ill be shared among the three levels of government—local, state and federal? A minimum care system for this population includes treatment services *plus* life support services such as shelter, clothing and food *plus* social support services such as rehabilitation. Complicating the issues of funding are issues of intergovernmental relations. The limitations of treatment provide another constant theme. The causes of the major psychotic illnesses are still not well understood. In the absence of scientific rationale, treatments have never done more than relieve symptoms and suffering but have effected few cures. Perhaps because precise modes of treatment have for so long eluded discovery, the proper locus of treatment has also been a recurring question. Normal community settings and family life have been seen at various times as causing mental illness and as essential factors in the therapy of mental illness. Finally, the role of leaders in improving the system and enlarging its access to needy persons has been an outstanding feature in the history of public mental health care in America.

Colonial Times

In the beginning, American public policies towards the indigent insane derived from English common law and did not distinguish among the poor. So long as demented persons posed no threat to peace and security they were treated as all other paupers. Those who belonged to the community—and the poor laws were explicit about residence requirements—were regarded as local responsibilities. Arrangements for their care were informal. If no relative or neighbor could take them in, they were housed in the local jail or almshouse. Historians note a sense of local social responsibility probably only seen in pre-industrial societies in the world today. "It was as unthinkable to allow the destitute to shift for themselves as to let commerce flounder or children grow up untrained. Thus, without second thought the colonists relieved the needy, the widows and orphans, the aged and sick, the insane and disabled" (Rothman 1971, p. 14). The acceptance of responsibility was strictly limited to local residents, however. Strangers were returned to their place of origin or merely chased out of town. The law was punitive to indigent "wanderers" without regard to their mental status. For example, the first house of correction in Connecticut was designed for "rogue vagabonds" and "other lewd, idle, dissolute, profane, and disorderly persons that have no settlement in this colony" (Ibid., p. 27). Undergirding this public policy was the colonists' view of insanity as an aspect of God's will. Although the relief of poverty and insanity was appropriate, these dire conditions were seen as an expression of divine will. People did not think of tampering with the preordained, and so did not consider treatment of the mentally ill.

Rational thought and humanitarian values spawned in the European Enlightenment gradually made their way to America during the last years of the eighteenth century. In particular, the ideas of Dr. Philippe Pinel and William Tuke excited the interest of physicians and public benefactors. In France, Pinel had literally unchained the insane and released them from dungeons, transforming two Parisian madhouses into hospitals for the mentally ill. In England, Tuke led the Quaker group that founded the York Retreat, where the mentally ill were treated with kindness and "plain talk." These men led the development of "moral treatment" for insanity, which was based on humanitarian and religious values. Nevertheless, a pseudoscientific theory was elaborated to help convince society's decision-makers that kind treatment in a decent environment would cure the insane.

The rise of moral treatment coincided with the social upheaval, industrialization and urbanization of America associated with the Jacksonian era (the 1830s). The turbulent times fostered a radical revision of the perceived cause of mental illness. God's will was not the cause; American society itself was to blame. In fact, society was the culprit behind a general moral decay. A sociobiological conception of insanity gained currency in which madness had an environmental cause. The high-flying economy and rapid erosion of social norms produced insanity. If chaos in the social order created mental illness (actual physical damage to the brain was hypothesized as a result of the pressures of swift social change), then the cure was respite in serene, orderly and dignified surroundings. Asylum in such an environment and kind, sustaining relationships were the elements of so-called moral or psychological treatment. Advocates felt that these utopian communities could serve as examples to the society at large. A sense of therapeutic optimism pervaded the efforts of the medical superintendents who ran the early asylums. Indeed, during the 1840s superintendents vied with one another in reporting the highest cure rates, giving rise to what historians now call the cult of curability.

Meanwhile, custom was slow to change among the authorities responsible for providing the upkeep of the poor who were also deemed to be insane. Although the growing number of asylums, including a few public institutions, provided care at cut rates for these dependent persons, the cost was higher than maintaining them in poorhouses and jails. Mentally ill persons without resources of their own, especially including a rapidly growing number of immigrants, continued to be locked up and shut away without regard for their clinical condition. But America's social conscience was stirring, and this situation was soon to change.

Dorothea Dix and the Reform Movement

The moral treatment movement was led by a small band of physicians who formed the first specialty medical society in America, the Association of Medical Superintendents of American Institutions for the Insane, and published their own journal, the American Journal of Insanity. They were a part of a wider reform movement of which the most effective spokespersons were Horace Mann and Dorothea Lynde Dix.

A Sunday schoolteacher from Cambridge, Massachusetts, Dorothea Dix began her prodigious career by petitioning the city for heat for the inmates of the local jail, several of whom were obviously mad. She visited poorhouses and jails throughout the Commonwealth, found deplorable conditions, and lobbied the state legislature to enlarge the existing state asylums. She won the day by arguing that treatment would be both humane and, in the long run, cheaper to society than lifelong maintenance of the mad. The Massachusetts legislators had heard the medical reports of the successes of moral treatment and took them as evidence of the long-term economies to be realized when sick people were cured and restored to productive activity. They were further persuaded to Dix's point of view by the "economies of scale" argument. It would be cheaper to fund in one financing package not only treatment but also food, clothing, shelter, perhaps even vocational rehabilitation and other social services (Sharfstein et al. 1978). Over her forty-five years of advocating decent care for the mentally ill poor, Dix led a movement which succeeded in establishing asylums in twenty-eight of the thirty-three states of the republic. The talented and tireless Dix was personally involved in the founding of thirty-two public mental hospitals.

Her most interesting and, in some ways, most important effort was her near miss in getting the federal government to assume responsibility for the development of mental hospitals. In the 1840s the federal government raised revenues through land sales. Precedents of such sales aiding the ill and dependent existed, including two schools for the deaf and mute which had been funded in this manner. For seven years, from 1847 to 1854, Dix and her allies (she enlisted the former President Millard Fillmore in the cause) lobbied the Congress for a bill granting the proceeds of a federal land sale for the building of public mental hospitals. The "12,225,000 Acre Bill" passed the Senate in 1851, the House in 1852, and both houses of the Congress in 1854 by a greater than 2-to-1 margin. It was then sent to President Franklin Pierce for his signature.

Pierce had a major decision to make. Enactment of the bill would alter long-standing public policies. Even more significant, it would raise constitutional issues of federalism. The president backed away from such a course. He chose instead to veto the bill, citing James Madison's statement that the powers of the federal government were few and specific while the powers of the states were many and general. Although decent care for the mentally ill was a worthy goal, he wrote, it was the responsibility of the states, not the federal government.

The situation wherein America's federal system of government reveals points of tension and opportunity repeats itself often in the story of madness and government. In this first instance, the president stood on solid constitutional and political ground that was at variance with the moral choice expressed by the Congress. Pierce feared that the bill might set a dangerous precedent by which "the whole field of public beneficence [would be] thrown open to the care and culture of the federal government" (Reichenbach 1977, p. 13). In short, if the federal government took on the responsibility of caring for the mentally ill poor, it might have to take care of all the poor. Thoroughly disappointed, Dorothea Dix went to Europe to rest and recover. On her return she resumed her intense lobbying on a state-by-state basis which was, as we know, extraordinarily successful. Had she managed to get the bill through both houses of Congress two years earlier when Millard Fillmore was president, federal support for the mentally ill might have begun 100 years earlier.

Descent into Custodial Care

The idea of institutions to provide asylum for the mentally ill was in tune with a broader social interest in developing institutions for a variety of public problems. Correctional and ameliorational institutions such as orphanages, reform schools and settlement houses all had popular approval during this period, as much for their reputed benefits to their clients as for their provision of social control. The waves of immigrants, with poor and insane persons among them, alarmed the native-born Americans. Aliens were threatening to social order and public institutions were seen as appropriate remedies. Most of these institutions were funded at the state level of government because of the states' superior revenue-raising powers vis a vis local communities. Local communities also insisted on their poor law residence requirements, and for the most part did retain responsibility for their own mentally ill poor. Thus did the responsibility for the foreign-born, as well as for persons displaced by the social upheaval characteristic of the period, evolve upward to the next higher level of civil organization, state government.

Yet even as state care systems for public mental patients were being built throughout the country during the latter half of the nineteenth century, state mental hospitals were deteriorating into human warehouses where long-term and even lifetime stays were the norm. The decline of the asylums from would-be therapeutic to frankly custodial institutions disabused decision-makers and ordinary citizens of the notion that mental illness was amenable to moral treatment. The stark reality of the institutions reinforced the estrangement of the mentally ill and those who cared for them from the mainstream of community life and general medicine.

Desperate conditions became commonplace as the decades passed. Funding was chronically inadequate to the need. Crowding and overcrowding became endemic. An upper limit of 250 patients had been recommended in the early years. Although raised again and again in the ensuing decades, few hospital superintendents could comply with such recommendations. In time, some state hospitals were keeping confined as many as 15,000 inmates. The social control function of the hospitals, in contradistinction to their treatment function, became increasingly evident as the proportion of foreign-born inmates climbed to more than half. The close personal relationships called for by the methods of moral treatment were impossible when caretakers and patients had disparate cultures and languages. Treatment was tacitly replaced by restraint and confinement.

Other physicians publicly criticized hospital superintendents for their indifference to treatment and research, and the press sensationalized claims that some people were railroaded into state hospitals. Journalists exposed the wretched conditions they had witnessed while posing as patients. Yet the general outcry about how asylums were run was somewhat unfair because there was no way anyone could provide moral treatment for the legions of sick people committed to state hospitals. The superintendents' own standard of success, and that of their political masters, "was not related to the proportion of recoveries, but rather to the degree of efficiency and economy with which they managed their hospital" (Grob 1966, p. 356).

The idea of institutions to provide asylum and treatment for the mentally ill was itself strongly challenged by a new reform movement that rallied around Clifford Beers following the publication of his autobiographical *A Mind That Found Itself* in 1908. Clifford Beers was a young man who had suffered a severe mental illness soon after graduating from Yale University and had become a patient in a string of private and public hospitals. Beers eventually recovered to tell the tale. His account did more than document the inhumane conditions, for he argued persuasively that earlier treatment in the community could have prevented his illness from running its devastating course. Encouraged and actively assisted by such luminaries of psychology and psychiatry as William James and Dr. Adolf Meyer, Beers founded the National Committee for Mental Hygiene in 1909. The group is today known as the National Mental Health Association and is the largest voluntary organization in the field, with more than a million members.

The mental hygiene movement advocated early treatment and community care, preferably in outpatient clinics. Preventing afflicted persons "from passing into the insane state" was the foremost requirement, and it could be met by "psychiatric institutions in connection with general hospitals and psychiatric clinics better than by the familiar types of hospitals for the insane existing in this country" (Beers 1925, p. 280). However, the mental hygiene movement was fifty years ahead of its time in proposing a community-based alternative to the state institutional system. That system remained dominant even though it gave rise to hospitals which were called "the shame of the states."

The Turn of the Tide

Society's pessimistic view of the effectiveness of treatment began slowly to shift early in the twentieth century. One factor was the wide circulation achieved by Beers' story of recovery from severe mental disorder. Other developments occurring in medicine and science shed light on the nature of at least certain types of acute psychotic illness and behavioral aberration. Medical conditions such as advanced syphilis and pellagra were shown to produce mental disturbance. In Austria, Sigmund Freud's studies of hypnosis and dreams, his insights into the psychopathology of everyday life, and his formulation of psychoanalysis were, in time, radically to alter everyone's view of individual mental life. In Russia, Ivan Pavlov's animal experiments, which yielded predictable, reproducible results, attested to the profound influence of environment on behavior. The psychiatric profession, in common with other medical specialties, became convinced that development of a scientific base would lead to effective treatment for previously unreachable patients. Psychiatry began moving gingerly toward the medical mainstream; the first general hospital psychiatric unit opened at the Albany Hospital in New York in 1902 (Lipowski 1981).

What was probably the most persuasive news about mental illness came out of the First World War. As usual, there was good news and bad news. On the positive side, military medics discovered that the minds of soldiers deranged by battle conditions could often be helped to heal. Early intervention and active treatment were cited as factors in the successes, as was removal of disturbed soldiers to nearby noncombat areas.

The bad news was the high proportion of young men judged to be psychiatrically unfit to serve in the armed forces. Even after the conscripts had been screened and trained, military officers found them wanting. In 1918, General John J. Pershing cabled the Army chief of staff: "Prevalence of mental disorders in replacement troops . . . suggests urgent importance of intense effort in eliminating unfit . . . prior to departure from U.S . . . ." (McDonald 1982).

On balance, Americans were getting ironically complementary messages about mental illness in the wake of the Great War. There was reason to think that effective treatment of mental illness was possible, particularly if the illness was of recent origin. There was also clear evidence of a greater incidence of illness than had been supposed. The whole idea which emerged was that the nation could and should take steps to improve the mental health of its people if only to assure its defense against hostile foreign forces.

It was narcotics addiction, not mental illness per se, that provoked the first national action against threats to mental health. Criminal justice rather more than clinical or humanitarian considerations prompted the passage of the Harrison Narcotics Act of 1914, which authorized the first federally funded studies of addiction, crime, delinquency and the emotional consequences of immigration. Medical and psychological aspects of addictive behavior revealed in these studies eventually led in 1929 to passage of legislation authorizing the construction of two federal hospitals for treatment of persons addicted to drugs, and the establishment within the Public Health Service (PHS) of the Narcotics Division to conduct research on addiction and rehabilitation. Within two years Congress enlarged the research mission to include studies of the prevalence, prevention and treatment of mental diseases, and renamed the office the Division of Mental Hygiene to give emphasis to the new focus. These changes reflected the steadily growing confidence of the psychiatric profession in the possibilities for more effective techniques and settings to treat mentally ill persons.

Although the long night of custodial care for mentally ill public patients lingered until the mid-1950s, the experience of the economically depressed decade of the 1930s deeply if indirectly affected American attitudes about the proper disposition of the mentally ill poor. The Depression brought home to millions of people that individual effort is tempered by social interdependence, and that the federal government has a rightful role in solving problems perceived as national in extent. The social welfare legislation that would benefit the mentally ill poor in years to come had its roots in the New Deal programs of President Franklin Roosevelt.

More concretely, in the late 1930s the director of the Division of Mental Hygiene, Dr. Lawrence Kolb, Sr., was talking out the idea of a national neuropsychiatric institute that would administer both clinical and basic research programs. The idea was drafted into a bill to be introduced to Congress, but the advent of the Second World War tabled congressional consideration as the nation swiftly turned to meet the challenge. Once again, beginning in January 1942, the conscription of men for the armed forces revealed an intolerable degree of mental and emotional disorder in the country: 12 of every

100 men examined were rejected for neuropsychiatric reasons (McDonald 1982).

By the time of the war's end, public revulsion against state mental institutions and concern about the extent of mental disability in the country coincided with a favorable view of psychiatry. National mental health leaders determined to seize their advantage. These leaders were committed to replacing the few score state mental institutions with a system in which any number of small communities would provide comprehensive mental health care services to their local populations. Knowing that political leverage was needed to carry a social and public policy change of this magnitude, they proceeded methodically to cultivate political power for the purpose of developing a national mental health enterprise which would stimulate and support the radical rebalance they hoped to effect.

The remainder of this book tells the story of what happened next. Its objectives are several and interwoven. Primarily, the narrative presents a case study of the interaction of political, social and clinical factors in public policy decisions affecting the dependent mentally ill since 1945. The focus is on the role of the federal government in providing leadership and direction to our society's efforts to understand and ameliorate a major social problem. Specifically, the narrative explores in depth the origins and development of federal community mental health programming. The questions and themes noted at the beginning of this chapter continued to figure prominently in the recent history of madness and government—the issues of financial responsibility and intergovernmental partnerships, the limitations of treatment and the appropriate care settings, and the role of leadership in improving the system of public mental health care. The political dynamics and social reform movements, the shifting clinical issues arising from new policies, the individual actors who made things happen are all part of the story, but the two main "characters" are present only by implication. One is the mentally ill; this population is described in Chapter 6. The other is all the rest of us.

Who cares for the mentally ill? Each individual American makes that decision. Today each of us faces a moral choice of whether to care for the dependent mentally ill in our communities. If we answer in the affirmative, then the political questions are how to use our resources most effectively and how to apportion responsibility for mental health and related support services among the levels of government. In the end it is individuals in local communities who must insure the provision of care for the dependent mentally ill through human and financial resources solicited from government. It is each of us directing our government and defining the extent of government's intervention.

CHAPTER TWO

Learning the Political Arts
(1946-1960)

The Leadership Emerges

Big Brother: The Washington Health Syndicate

Achievements of the Mental Health Enterprise

Mobilization for Consent

A National Study Is Launched

*I*f we are to ... reduce mental illness and improve mental health, we must rise above [allegiances to] different professions ... different social classes ... different economic philosophies ... and [work] together out of mutual respect for our fellow man. We each have our ... sense of obligations, but also we each have one ... responsibility that ... transcends all others. This is our responsibility as citizens of a democratic nation founded out of faith in the uniqueness, integrity, and dignity of human life.

Jack R. Ewalt, M.D.
Action for Mental Health, 1961

CHAPTER TWO

Learning the Political Arts
(1946-1960)

The men and women who initiated the development of a federal base of support for mental health were strongly committed to providing better care for the mentally ill. This commitment bound them to an alliance in which each represented a constituency vital to their common goal. Psychiatrists and other physicians (those in federal service and not), members of Congress, philanthropists and reform-minded activists—these were the key groups that pooled resources to effect a radical rebalance of the nation's system of care for the mentally ill poor. By the post-war 1940s, when these groups were beginning to coalesce, America was ready to accept their views and take their advice. The magnitude and urgency of the problem were acknowledged by all, and Americans were almost as unanimous in believing that technical experts—that is, physicians and scientists—could solve the problem if given the resources to do so.

The Leadership Emerges

The first leader to emerge was a psychiatrist in federal service, Robert H. Felix, who was committed to ensuring humane care for the mentally ill and trained in the technology to carry out his purpose. Robert Felix had grown up with William and Karl Menninger on the Kansas plains. He graduated from the University of Colorado in 1930. As a resident in Colorado under psychiatrist Dr. Frank Ebaugh, he came to share his mentor's commitment to community care and revulsion against the condition of state mental hospitals. In 1933 Felix joined the Division of Mental Hygiene of the Public Health Service, headed by Dr. Walter Treadway. He served at the government's first hospital for narcotic addicts near Lexington, Kentucky, and moved up the ranks. By 1942 he had completed his Master of Public Health degree at the Johns Hopkins University with a thesis on the organization of a national mental health program. "More a dream than a thesis" is how he thought of it at the time, but the revelations of the Second World War transformed this man's dream into a vision shared by many.

Aside from the high incidence of psychiatric disorders resulting from the war itself, more men were rejected for the services due to psychiatric disorders than the total number fighting at the peak of the war in the Pacific. In addition, the demand for psychiatrists for the military services had so reduced their numbers in state mental hospitals that care was more inadequate than ever. The war had also hastened the development of crisis intervention techniques, enabling medics to provide effective treatment for many of the psychiatric wounds of battle.

In 1945 the chief of the Public Health Service, Surgeon General Thomas Parran, asked Felix to design a national mental health program. Felix, then assistant chief of the PHS Hospital Division, met with the chief psychiatrists of the military services, Dr. William Menninger, Dr. Francis Braceland and Dr. Jack R. Ewalt. The four were friends as well as colleagues in the nascent Group for the Advancement of Psychiatry (GAP), the radicals of the American Psychiatric Association; GAP, wanting more than just the improvement of the state mental hospitals, promoted community care (Interview 1972d.,g.,i.). Together, they reworked Felix's Hopkins thesis into a draft legislative bill in a few short months. Just before the war, Felix's chief at the Division of Mental Hygiene, Dr. Lawrence Kolb, Sr., was preparing to submit to Congress a bill establishing a national neuropsychiatric institute which would conduct and support research. The GAP fellows built on Kolb's foundation, but they went further by calling for federal support of training as well as research and federal grants to the states to assist them in improving services through the use of "the most effective methods of prevention, diagnosis and treatment."

The fruit of their labor, the National Mental Health Act, was introduced to the Congress in the spring of 1946 by Representative J. Percy Priest (D-Tenn), chairman of the Subcommittee on Public Health of the House Committee on Interstate and Foreign Commerce. Democrat Lister Hill, the junior senator from Alabama, obtained the cosponsorship of distinguished senators from both parties for the Senate's version of the bill. Senator Claude Pepper (D-Fla), chairman of the Subcommittee on Health and Education of the Senate Committee on Labor and Welfare, held the hearings in the Senate and managed the bill through that chamber.

In both Senate and House, much of the evidence was presented by psychiatrists still in military uniform. Their testimony focused on the large number of wartime psychiatric casualties and the acute shortage of people, notably psychiatrists, trained to care for them. Much testimony was heard in praise of the new, more effective methods of care developed during the war. Early, active treatment was stressed, as was the value of providing care in normal rather than institutional settings. Only a very few raised opposition to the bill, specifically to the enlargement of the federal role: Senator Robert A. Taft (R-Ohio) wished to delete the provisions for direct aid to the states. Also worth noting is that, although psychiatrists predominated and uniformly testified favorably for the bill, the absence of a representative of the American Medical Association (AMA) indicated that organization's tacit disapproval (Reichenbach 1977). The National Mental Health Act was signed by President Harry S. Truman on July 3, 1946.

The Act established the National Institute of Mental Health (NIMH) as the national focal point of concern, leadership and effort for the mentally ill. The legislation authorized $7.5 million for the purposes of (1) fostering and aiding *research* related to the cause, diagnosis and treatment of neuropsychiatric disorders; (2) providing for the *training* of personnel, for the award of fellowships to individuals, and for grants to public and nonprofit institutions; and (3) *aiding states* in the prevention, diagnosis and treatment of neuropsychiatric disorders through grants and technical assistance (see below).

The precedent for federal support of health research had been set in 1937 with the establishment of the National Cancer Institute. The provision for direct financial aid to states for the purpose of encouraging use of new methods of care was consistent with previous legislation in that grants-in-aid to the states was a type of support already in use in two public health programs, venereal disease control and tuberculosis control. The Act broke new ground, however, in its provision of training grants to institutions as well as training stipends and fellowships to individuals.

The law also provided for the creation of a National Advisory Mental Health Council charged with responsibility for recommending applications for research grant awards, and for advising the surgeon general on all public health service programs involving mental health matters. The council was to have the supportive service of study groups organized by psychiatric and social scientific disciplines. The surgeon general, chairman of the council, was to appoint six members from among the leading medical and scientific authorities in the study, diagnosis or treatment of mental disorders. In later legislation, membership was expanded and, critically, opened to nonprofessional citizens.

Over the next decades the council served both to direct the development of federally funded mental health technology and to link the NIMH professionals with their colleagues in universities and professional organizations and with their supporters among philanthropic interests and citizen groups. After observing the council's operations for nearly a quarter century, a retired Felix concluded that it had produced a more significant effect on the direction and growth of the mental health program than any other provision of the 1946 legislation: "The quality of individuals selected to serve on this group, their dedication and sound advice from the very beginning, have involved the professional and nonprofessional public and have brought their concerns into the institute's plans and operations" (Felix 1971). The council evolved into a professional-citizen constituent base for NIMH as members of all the major mental health interest groups came to serve on it (the American Psychological Association, American Psychiatric Association, National Committee Against Mental Illness, National Association for Mental Health, universities, and state mental health authorities), and key supporters and advocates of mental health were among the citizens to serve on it. The evolution was abetted by the institute's use of fiscal patronage provided by a coalition of politically powerful and wealthy Washington health leaders.

Big Brother: The Washington Health Syndicate

President Truman signed the National Mental Health Act the day before the Fourth of July holiday in 1946, and Congress adjourned the next day without appropriating funds to implement the new law. Not to be delayed, Felix obtained a grant of $15,000 from the Greentree

Foundation to enable the council to meet and initiate the program. Dr. Stanley Yolles, Felix's successor, commented recently: "It has always seemed particularly significant that the National Institute of Mental Health, which awarded [public] funds to so many grantees for training and research purposes and to assist the states—had its origin in a grant made by private philanthropy" (McDonald 1982). Congress enacted the first appropriation in 1947. In April 1949, NIMH became fully operational when the Division of Mental Hygiene of the Public Health Service was abolished and NIMH became an institute of the National Institutes of Health (NIH) in the Department of Health, Education, and Welfare (HEW).

These years also saw the beginning of a sharp rise in the influence of professionalism in government. Nowhere was this more clear that at NIMH, which Samuel Beer has termed "a professional-bureaucratic complex" (Beer 1976). Felix headed the leadership of this professional-bureaucratic complex, which worked in close cooperation with certain interested legislators in the Congress—especially the chairmen of the relevant specialized subcommittees, Senator Lister Hill and Representative John F. Fogarty (D-RI)—and with spokespersons for the groups that benefited from programs initially conceived by the professionals and passed into legislation by the politicians. To persuade Congress to appropriate more and more money to NIMH for research, training, and demonstration service programs, Felix worked primarily with the leadership of the American Psychiatric Association and three key lobbyists, Florence Mahoney and Mary Lasker, both wealthy philanthropists, and Mike Gorman who, as a newspaper reporter, had written of the state mental hospitals as snake pits (Gorman 1948). This alliance of mental health interests focused on drastic reduction of the role of state mental hospitals in the public mental health care system by means of a vastly expanded federal presence in the system.

The mental health alliance overlapped another, much broader association, a group of well-placed individuals whom the journalist Elizabeth Drew described as "Washington's Noble Conspirators" (Drew 1967). The media referred to them collectively as "the health syndicate." Their aim was to expand the federal support of medical research. Together, the mental health alliance and the Washington health syndicate were effective in convincing Congress to expand funding for mental health and for other categorical health programs of the NIH.

The Washington health syndicate was composed of men and women in positions of great power. Among them were Dr. James E. Shannon, director of NIH; Senator Hill, chairman of the key Senate committee and Representative Fogarty, chairman of the key House committee; and philanthropists Mary Lasker and Florence Mahoney, who contributed to the campaigns of politicians favoring medical research. The philanthropists also supported Mike Gorman; the journalist had become a highly skilled lobbyist and was executive director of the National Committee Against Mental Illness, a reform-minded citizens group. Gorman developed data that compared the cost to the national economy of various diseases to the cost of concerted research efforts to overcome them. In addition, Gorman provided valuable staff work to congressional allies. He became known for doing his homework.

Shannon combined his professional standards and collegial interests with his native political instincts for the stated purpose of expanding "the obviously inadequate federal medical research base in the early 1950s" (Interview 1972n.). In 1953 he joined forces with Fogarty and Hill to double the NIH budget. From that year on, the three men drew up budgets deemed appropriate by the professional elite in the NIH, Felix among them. Shannon included technical information in his reports to committees, which justified increased appropriations. He marshalled medical scientists to testify and in other ways support existing and new programs.

Strategically, Fogarty and Hill proceeded in this fashion: Fogarty castigated the White House, the Bureau of the Budget and HEW for submitting a budget request for NIH lower than that which NIH had suggested. He elicited from the NIH professionals the amount they had initially requested (and corresponding to the one he had before him). He called for the experts.

On his part, Gorman recruited as witnesses such well-known physicians as Michael DeBakey and Karl Menninger. They offered "professional judgment budgets," which were, in most instances, even higher than NIH's. The budgets were promoted by Mahoney, Lasker and Gorman, who lobbied all the members of the appropriation committees in both houses. Fogarty could then raise the NIH budget. His stature as an extremely knowledgeable appropriations chairman assured that he would be successful when the bill came before the full House.

Assisted by the same Mahoney-Lasker-Gorman lobbying routine in the Senate, Senator Hill's tactic was to raise Fogarty's inflated budget still higher. Where new NIH programs could be funded under existing legislative authority, the tactics became specific. In "year one" the NIH directorship would suggest that a specific program might be promising, but not request money. Hill and Fogarty would ask for a technical report on the idea in "year two." In "year two" the NIH director would submit the report, and Fogarty and Hill would appropriate the money for "year three" (Ibid.).

The Bureau of the Budget and HEW never publicly admitted that this strategy checked the fiscal control of the president. It was important that Lasker and other wealthy campaign contributors were supportive to executive and legislative leaders alike. In Shannon's judgment, "there was no conspiracy . . . generally the secretary of HEW was as dissatisfied with Budget's proposal as was the director of NIH" (Shannon 1974).

From 1953 to 1960, the Washington health syndicate expanded financing of medical research, including mental health research, nearly sevenfold, from $59 million to $404 million. The funding strategy of the health syndicate shaped NIMH into a pluralistic establishment. How pluralistic will become clear when the incentives Felix used are enumerated.

Felix and NIMH cooperated in and benefited from the strategy of the health syndicate. That is, Felix had to negotiate with members of the syndicate in order to obtain increased appropriations. For example, compromises were struck with Mahoney, Lasker and Gorman. Lasker pushed NIH directors to translate basic research into applied services. The fact that Felix designed and maintained a research organization that promoted applied research and demonstration services was consistent with her aims. Gorman empathized with Felix's revulsion toward traditional care in state mental hospitals. "My hidden agenda," he said in retrospect, "was to break the back of the state mental hospital" (Interview 1972j.).

Two major events in NIMH's program development illustrate how Felix had to accommodate his interests to those of Mahoney, Lasker and Gorman. The first event concerned drug research. European physicians were using new "tranquilizing" drugs to treat mental illness—with great success. Reports of their work stimulated clinical trials in this country, and many of the psychiatrists to try the new drugs observed remarkable benefits. Mahoney, Lasker and Gorman were persuaded that this discovery could be exploited simultaneously in both basic and clinical research fields—it represented an opportunity tailormade to their interests. They pressured Felix to undertake a massive NIMH study to evaluate this new modality. However, Felix was representing the interests of NIMH scientists, who were skeptical of the claims. Felix himself may have had reservations, because the institute had been decreasing its work in psychopharmacology before the new drug breakthrough, which occurred in 1956. Despite Felix's failure to back a major psychopharmacology effort, Gorman gained the support of Hill and Fogarty.

In the 1956 appropriations, Congress earmarked $2 million in additional funds for NIMH for the purposes of psychopharmacology. Gorman's witnesses in the congressional hearings had urged the funding of a multihospital, nationwide evaluation of the new drugs. With the earmarked funds, Felix established a psychopharmacology service center. By 1960, when the effectiveness of the drugs had been demonstrated, Felix was an ardent supporter of the program because it was providing the clinical data needed to demonstrate that patients could be cared for in the community. In 1956, however, he had to be talked into the compromise of additional funds for psychopharmacology research with no redirection of NIMH's current funds.

In the second event, Felix did accept the redirection of training funds to nonpsychiatric personnel. Gorman wanted more funds for training psychologists, nurses and psychiatric social workers, and for psychiatric training of general practitioners. Felix, the Public Health Service officer, may not have disagreed, but he faced contrary pressures from within the institute and from the American Psychiatric Association. Despite those pressures, Gorman's lobbying convinced Congress to direct NIMH to fund training of all mental health personnel, not just psychiatrists.

By thus working out differences behind the scenes, Felix and the other syndicate members presented a solid front to the members of Congress. By 1963, NIMH was the fourth-ranking institute in appropriations.

The political successes of the health syndicate generally and NIMH particularly were expected phenomena for the period. In those years Americans believed that science was power, and that its power could be cultivated and channeled into whatever ends society sought and was willing to pay for. The sciences that deal with human mental and emotional life shared in the deep respect accorded all technical expertness. What Veroff and his colleagues have called "an era of psychology" was manifesting around the mid-1950s (Veroff et al. 1981a, p.7). Freud's breakthrough, psychoanalysis, was at its center.

His was the first form of psychic healing to isolate the patient from family and other relationships and treat the illness through discussion, interpretation and analysis. In these characteristics of isolation, detachment and intellectual analysis, Veroff has observed, "psychoanalysis represents quintessential science. Its popularity marks the movement of the scientific revolution to the last frontier—the sphere of human behavior and the thickets of the human soul—and represents, above all, a remarkable faith in and optimism about the powers of science (Ibid)." Felix, Shannon and many more were the technician-experts; Lasker, Mahoney, Gorman and others understood and selectively promoted their ideas; Hill, Fogarty and others bought these ideas for improving the nation's health and selectively funded them. In effect, this mental health professional and political leadership functioned like a technocracy under whose writ the National Institute of Mental Health was established and handsomely endowed.

Naturally, the public expected a return on its investment. Felix and his top staff had to manage the institute's resources so as to produce meaningful advances in order to maintain credibility among the public and their peers. In this, they were only partly successful. The extravagant claims of enthusiasts—that new treatments were highly effective, that all future potential victims of mental illness and their families would be spared the suffering, that great economies of money would soon be realized—were allowed to pass unchallenged by the professional side of the professional-political leadership. Promising more than could reasonably be delivered became a way of life for this leadership, as it had been for Dorothea Dix and her allies in the nineteenth century. In any event, Felix and the NIMH staff wasted no effort in using the congressional endowment to build a technological base composed of myriad bits of scientific data. From this base, in time, the power to effect the desired changes was to be generated.

Achievements of the Mental Health Enterprise

The National Institute of Mental Health under Felix's leadership satisfied its legislative mandate by meeting its three program objectives—the promotion of research, the development of personnel training, and the demonstration of new services. This was achieved through its authorized use of grants and contracts. Research, training and services formed NIMH's three-legged stool, a metaphor that came into use to point up that, unlike the other categorical health institutes of NIH, NIMH's responsibility extended well beyond research. In 1962, 85 percent of the total NIMH appropriation supported grants for research, training and assistance to nonfederal settings such as universities, research and training institutions, and state and local mental health agencies and institutions (though not mental hospitals — see below). The program activities of these organizations depended upon NIMH more or less heavily for part of their financial resources. Through the grant use of the federal dollar, Felix thus directed the development of a national mental health enterprise, drawing into the mental health field diverse disciplines from the biological, clinical, behavioral and social sciences. Their collaboration was immensely productive. Series of improvements in the care and treatment of mental illness emerged in a remarkably short period of time. The mental health enterprise could show tangible results to its investors.

During its first fifteen years (as of the end of fiscal 1962), the institute supported nearly 3,000 research projects, a total of over $120 million in awards, in the substantive areas of mental retardation, child mental health and development, schizophrenia, depression, alcoholism, aging, drug addiction and psychopharmacology.

NIMH was also tied into the Hill-Burton program, which could authorize the construction of special facilities for chronic disease, including mental illness. Although in the period 1947-62 the total federal expenditure under the Hill-Burton program was approximately $1.8 billion, only about 3 percent, or $59.6 million, had been used for construction of beds and facilities for care of the mentally ill. The Hill-Burton program had been authorized primarily to assist general hospital facilities, with only minimal support to mental health facilities. In large measure, what construction support provided was limited to psychiatric wards in general hospitals.

During the same period the institute directed a major portion of its total effort to the problem of mental health personnel. The institute at first supported only graduate training of the core professional groups—psychiatry, clinical psychology, psychiatric nursing and psychiatric social work. Faced with evidence of continuing shortages of trained personnel, and with public pressure as reflected in congressional mandates, Felix agreed to expand the training program to general practitioners (promoted by Mahoney, Lasker and Gorman), occupational and recreational therapists, the clergy, psychiatric aides and mental health attendants. As of 1962 the institute had supported 1,500 training projects whose awards totaled approximately $185 million. Eighty percent of the awards were made to colleges and universities and about half of that sum went to their affiliated medical schools. Every major medical school's department of psychiatry, all the major graduate departments of psychology and graduate schools of social work and of nursing received some support through a training grant from the institute. It is not surprising that, given such a financial impetus, the number of persons in the core mental health professions increased nearly ten times faster in the 1950s and '60s than the total number of all other health professionals. Although this difference has since narrowed, the growth in number and rate per 100,000 population of mental health professionals continued at least until 1980 (Sharfstein 1982; see Table).

Growth in Number and Rate of Mental Health Professionals, 1955-1980

Group of Professionals	1955	1980	Percent Increase
Psychiatrists[a]			
Number	10,600	30,023	183
Rate per 100,000 population[b]	6.4	13.7	114
Psychologists[c]			
Number	13,500	56,933	322
Rate per 100,000 population[b]	8.1	25.9	220
Social workers[d]			
Number	20,000	83,000	315
Rate per 100,000 population[b]	12.1	37.8	212

From: Sharfstein 1982.

[a] Data until 1960 included American Psychiatric Association membership plus filled psychiatric residency positions. 1960-1980 data also included nonmembers of the American Psychiatric Association who reported their specialty as psychiatry to the American Medical Association. Approximately 10% of all psychiatrists in 1980 were child psychiatrists.

[b] Source for civilian population of the United States: U.S. Bureau of the Census: *Current Population Reports,* Series P-25, numbers 802 and 888.

[c] Data based on membership in the American Psychological Association. Until 1980, 37% of all psychologists were in clinical counseling or guidance psychology. In 1980 between 26,000 and 28,000 (52%) were licensed or certified health science provider psychologists.

[d] Data based on membership in the National Association of Social Workers. Approximately 20% to 25% of all social workers were in mental health practice. In 1980, 11,000 were on the register of "certified clinical social workers."

The crucial political aspect of the institute's grant and contract power was that it provided NIMH with constituencies in the universities and the professions. The institute also used grants and contracts to build constituencies in support of its "third leg," the services demonstration programs. State mental hospital leaders were not among them, as we will soon see.

Felix recruited a staff to work with representatives of public and private mental health organizations. The staff's function was to communicate research findings and to advise and assist in the application of these findings to treating mental illness. Collectively, these consultants served as a bridge between the research laboratories and training facilities and the mental health practitioners, both direct-care providers who worked with patients and those engaged in the administration of clinics, general hospital psychiatric units, day centers, and other community facilities concerned with the care of the mentally ill. New knowledge from research that might be put into clinical practice or used to improve mental health services administration was critically analyzed. The most promising new information was translated into mental health treatment practices, which were then further evaluated in clinical settings. Demonstrations focused on the translation of new knowledge into treatment practices and the application of recently developed treatment practices in new settings.

Special techniques were developed to disseminate new information. Intensive workshops called technical assistance projects were begun in 1955. They were designed to present to health professionals and state mental health representatives new information on the application of modern principles and methods of administering mental health service programs. The institute, which financed these projects and guided their planning, focused them on programmatic elements of community mental health: short-term inpatient care, outpatient care, partial hospitalization, emergency services, and consultation and education for caregivers in the community. These elements were suggested as the core of comprehensive community mental health services.

Another set of incentives available to Felix beginning in 1948 was the grant-in-aid to states, administered under authority of (former) Section 314(c) of the Public Health Service Act. Federal grants that states must match dollar-for-dollar were made to the agency in each state designated as the "mental health authority." Funds were made available to assist states in establishing, maintaining and expanding community mental health services. It is important to note here the guidelines promulgated to implement the law which authorized NIMH to make these grants. In keeping with the intent of Congress, the guidelines favored active, community-based services over custodial, institution-based services. The guidelines stated that federal funds could *not* be used to train personnel or obtain equipment for state hospitals, to undertake surveys or research on institutional programs, or to provide domiciliary care and subsistence. Appropriate use was for central administration, professional services, psychiatric clinics, training personnel to work outside of state hospitals, and prevention and education activities.

While Felix was making the federal government the prime mover in research and training and a vigorous proponent of innovative, community-based services, news of the development in Britain of "open hospitals" began to effect changes in the way state institutions were run in America (Gruenberg and Archer 1979). These changes aimed at reforming the hospital's social organization, restructuring the custodial institution into a therapeutic community. Locks were removed and physical restraints eliminated by the British doctors. They replaced long-term hospital stays with short-term hospital care followed by long-term community outpatient care with hospital care readily available in times of crisis. The U.S. open hospital movement sharply accelerated after the discovery of the tranquilizing antipsychotic drugs, for these and the other psychotropic medications which followed made it possible to maintain many patients in their communities who otherwise might have needed to be hospitalized for years. By the early 1960s, many state hospitals in the U.S. were operating as open hospitals, and a few were providing service in communities for their patients.

The trend toward state-hospital-based community care for patients with serious and chronic mental illness was funded in part by the federal "seed money" for planning community-based mental health services. For example, a commission was established in 1949 by New York to administer the federal grants for planning community mental health services. Five years later the state legislature enacted a law based on the commission's work. New York's Community Mental Health Services Act of 1954 returned to local governments some of the responsibility for operating mental health services and authorized state financing for up to half of the cost to local governments of outpatient clinic services, inpatient services in general hospitals, rehabilitation, and consultation and education services. Fourteen other states followed this lead and had enacted similar community mental health legislation by 1963 (Beinecke 1979, p. 19).

In fiscal 1948, a minimum grant of $20,000 was made to each state, with all states expending a total of $1.6 million of grant-in-aid federal funds. In a number of states community mental health programs did expand, and additional funds were appropriated to stimulate more state interest in providing community mental health services. The minimum grant to each state was reduced in fiscal 1955 during the Eisenhower administration, although more states participated and the total amount expended by states increased to $2.3 million. An increase in grant appropriations made in 1962 during the Kennedy administration enabled the minimum grant to be raised to $65,000, and the total of grant funds expended by states to $6.6 million. As noted, states utilized these so-called formula grant funds primarily to plan, develop, and assist the operation of community mental health services. The foundations of a national community mental health services program were in place.

·Mobilization for Consent

Psychiatrists were Felix's older, senior constituency. Their ethical and scientific perspective held sway at NIMH under the guidance of the National Advisory Mental Health Council. As noted earlier, council membership included among the psychiatrists a number of "prominent citizens"—that is, knowledgeable, sophisticated advocates of mental health, untrained in psychiatric practices per se—and this professional-citizen alliance, in collaboration with the Washington health syndicate, justified the launching of a national mental health enterprise to the key congressional health leaders, who then authorized and appropriated federal dollars to underwrite the venture.

"State mental health authorities" were Felix's newer, junior constituency. Its existence was made possible by the provision for grants-in-aid to the states in the National Mental Health Act. Through these grants Felix was able to stimulate many states to set up a separate mental health authority which would control the grant dollars. New York State's mental health commission was such a one, and most states moved with purposeful alacrity to follow the national leadership and accept federal financial support. The formal organization through which the newly created mental health authorities related to Felix was the Council of State and Territorial Mental Health Authorities. The council convened annually to advise Felix and also to obtain his direction. Understandably, it was not as potent an advisory body as the National Advisory Mental Health Council. Yet it too gradually became the nucleus of a professional constituency. Effective representation of the interests of this constituency was critical to Felix's long-range goal. If community mental health services were to become a reality, state governments would have to be persuaded to rebalance their health budgets in favor of community care.

During the decade 1946-56, as these two key constituencies were growing in political effectiveness, Felix successfully mobilized their technical and public relations skills to shape congressional and public attitudes to an acceptance of a national mental health program with community mental health as its centerpiece. The process was an additive one of continuing education and improved communication. Congressional testimony in the late 1940s reflected widespread public emotionalism and ignorance about the nature of mental illness and the role of psychiatry. During the 1946 hearings, for example, extremely conservative citizens groups sent letters opposing the bill because of their distrust of psychiatry and "overzealous psychiatrists who . . . [may] . . . use government agencies to force their views upon the individual" (Reichenbach 1977, p. 36). Few in the Congress shared such suspicions, while almost all were appalled by what they understood of existing institutional conditions. Yet the early dialogues between the professional technicians and members of Congress went haltingly, hampered by the absence of a common language. The technical talk of mental health scientists bewildered lay people, whose questions, in turn, were often simplistic. To change that, Gorman's great gift for public relations, and his deep reservoir of heroic-hearted volunteers, used the valid technical information supplied by Felix and his psychiatric colleagues. By the mid-1950s, the communications impasse had cleared dramatically. The media grew increasingly knowledgeable and mental health, high in reader appeal, became a popular topic to cover. Voters were coming to understand that money must be spent to attack this public health problem. Congressmen, reacting to their constituencies, hired staff who could help to educate and inform their judgment of testimony. Testimony became more sophisticated; complicated statistical tables and research designs were routinely introduced as evidence. A scientific survey conducted in 1957 indicated that one in every four Americans felt the need for help with emotional problems, and one in every seven had sought that help (Gurin et al. 1960). The stigma of mental illness was still abroad, but mental health information had wedged an opening—room for tolerance and acceptance—into this problem area.

A National Study Is Launched

The mobilization of technical and promotional skills orchestrated by Felix paid off handsomely. By the mid-1950s, the lawmakers knew enough to know that they needed an objective, thorough, nationwide analysis of the public health problem of mental illness. Hill, Fogarty and Priest were ready to introduce a legislative proposal to that effect, fully aware that (thanks to Gorman) the National Governors Conference was ready to support it.

At the 1954 annual meeting of the American Psychiatric Association, association president Dr. Kenneth Appel issued a call for a report comparable to the Flexner study (see below) on the status of mental health research and training. In February 1955, Senators Hill, John F. Kennedy (D-Mass), and other cosponsors introduced a resolution calling for a mental health study act to fund a survey and reevaluation of the human and economic problems of mental illness. The proposed legislation had been drafted by the American Psychiatric Association and the mental health council of the AMA. It reflected the perceptions and interests of psychiatrists and, to a lesser degree, other concerned citizens. Only a few weeks earlier, the psychiatrists had taken the lead in forming a commission on mental illness and health, a joint undertaking supported by several citizen groups, notably the National Association for Mental Health. In introducing the measure to the Senate, Hill made it clear that the proposal was not to be construed as in any way interfering with or diminishing the more limited and specific programs and studies being conducted under NIMH authority; thus was Felix's institutional base protected. Hill also made the authorship of the resolution a matter of public record.

> The council of the AMA and the American Psychiatric Association are to be commended for the initiative and fine sense of public responsibility they have shown in formulating plans for this most important undertaking. The results . . . may well prove as important in the field of mental health as the Flexner Commission report was in the field of medical education at the turn of the century. [Reichenbach 1977, p. 54]

The Flexner Commission Report (1910) led to AMA accreditation of medical schools and vastly improved standards of medical education. Control over medical training standards, in turn, had made the AMA into a powerful medical monopoly. Able as it was to preserve the status quo over which it held dominion, the AMA acknowledged that it was now ready to explore new options, "fundamental departures from our traditional concepts and methods of dealing with mental illness" (Reichenbach 1977, p. 55). This new willingness to consider change (ten years earlier the AMA had remained mute during hearings on the first federal initiative, the National Mental Health Act) signalled the influence of the greatly increased number of psychiatrists who had joined the AMA ranks during the previous decade. Felix's senior constituency had grown sufficiently to persuade organized medicine to support its interests.

During the spring and summer of 1955 the congressional committees under Senator Hill and Representative Priest held hearings on the resolution to fund a nationwide mental health study. Felix testified to the progress of NIMH in research, training and community mental health programs (Hearings 1955a). Material on community mental health clinics from publications of NIMH was introduced into the record. Dr. Winfred Overholser of St. Elizabeth's Hospital spoke about the dim prospects of release for patients who resided overlong in mental institutions; he suggested that treatment of patients in the community could be economical: "It is not only a question of emptying the hospital or reducing the load, not only restoring the patient to his family, but making him again a productive unit in society" (Ibid., p. 16). Gorman stressed the dimension of the states' efforts and voiced the governors' concern that to maintain custody of patients, rather than to offer treatment, would soon lead to impossible budget situations. He noted that state expenditures for mental illness had increased more than 300 percent in ten years. Gorman also called attention to the cost of mental illness to the patient and his family as well as to public agencies (Ibid.). Dr. Leo Bartemeier, chairman of the AMA Council on Mental Health, challenged the concept of the mental hospital as the primary organizational focus for treating the mentally ill and pointed out new modes of treatment: halfway houses, community care, new drugs, family reeducation (Hearings 1955b, p. 34).

Dr. Daniel Blain, medical director of the American Psychiatric Association, introduced to Congress the concept of the community mental health "center." He described it as a new approach to organizing all mental health resources within a geographical area under shared-government authority. The center organized the services of the area's mental hospitals, general hospitals, outpatient clinics, and public health prevention activities (for example, active case-finding, "working back in the homes to pick up cases and treat them there"). He pointed out that such service delivery organizations had been tried in Canada and England, and suggested that the federal government fund experimental programs based on the concept (Hearings 1955a, pp. 75-76).

Organized medicine stated its objectives and hopes with clarity. Dr. David B. Allman, member of the board of trustees and chairman of the Committee on Legislation of the AMA, testified that both the AMA and American Psychiatric Association had concluded that a commission be formed with two basic objectives:

> (a) to make a national survey of all aspects of the present status of resources and methods of diagnosing, treating, and caring for the mentally ill and retarded, both within and outside of institutions; and
>
> (b) to formulate, on the basis of the survey, a feasible program for the fundamental improvement of our methods and facilities for diagnosing, treatment, and care of the mentally ill and retarded.

Dr. Allman declared, "What the Flexner Report did for medical education is what we hope to accomplish with the Joint Commission on Mental Illness and Health" (Ibid., pp. 104-105).

Spokespersons for the American Nurses Association and the National Association for Mental Health testified in support of the resolution, as did the American Psychological Association, whose spokesperson obtained a commitment that the bill specify that behavioral scientists would participate in the study—anthropologists, clinical and social psychologists, sociologists, political scientists and economists (Ibid., p. 146). Mental health leaders in the states and from organized labor also testified on behalf of the bill.

Issues of federalism were briefly raised in the Senate hearings but Bartemeier dissipated any latent concern about federal co-optation of states' responsibilities. He emphasized the limited, temporary nature of the federal program being proposed, and reiterated the AMA's "sincere conviction that the entire question of defining local and federal responsibilities in the public health field should be carefully analyzed by Congress" (Reichenbach 1977, p. 59).

After two months of consideration, all proposals related to a nationwide mental health study were reduced to the resolution passed by the House in April and reported to the full Senate by Hill's subcommittee in July. Without a dissenting vote, the 84th Congress passed the Mental Health Study Act (PL 182) on July 28, 1955, and President Dwight D. Eisenhower promptly signed it into law. The Act required NIMH to appoint a joint commission to Congress to plan and conduct a thoroughgoing reevaluation of the nation's approach to mental illness. Congress appropriated $1.25 million for this purpose. The general expectation was that this sum would be supplemented by contributions from the private sector. However, only $146,400 was contributed by charities and professional associations. Congress later added $160,000 to the original appropriation (Reichenbach 1977, p. 62).

Felix chose Jack Ewalt, then treasurer of the American Psychiatric Association, to be the commission's director. Ewalt and Felix chose the AMA-American Psychiatric Association-sponsored Joint Commission on Mental Illness and Health to conduct the authorized study. The selection of Ewalt was based partly on his previous work with the first Hoover Commission. From that experience, Ewalt had learned the importance of open communications and pluralism. Consequently, from the inception of the joint commission, Ewalt built in ways of communicating and implementing its recommendations (Interview 1972 g.). He expanded the number of interest groups to a broad range representing a cross-section of society and government, from the American Academy of Neurology to the United States Department of Justice (Joint Commission 1961, pp. 306-307) (Chapter Note 2-1). Ewalt intended to direct these pressure groups to influence favorable public opinion.

Commission members, each nominated by an interest group but acting independently within the commission, would travel around the country once a year, speaking to local and state constituents about the commission's work and obtaining their feedback. Equally important, each kept his respective memberships informed of plans and recommendations as they developed.

Ewalt wisely decided to solicit the help of the American Legion to defuse any charge that the commission's final report was part of a "commie plot." He obtained a grant from the Legion to publish the final report. In the congressional hearing in which Ewalt presented the final report, one congressman indeed raised such a charge. But since Ewalt could point out that the American Legion had paid for the publication of the report currently before the congressman, the charge was completely deflated (Interview 1972g.). Never again was the accusation raised about the work of the joint commission and its final product.

In his yearly progress reports to Congress, Ewalt highlighted ongoing policy formulations. He promised in the first report "a comprehensive view of the many facets of the problem [that will] permit the Joint Commission to recommend to Congress, the states, and the mental health professions a course of action best calculated to achieve maximum progress in the future" (Ewalt 1957). He went further in the second report, expressing the hope that the commission's recommendations would result in the development of a "rationally planned, cooperative, nationwide mental health program" (Ewalt 1958, p. 4). He regarded it as a commission duty to stimulate action at national, state and community levels.

> [I]n its scientific aspects, the Commission is concerned with theory, its testing, and its validation. In the area of moral or social responsibility, however, it is concerned with practice—what works for the improvement of mental health, what produces better results in treating mental illness, where we have failed, and what should be done next. [Ibid.]

Ewalt also broached the concept of the neighborhood mental health center, available to people on the basis of their residence, and staffed around the clock to give emergency psychiatric services when needed.

The commission funded studies on patterns of patient care, nonpsychiatric community resources for mental health, the role of schools in mental health, the role of religion in mental health, along with others, including some studies on economic issues. Nor did the commission overlook the views and opinions of the American people themselves. The commission believed that "the needs of the people—as they themselves feel them, come to understand them, and express them—ultimately determine [in a democracy] the ways in which organized efforts will be made to meet these needs" (Gurin et al. 1960, p. ix). In order to obtain this vital perspective, the commission funded a study by the Survey Research Center at the University of Michigan (Veroff et al. 1981a,b). All commission study findings were published in a monograph series.

Several commission members served on NIMH's National Advisory Mental Health Council and shared ideas with NIMH staff.

Through the five years of the commission's existence this process of cross-fertilization worked to create a common perception about what was possible, what was needed, and what it would all cost (Interview 1973). While the commission did its work, Felix was propagandizing; he tried to give the general public the impression that the commission's recommendations would lead to a nationally planned and coordinated public-private mental health system. In his third report to Congress, Ewalt cited European research centered on the care of mentally ill patients in the community (Ewalt 1959, p. 14).

The joint commission, which finished its work in 1960, achieved the three prime goals sought by the mental health alliance. First, the commissions's monograph series represented a coherent body of new syntheses of knowledge in areas impinging on mental illness and health. Second, partly for this reason, the commission attracted broad media coverage over a sustained period of time; from academic journals to the Sunday supplements, the whole society had been exposed to an education in mental health. And third, best of all, the commission process and leadership had created a grand consensus of professional and public mental health interests.

The spirit of the consensus lay in humanitarian and ethical principle: in Ewalt's words, "[T]he collective human minds of our people are the greatest national resource . . . we should nurture [their] development and treat and rehabilitate [them] when decompensated" (Ewalt 1979, p. 509). The specific recommendations materializing from this principle—the flesh and bone of the consensus—may be characterized in political and public health terms (somewhat simplistically) as follows. The interest of the AMA and American Psychiatric Association majority commission membership was in so-called secondary and tertiary prevention activities to combat mental illness—that is, in treating persons afflicted with acute mental illness in community-based clinics and in treatment and care of persons disabled by severe or chronic mental illness in specialized mental hospitals. In contrast, the main interest of commission members who represented volunteer citizen groups was in so-called primary prevention—that is, in preserving and promoting mental health through such activities as active case-finding in communities and consultation by mental health experts to all potential community caretakers (school nurses, officers of police and the courts, ministers, social case workers, among others). Commission members representing other professional mental health interests were invested about equally in secondary and primary prevention activities. In the joint commission's final report, it was the expert opinions of the AMA and American Psychiatric Association professionals that shaped the recommendations: secondary and tertiary prevention goals were endorsed; primary prevention goals were not, on the grounds that too little was known of effective techniques in this area.

It is useful to pause here and remark about the grand consensus that, although its recommendations were subject to extensive interpretation, the validity of its enspiriting principle was never challenged. For a brief moment in our history, before the combative, often divisive tactics of political compromise commanded all attention, an independent, congressionally sanctioned group of knowledgeable and concerned Americans was heard to express its moral choice about the care and treatment of society's mentally ill.

CHAPTER THREE

Winning Federal Support for Community Mental Health (1961-1965)

The New President

The President's Interagency Committee on Mental Health
NIMH Proposes . . .
Rallying Support

The Politics of Legislative Compromise
Dynamics of the House Committee on
Interstate and Foreign Commerce
. . . The AMA Objects

Final Negotiations

Completion of JFK's "Unfinished Business"
The AMA Retreats
NIMH Wins the Prize

The problem is mental illness cannot be limited to any one jurisdiction of government. The mentally ill person who breaks down in Rhode Island, Nebraska or California, or here in Illinois, is not only a citizen of that particular state—he is a citizen of this entire country, and his loss is a loss to all of us. In these crucial times, our country can hardly afford the staggering losses of manpower exacted by mental illness.

John F. Fogarty
Address to National Governors' Conference on Mental Health
Chicago, 1961

CHAPTER THREE

Winning Federal Support for Community Mental Health (1961-1965)

The final report of the joint commission was good news to start off a new decade. 1960 was also a presidential election year. For the mental health alliance, the times could hardly have been more propitious to begin the next phase, the gratifying task of fashioning a national program from the commission's goals and recommendations.

The commission's proposal for a national mental health program envisioned two major lines of defense and attack against mental illness. Its boldest recommendation came in the area of secondary prevention: "If the development of more serious mental breakdowns is to be prevented . . . one fully staffed, full-time mental health clinic [should be] available [in their community] to each 50,000 of population" (Joint Commission 1961, p. xiv). (In 1960, that would have amounted to some 3,000 clinics.) These community mental health clinics could be operated as outpatient departments of general or mental hospitals, as part of state or regional government systems, or as independent agencies. Such clinics, the commission asserted, "are a main line of defense in reducing the need of many persons with major mental illness for prolonged or repeated hospitalizations" (Ibid.). What made this proposal so bold was its unstated assumption that the 1948-1961 pattern of a fifteen- to twenty-fold increase in the number of community mental health service providers could be sustained in the future and repeated on a national scale. With respect to the second attack line (tertiary prevention), the commission

41

recommended that state mental hospitals be reformed along the lines of the Veterans Administration (VA) and general hospitals (which were smaller and offered active treatment), and that they eventually include outpatient and aftercare as well as inpatient services. The reformed hospitals would progressively become chronic disease centers for long-term illnesses of all kinds (Ibid., p. xvii). (As noted earlier, the commission failed to endorse any primary prevention goals.)

On the critical issues of financing and staffing a national program of this dimension, the commission declared that federal, state and local governments' spending for public mental health services should be doubled in five years and tripled in ten; and that government loans, scholarships and tax relief should be granted immediately to encourage the pursuit of higher education by young people, particularly in the health professions. The commission therefore recommended that the states and the federal government "work toward a time when a share of the cost of [public] patient services will be borne by the federal government, over and above the present and future program of federal grants for research and training" (Ibid., p. xx). With these words the commission implicitly repudiated President Pierce's 1854 "hands-off" federal policy regarding financial responsibility for treatment and care of the mentally ill.

In recommending this fundamental departure in public policy, the commission advanced "certain principles" to be followed by "a federal program of matching grants to states for public mental health services" (Ibid., p. xxi). With respect to the proportion, timing and absolute size of the federal financial responsibility, "the federal government, on the one side, and state and local governments, on the other side, should share in the cost of services to the mentally ill. . . . the total federal share would be arrived at in series of graduated steps over a period of years, the share being determined each year on the basis of state funds spent in a previous year" (Ibid.). With respect to control of the awarding of federal grants, recipients should be selected "according to criteria of merit and incentive to be formulated by an expert advisory committee appointed by the National Institute of Mental Health" (Ibid.).

To Felix and the NIMH, the recommendations of the joint commission must have posed a bit of a predicament. By focusing on acute and chronic mental illness but eschewing recommendations on mental health promotion, Felix's senior constituency had overridden interests close to the hearts of the other professional and citizen groups. Moreover, Felix's bureaucratic superiors were doubtful about the commission's emphasis on reformation of state mental hospitals. Within weeks of the commission's final report, in top-level discussions at HEW, officials decided that a large-scale federal program directly supporting hospital care of mental patients would violate what they considered to be the intent of Congress in 1946—that is, not to fund care of state hospital patients (NIMH Task Force 1962). They also considered the proposal too expensive. On the other hand, the recommendation of mental health clinics in local communities was thought to be on the right track. The other professional and the citizen groups would support the development of such "clinics" if they offered comprehensive mental health services—including services for both the preservation and promotion of mental health and the treatment, care and rehabilitation of mentally ill persons. The NIMH was charged with the responsibility for designing a national program along these lines; to the extent possible, the institute was to utilize existing legislation and models of federal-state relations.

The institute staff found this direction compatible and set to work. In a series of internal documents, they developed the position that the proper goal for any publicly supported program of this nature should be the improvement of the mental health of the people in the country through a balanced continuum of services; emphasis on the rehabilitative aspects of mental illness, which was a primary theme of the commission's recommendations, was improper because it would unbalance the services continuum. On the question of financing, the institute endorsed the commission's principle that significant levels of new federal financing were needed.

But the institute's National Advisory Mental Health Council and its parent agency, NIH, were less sanguine about the federal government sharing in the cost of services to the mentally ill (NAMH Council 1961). A federal role in direct-care patient services involved a social policy change with broad ramifications. Such a change had to be decided upon by the political, not the health professional, leadership. Shannon, NIH director, declared that any program recommended as feasible by the NIMH staff would have to be consistent with current public policy (Shannon 1961). The mental health leadership must have accepted this decision with equanimity. If decision-making at the presidential level was the missing element, by the summer of 1960 they knew that they had not long to wait.

The New President

The joint commission's report, through the efforts of Mike Gorman, generated a significant political response from the Democratic party. Meeting in Los Angeles in July, the delegates made this a plank of their platform:

> Mental patients fill more than half the hospital beds in the country today. We will provide greatly increased Federal support for psychiatric research and training, and community mental health programs to help bring back thousands of our hospitalized mentally ill to full and useful lives in the community. [Democratic Party 1960]

John F. Kennedy, the party's nominee for president, would have the task of formulating a policy responsive to the plank. The leadership of NIMH thought themselves lucky in the choice of Kennedy. He seemed to be the right person in the right place (Interview 1972q.).

Once elected, however, Kennedy's task was complicated by the fact that his family, especially his sister Eunice Shriver, wanted federal investment in the care of the mentally retarded to be separate from a mental health program. Shortly after taking office in January 1961, the new president appointed a panel on mental retardation and asked the distinguished researchers to study the issues. During its deliberations many members of the panel argued against the participation of the psychiatric discipline in any program they might design because, in their view, mentally retarded persons had received second-rate service from the psychiatric profession in the past. Specifically, they did not want NIMH to administer any retardation program. Aware that the influence of some panel members implied budgetary cutbacks to NIMH, Felix helped to maneuver such programs into other parts of HEW, especially the National Institute for Child Health and Human Development, which was established under NIH in 1963 (Interview 1972 i.,e.).

When the panel on mental retardation was well underway, in the winter of 1961, the president asked his staff for an assessment of the panel's effort vis a vis the recommendations of the joint commission. This was evidence that the lobbying activities of the mental health interest groups had been successful. Mahoney, Lasker and Gorman had access to the president (Interview 1972k.); Kennedy had read *Action for Mental Health*. Guided by discussions with Meyer Feldman of the White House staff, the president decided that a cabinet-level interagency committee would formulate his response.

The President's Interagency Committee on Mental Health

With consummate political skill Kennedy and Feldman appointed a committee chaired by the secretary of HEW and including the secretary of labor and the administrator of veterans affairs. They requested two other executive branch agencies, the Bureau of the Budget and the Council of Economic Advisors, to assist in the work.

The president charged the committee to answer five questions about appropriate federal action:

• What should be the federal role in mental health and what responsibility should remain with the states, localities, and private groups?

• If broadened federal activity is warranted, through what channels should it be directed?

• What emphasis should be given to federal activity in mental health in relation to support for more general health programs?

• What rate of expansion in public programs for mental health services and research is consistent with the present and prospective supply of trained manpower?

• In the mental health field, should relatively greater encouragement be given to strengthening institutional services or noninstitutional programs, including means for bringing the cost of noninstitutional services within the financial means of a larger number of people? [Celebrezze et al. 1962, p. 1]

The chair of the committee was unofficially delegated to Boisfeuillet (Bo) Jones, a special assistant in the office of the assistant secretary for health and medical affairs in HEW (Interview 1972p.). Jones, in turn, included the NIMH leadership in committee deliberations, and asked the NIMH to develop specific proposals for consideration. Felix told his staff in the spring of 1962 that assisting the president's interagency committee was the most important job the institute faced (Felix 1962).

Boisfeuillet Jones was a medical administrator of renown. He had created and organized the medical center at Emory College, from where he was on leave from his post as vice-president and administrator of health affairs. In Eisenhower's second term, he had served on the National Advisory Health Council. A few months before his appointment as special assistant to the Kennedy HEW secretary, he

had chaired the consultant group that produced a report entitled
Federal Support of Medical Research, called the "Jones Report," for
the Senate appropriations committee. The other members of the task
force were Daniel P. Moynihan, representing the secretary of labor;
Robert Manley, the Veterans Administration; Robert Atwell, the
Bureau of the Budget; and Rashi Fein, the Council of Economic
Advisors. Invited by Jones to assist the committee were Felix and his
deputy, Dr. Stanley Yolles.

The membership of this committee may be divided into two types.
Felix, Yolles, Manley and Atwell were professional bureaucrats, while
Jones, Moynihan and Fein were political advisors. In his government
work in New York under Governor Averell Harriman, Moynihan had
witnessed the decline in admissions to state mental hospitals that
began in 1956; he thought there was a need for treatment programs in
the community (Interview 1972m.). Fein, an academic economist,
had written one of the joint commission's monographs, *The Economics of Mental Illness.* He had argued that society could not refuse
to spend on mental illness and health and that the proportion of the
gross national product that could be directed to the support of public
mental health services depended upon the will of the citizenry (Fein
1958).

A critical contribution to the committee was made by Robert
Atwell, who was budget examiner for NIH. The Bureau of the
Budget's mission was to coordinate the monetary requests of various
federal agencies and, after modifications by the president, present to
Congress a budget detailing proposed expenditures and sources of
income. The bureau was authorized to "revise, reduce, or increase"
requests. Staff of the bureau advised the president on matters of
administrative organization, supervised financial programs, con-
trolled rates of congressionally authorized expenditures, reviewed
agency programs and proposals before Congress for compatibility
with presidential policy, and prepared veto messages for financial
bills unacceptable to the president. Powerful in respect to agencies'
budgets, BOB staff were unusually knowledgeable about agencies'
programs. Atwell was no exception—he had read the joint commission's complete studies. In his judgment, those studies totally dis-
credited the system of state mental hospitals, while the commission's
report emphasized improved institutional services and gave scant
attention to noninstitutional services. Atwell agreed that the improvement of institutional services was extremely important, but he

was convinced that it was even more crucial to develop new noninstitutional services. A way would have to be found to make the cost of noninstitutional services affordable to a much larger proportion of the population than currently (Interview 1972a.).

In committee deliberations, Felix consistently represented the professional concerns of psychiatrists, while Yolles urged a comprehensive community mental health program. The NIMH career professionals were responsible for the technical aspects of this presidential political initiative. The committee relied on these professionals for information and advice on the clinical issues: what was professionally appropriate in the care of the mentally ill? (The committee did check NIMH views with independent experts, however; these others agreed that NIMH proposals were both desirable and, in terms of medical knowledge, feasible [Interview 1972m.].) Political and financial concerns were the provinces of other members. In politics, they were Jones and Moynihan; on budgetary matters, Atwell; and on financing, Fein. Felix appreciated that others could best judge what the nation would support.

An institute study group under Yolles' direction worked to develop a comprehensive program for committee consideration. Members of this group were almost all officers in the Public Health Service (indeed, there were more staff members holding Master of Public Health degrees in NIMH in 1959 than in any other division of the Public Health Service). Imbued with the public health philosophy, they believed in a balanced continuum of mental health care to patients in the community, care provided within the health care mainstream and (drawing on the British experience) available to the general population in specific geographic zones. Moreover, many of the study group, notably Dr. Bertram S. Brown and Dr. Allan Miller, had personal experience of a model demonstration community mental health program that had been operating since 1949 in Prince George's County, Maryland. Also, they were familiar with the research findings of the institute's Community Services Branch.

By 1960 the bits and pieces of the concept of the community mental health center were coming together. It was Yolles who developed the position that the mental health center was to be the major service delivery organization funded by the federal government. The financing would be in the form of permanent subsidies, not in the form of seed money. Thanks to the leadership of Gorman, Ewalt and Dr. George Tarjan (who served the Kennedy family in the White House), the National Advisory Mental Health Council collaborated with Yolles in the design of the community mental health centers proposal. The council considered that the community mental health centers program would become an essential component of the National Institute of Mental Health.

NIMH Proposes . . .

In mid-April 1962, the president's interagency committee considered the community mental health centers program drawn up by the NIMH study group. The institute had concluded, said Felix and Yolles, that the mentally ill could be better served through community mental health centers than through state mental institutions isolated from community life. There would always be patients who would need institutional care, but it was felt that populations of these institutions (at that time about 505,000 patients) could be drastically reduced in the next generation. The substitute for the state mental hospital was to be the *comprehensive* community mental health center (CMHC), including a general diagnostic and evaluation service, an acute inpatient service, outpatient services, day-care services, night-care services, emergency services, rehabilitation services, foster-home supervision, consultation, public information services and education services.

All of these services were to be administered by a single entity, an individual CMHC, which could be attached to the psychiatric ward of a general hospital, or be under the auspices of some other nonprofit community agency. These decisions would be the option of the local community, consistent with a state plan and subject only to the requirement that there be a continuum of services—that is, from the point of view of the recipient of the services, an integrated program fully accessible through any one of its many service points of entry. Each of these centers and their affiliated programs typically would be staffed full-time by some 100 psychiatrists, psychologists, social workers, nurses, therapists, counselors, and supporting staff and clerical workers. In addition, psychiatrists, psychologists and other professionals in private practice would offer part-time services to the center on a fee basis, in exchange for which they might be required to perform certain emergency functions for the center without compensation, in much the same way that the physicians in a community staff the emergency units of general hospitals on a rotating basis. The proportion of staff and private practitioners would vary according to the desires of the community and the management of the center (Yolles 1962).

In the ensuing discussion, Manley of the VA thought the proposal very good, the best thing so far, and hoped it would all come about. Atwell felt that the community mental health center concept was a good departure from the final joint commission report, and hoped for a funding pattern different from the state-oriented Hill-Burton formula. Fein was concerned as to how to maintain state financing. He also viewed the center concept as more beneficial for the patient and the nation's economy. Felix advocated federal and state matching of financing based on the Hill-Burton formula. The political appointees and Felix agreed that the states had to be involved. Hill-Burton financing was the appropriate mechanism. Felix suggested using guidelines and regulations to control program development. Atwell expressed the need for standards of some sort to evaluate the program as it developed. Moynihan was interested in the challenge of eliminating mental hospitals and developing new types of mental health personnel. There would never be enough psychiatrists. Blue-collar workers could not afford them. Felix agreed to Moynihan's points. Atwell was interested in coordinating their work with the concurrent effort of the mental retardation panel. He felt that the personnel question was the critical problem. Jones thought that the program envisioned totally new community health legislation. Jones, Moynihan and Fein accepted the idea that NIMH knew what program was needed. In their own minds, "the CMHC program was reasonable" (Interview 1972h.).

The public administration issue was whether to bypass the states completely or to give them assistance. Jones, Felix and Moynihan argued that it was politically and professionally inappropriate to bypass the states: politically inappropriate because such an action would run counter to current federal-state relations; professionally inappropriate because states would have to continue to support their institutional services until the proposed total number of CMHCs— 2,000, or 1 per 100,000 population—was reached. Atwell argued that the states should be bypassed because they were an obstruction. Fein argued that the states could ill afford to support the treatment and care of mental patients; he concluded that a permanent federal subsidy might be warranted.

The strategy of the mental health alliance was to de-monopolize the states' position in favor of shared-government support (federal, state, local) for mental health services. Their intention was to obtain a degree of control over the renewal and expansion of the system of public mental health care.

The president's committee agreed to a strategy. The comprehensive community mental health center approach was to be the cornerstone of the president's program. The committee would recommend a two-part proposal: a program of federal grants-in-aid to assist in the construction of comprehensive community mental health centers (with the goal of establishing 500 such centers by 1970); and decreasing, matching federal dollars to cover the centers' initial operating costs. The committee reasoned that, without the operating grants, states and local governments would not build the centers because: (1) they could not afford to run them; or (2) if they built them, they would not provide comprehensive services; or (3) in the operation of a comprehensive program, they would screen out "charity patients" into the state hospital; or (4) they would run the comprehensive program but only by robbing other sectors (for instance, education).

The committee would also recommend to the president:

• Additional grants to states for the planning of comprehensive community mental health programs;

• Federal support to raise the level of patient care in state mental hospitals through grants to states for (a) demonstrations of new and improved techniques of patient care, (b) upgrading of facilities (the hospital improvement program), and (c) inservice training for the staff of these institutions (hospital staff development program);

• Federal stimulation of and reinsurance for private sector insurance programs covering the costs of mental illness;

• Federal support for the training of the additional professional and paraprofessional personnel necessary for the proposed large-scale attack on mental illness; and

• Continued increase in federal support of research in mental health.

The committee proposed these actions in order to eliminate, within the next generation, the state mental hospital as it then existed (Celebrezze et al. 1962). Clearly not bound by the final report of the joint commission, the committee departed from it in this major respect: that there be an intensive effort to effect a radical rebalance, within a generation, of the nation's public system of care such that state mental institutions would be replaced by comprehensive community mental health centers. In this way, the president's interagency committee struck a professional and political compromise between a massive effort to upgrade the quality of care in the nation's system of state and county mental hospitals—and doing nothing for the hospitals by putting all new federal resources into the community mental health centers.

The committee's work raised certain issues that, while neither mitigating the need for the program nor seriously disputing its feasibility, required resolution by the president. Did the CMHC legislative proposal adequately address the issues involved in paying the costs of operating such centers? Secretary Anthony J. Celebrezze thought not. Was the proposal feasible in terms of the supply of personnel? Michael March of the Bureau of the Budget thought not. The president himself resolved these issues. With respect to operating costs, HEW professionals envisioned a diversity of state, local and private sources rapidly taking the place of temporary federal subsidies. To staff the facilities, they proposed that federal training outlays be more than tripled (Chapter Note 3-1).

The president disagreed with HEW Secretary Celebrezze's position that, from the beginning, the states should pay to operate their programs; the president instructed him directly to put provisions for initial operating costs into the proposed legislation. As for the other issue, in a White House meeting with March and his agency superior, Hirst Sutton, Feldman acted on the president's wishes by deciding in favor of raising the funds for the training of psychiatric professionals (Interview 1972h.,k.).

Rallying Support

The key political question was whether the country was ready to accept the extension of the federal government's role in providing services for the mentally ill. Most certainly, the approval of the states was essential. In November 1961, Felix, Blain of the American Psychiatric Association and Gorman served as consultants to the policy committee of the Governors' Conference on Mental Health meeting in Chicago. Attending on behalf of President Kennedy, Jones assured the governors that Kennedy and his administration were closely considering the joint commission's recommendation that the federal government pay part of the cost of care for the mentally ill. He told the governors that their deliberations would be extremely useful in helping the administration shape the legislative proposal under current discussion. Fogarty then gave the congressional mental health perspective. His speech reflected several themes that the mental health alliance was emphasizing during the period just prior to the introduction of the CMHC legislation:

- In drafting mental health legislation from 1946 to 1960, the Congress had carefully restricted the role of the federal government to a stimulative one, by emphasizing research, training and matching clinic grants to aid the states in developing additional ammunition for an all-out fight on mental illness.

- Testimony before congressional committees indicated that the recent trend of declining mental hospital populations resulted from the introduction of new drugs, the increased numbers of psychiatrically trained personnel in state hospitals, and the increased availability of new psychiatric facilities designed to serve patients in the community.

- The care of the mentally ill continued to place a heavy load upon the states. Fifty states were spending approximately $1.2 billion annually for the maintenance and treatment of patients in state institutions for the mentally ill and mentally retarded.

- The joint commission reported that only 20 percent of the mentally ill were housed in hospitals that provided active treatment rather than mere custodial care. Americans were spending too little on the treatment of the mentally ill in state mental hospitals; for four or five dollars a day there would be no therapeutic miracles.

"Most of all," Fogarty declared, "the Joint Commission report stated over and over again that to improve the care of the mentally ill, all levels of government—federal, state, and local—must join together in a united effort. In the years ahead, I want to see this problem of mental deficiency licked, and I don't care who...does it—the federal government, the state government, private research foundations. However, I have a strong suspicion that it is going to take all of these to do the job. ... The problem is mental illness cannot be limited to any one jurisdiction of government. The mentally ill person who breaks down in Rhode Island, Nebraska or California, or here in Illinois, is not only a citizen of that particular state—he is a citizen of this entire country, and his loss is a loss to all of us. In these crucial times, our country can hardly afford the staggering losses of manpower exacted by mental illness" (Fogarty 1961).

The governors were in accord with this view. Moreover, they asserted, a modern approach required new public investment in research, training, prevention and treatment, and this added investment should be borne not only by the states, but increasingly by local governments—where the problem must be met—and by the federal government, which must regard the conservation of productive life as fostering its greatest natural resource. The governors' policy statement, originally drafted in NIMH, called for federal, state and local financing of community mental health services. This line of states' policy was affirmed two months later, in January 1962, by state and territorial mental health authorities who were meeting in annual council with the surgeon general.

In addition to the states' concurrence, the mental health alliance needed at least neutrality from the AMA. Presidential interagency committee chairman Bo Jones was the perfect spokesperson to win over the AMA. In the fall of 1962 Jones met with the AMA's Council on Mental Health, which was challenging the committee's staffing grant proposal as government intrusion into the reimbursement pattern of physicians. In the finest traditions of political art, Jones used word-magic to disarm the opposition. To the charge of "socialized" medicine Jones answered that the choice of public or private operation of the centers was entirely for the local community to make. The proposed CMHC program, in a very real sense, was an entirely "desocialized" alternative to, and substitute for, the state mental hospitals. There would be less socialistic flavor in the CMHC program because of its pluralism and democratization. Further, a large number of the centers would be privately operated—albeit publicly subsidized and consequently under some degree of (enlightening) public control. Jones further argued that, because local communities would overtax themselves trying to finance the initial years' cost of centers operation, the federal government's assumption of this responsibility, including physicians' salaries, was both reasonable and proper (Interview 1972k.). Convinced, the AMA council accepted his position and voted unanimously to support the staffing grant provisions in any proposed legislation.

The mental health alliance chose Gorman, the spokesperson for the philanthropists and for reform-minded citizens, to be the coordinator for the legislative effort when it reached Capitol Hill. In several meetings during the spring of 1962, in the West Room of the White House, Gorman encouraged Feldman and the president to propose legislation to satisfy Senator Hill, who wanted action in response to the joint commission's report. He pointed out that, even as they were talking, Hill and Fogarty were appropriating additional funds to NIMH for allocation to the states, which were to use them to plan comprehensive state mental health services with emphasis on care in the community. Resisting this argument, Feldman reminded Gorman of the need to temporize. "We had to hold off," Gorman has said in retrospect, "because Jack Kennedy and Eunice Shriver, through Mike Feldman, said that there would be no presidential initiative until after the panel on mental retardation reported later in the year" (Interview 1972j.). That was as well for other areas of political mobilization, as it turned out. More time was needed for the concurrence of the National Advisory Mental Health Council, which was not yet fully agreed on the design of the CMHC legislation to be proposed.

The Politics of Legislative Compromise

In the fall of 1962 the panel on mental retardation made its recommendations, and the executive branch completed the design of the president's legislative package (Chapter Note 3-2). On December 11, mental health and mental retardation leaders met in the White House for the major discussion of both a special message to Congress and the bills. The White House staff was represented by Theodore Sorenson, Feldman, and Richard Donohue; the BOB by Daniel Bell, Philip S. Hughes, Hirst Sutton and Michael March. HEW was represented by Secretary Celebrezze, Wilbur Cohen, Rufus Miles, and Jones; the Public Health Service by Dr. Luther Terry. The Council of Economic Advisors was represented by Walter Heller and Rashi Fein. Cohen briefed Kennedy on the total legislative package in Florida on December 28 (Interview 1972f.); the proposals represented a major departure in the national approach to mental illness and would involve considerable input of federal resources in the years to come. Committed to paying the political cost of supporting these proposals in the Congress, the president was now ready to move. For Kennedy, the package had the appeal of raising minimum legislative difficulties in contrast to the controversial idea, then being discussed, of financing medical services under Social Security. Most of the retardation panel's recommendations could be put into effect without new legislation. The difficulties would arise over new federal authority for construction of mental health facilities and the cost of their operation.

Kennedy's January 1963 State of the Union message spoke of a new moral resolve about mental illness and retardation: "I believe that the abandonment of the mentally ill and the mentally retarded to the grim mercy of custodial institutions too often inflicts on them a needless cruelty which this Nation should not endure." He promised to unfold a new program in a special message to Congress. He did so in February, presenting the first presidential special message on mental health (Appendix A). In it, Kennedy emphasized that the new knowledge and new drugs developed in recent years made feasible a national mental health program to treat the mentally ill in their own communities and return them to a useful place in society. He alluded to the fact that the Joint Commission on Mental Illness and Health had documented the obsolescence of state mental hospitals. He recommended a national program of community mental health centers. Now it was up to the Congress.

But first it was up to congressional committees to legitimize the executive initiative. Congressional committees have a legendary power of life or death over an administration's legislative proposals. Commenting on the power of the committees before he himself was to have a president's experience with them, Woodrow Wilson had written:

> It is evident that there is one principle which runs through every stage of procedure, and which is never disallowed or abrogated—the principle that the Committees shall rule without let or hindrance. And this is a principle of extraordinary formative power. It is the mold of all legislation. [Wilson 1956, p.66]

In 1963, two committees were crucial in the molding of CMHC legislation: the House Interstate and Foreign Commerce Committee and the Senate Committee on Labor and Welfare. The dynamics of each committee's role system, against the backdrop of its relationship to the president in 1963, shed light on why each committee acted as it did to produce the final outcome.

Although President Kennedy exerted more effort than his immediate predecessor to establish rapport with committees, particularly their chairmen, his day-by-day congressional relations were difficult. In 1963 he was the executive over an HEW that was proposing a panoply of health bills. In addition to the mental retardation bill and the mental health bill, HEW's New Frontiers proposals included the health professions education bill; revision of hospitals and medical facilities; construction of group practice facilities; specific project grants for improving public health; protecting against environmental hazards; prevention and control of dental diseases; air pollution control; Public Health Service reorganization; health insurance; and maternal and child health care. To Wilbur Cohen and other HEW administrators, "1963 was our weak point; we did not have a hot, effective majority [in Congress]. Our thinking was, if Goldwater runs in 1964, that will be our year!" (Interview 1972f.). In short, in 1963 an innovative president faced a moderate Congress, a Congress especially wary of legislation that called for further federal involvement in the nation's health sector, a move generally opposed by the AMA.

On February 11, Senator Hill introduced the administration's CMHC proposal, which was referred to the Committee on Labor and Welfare of which he was chairman, and Representative Oren Harris (D-Ark) introduced an identical bill in the House, which was referred to the Committee on Interstate and Foreign Commerce of which he was chairman.

On the face of each bill was its purpose: "To provide for assistance in the construction and initial operation of community mental health centers." Both bills proposed that federal matching money would be provided for a period of five years for the construction of community mental health centers including, as a minimum, diagnostic services, inpatient care, outpatient care, and day care for mentally ill persons. Funds would be allotted among the states on the basis of population, the extent of need for community mental health centers, and the financial need of the respective states. The percentage of matching would be roughly similar to that in the Hill-Burton program, with 45 percent as the minimum federal contribution and 75 percent as the maximum. No mention was made of a goal of establishing 2,000 community mental health centers.

Both bills also provided for limited federal participation in the operating costs of the centers for approximately four years. For the first fifteen months of the center's operation, the federal grant could not exceed 75 percent of the staffing costs of the center; for the ensuing three years, the federal participation in such costs could not exceed 60 percent, 45 percent, and 30 percent, respectively.

In developing plans for these new services, the president's program called specifically for the participation of all agencies and organizations, both governmental and nongovernmental, which had an interest in mental health. It also stipulated that a state advisory council, made up of representatives of nongovernmental organizations and groups of state agencies, should provide consultation to the state agency developing a state plan.

The one factor certain to be raised in the Congress was the cost of this new legislation. No specific dollar figures had been included in the two bills, since the federal contribution would depend upon just how many states got into the program. For the fiscal year beginning July 1, 1963, the president proposed $190 million for NIMH, approximately $45 million above the level of expenditures for that year. Rough projections of the cost of the legislation indicated that by 1968 the NIMH budget would nearly triple to about $540 million.

In the Senate, although Gorman had sought to ally the mental retardation interests with those of the joint commission, the retardation groups declined, wanting any new appropriations to be directed primarily to mental retardation programs. Senator Hill did not agree with them, but was willing initially to consider the mental health and mental retardation proposals separately. Hill soon changed his tactics and consolidated the bills, however, deciding that the popularity of the mental retardation legislation could overshadow the potentially controversial staffing grant provisions of the centers legislation. Years later, Eunice Shriver described it as "of great interest at the time and now to have seen the passage of the CMHC Act dependent upon the mental retardation components. [The support] for the mental retardation legislation was much more extensive than that for the mental health legislation" (Shriver 1974). Hill moved quickly to forestall opposition from any quarter.

Hearings, held early in March, contained the following themes. For nearly twenty years medical leaders in government and the private sector had extensively reappraised the concepts of the care of the mentally ill and mentally retarded. Leaders in other professions had been contributing their knowledge and skills to these studies. The federal formula grant program for state development of comprehensive mental health services had been a beacon encouraging further exploration in those areas since 1946. The joint commission report pointed up the difficulties of state mental health programs, the acute shortage of personnel, the excessive costs of the current programs, and the need for federal action. Hill made no assertion that state and local governments had failed in programming or financing. Rather, the positive was accentuated: that significantly increased federal funds over a limited period would enable the states and local communities to transfer the organizational locus of caring for the mentally ill from state hospitals to local community mental health centers.

The strategy of the mental health alliance on the staffing grants was that the proposition was for temporary federal aid phased over the period of greatest financial impact, the initial four years. In the longer term, financing would become the responsibility of the CMHCs, and they would have state, local, and private support. Each community in America would thus be afforded the opportunity to undertake reasonably prompt comprehensive programs and yet to have a reasonable lead time to develop long-term, nonfederal, continuing sources of support. (When Senator Frank J. Lausche [D-Ohio] raised the possibility that CMHCs would be permanently subsidized by the federal government, Hill bypassed the question completely [Interview 1972b.].)

Hill solicited favorable testimony from the American Psychiatric Association and the Mental Health Council of the AMA, the Conference of Governors, the American Hospital Association, the National Association of State Mental Health Program Directors and the National Association for Mental Health. Hill told the president that the centers bill was acceptable to the Senate, but perhaps not to the House. He felt that the president should "jump in" or the program would be weakened (Notes 1963).

Dynamics of the House Committee on Interstate and Foreign Commerce

House committee chairman Oren Harris was considered one of the most powerful southern leaders. Gorman, not Felix, was the mental health alliance's liaison to Harris, because Gorman was better known to the committee members. Gorman's strategy was, in his own word, to "tangibilate." He would have the witnesses in committee hearings point, as tangible targets, to the archaic state hospitals offering ineffective, inhumane care costly to all the states. Coordinating the lobbying activity, Gorman advised the mental health lobbyists to: (a) know and stick to the facts of the situation with which they were dealing; (b) be courteous in all their discussions with members of Congress, whether the members happened to agree with them or not; (c) know the opposition and the kinds of arguments being advanced by the opposition.

Gorman stressed an agenda that would establish a good line of communication to the representatives, especially the members of the Committee on Interstate and Foreign Commerce. He urged that the interest groups use these tactics:

1. Relate the broad purpose of the legislation to the representative's constituents by providing specific information on the status of the delivery of community mental health services in the representative's district.

2. In the campaign, involve local doctors on whom Congress members relied for advice in health matters. (The lobbyists were to remind the doctors of two facts: the president's message stressed the role of the private physician in treating his own patients in the proposed community mental health centers; and the AMA supported multiple-source financing for community mental health services and accepted the need to expand this financing).

3. Representatives of the local mental health associations, civic organizations, and the medical society either should come to see their representatives in Washington or see them back in their districts.

4. If the bill became bottled up in the Interstate and Foreign Commerce Committee, they were to devote particular attention to the thirty-three members of that committee. If a good line of communication was established, their telegrams might help in turning the tide. Telegrams would be of little use if the representatives had not been educated previously on the issue.

5. If representatives said that they were for the program but that the budget deficit precluded this new expense, they were to respond with the economic argument development by Fein and adopted by the president: mental illness and mental retardation yearly cost the taxpayers $2.4 billion in direct public outlays, with indirect public outlays (welfare costs and the waste of human resources) running even higher (Gorman 1963).

Some years later, discussing a particular incident, Mike Gorman told an interviewer: "I can only say in all fairness that all of the testimony before the congressional committees, including my own, had little or no effect on the final decision made by the Senate to increase the NIMH training funds. The decision was reached after a number of meetings with key Senators which involved considerable lobbying, some hand-to-hand combat, and a delicate adjustment of the needs of NIMH to the competing needs of all the other institutes. None of this, I assure you, was performed in a public forum" (Felicetti 1975, p. 93).

The members of Representative Harris' committee and their staffs were aware that there were demonstrably positive results of patient care in the community, in contrast to warehousing of the patients in state mental hospitals. They knew that the joint commission and the president's message had alerted the electorate. They believed that mental health centers should be available to virtually everyone. They were familiar with the Hill-Burton type of funding for the construction of the centers. They were also well aware that, should they authorize the CMHC program, it would be fully funded by Fogarty in the appropriations process if past successes in funding NIH and NIMH were any guide.

The AMA position also seemed clear to them. Authorized by its board of trustees and house of delegates in the summer of 1962, the AMA concurred with President Kennedy's stress on comprehensive care of mental patients at the community level rather than in large, remote state institutions. The AMA "Statement of Principles on Mental Health" and comment on the president's legislative package supported matching grants to the states by the federal government for construction of community mental health facilities. Dr. Gerald D. Dorman, an AMA trustee, had recently approved publicly: "I am hopeful that this, the Kennedy Administration's mental health program, marks the beginning of a truly nonpartisan, nonpolitical attack on mental illness." Another point of agreement encompassed in the president's message, Dorman said, was the recommendation that services provided by the CMHCs should be financed through individual fees for service, individual and group insurance, other third-party payments, voluntary and private contributions, and state and local aid (AMA 1962). Dorman here was speaking of longer term financing; he made no mention of federal grants for initial staffing.

House subcommittee hearings were chaired by Representative Kenneth A. Roberts (D-Ala), with Harris participating. The mental health and mental retardation bills were considered together because Harris judged that combining their interests would help to neutralize a negative reaction on the staffing grant provisions. The burden of the substantive testimony on the president's CMHC program fell to Bo Jones, who made several critical points:

- Special legislation was required for construction and initial staffing of the centers because the necessary authorization for funds exclusively for services programming did not exist under the Public Health Service Act.
- The matching formula for the construction grants used the pattern of the Hill-Burton program, but at a higher level (45 to 75 percent versus 33⅓ to 66⅔ percent), to provide an additional stimulus to communities and states to develop the center facilities. This part of the program would be coordinated through the Federal Hospital Council, the statutory advisory council for the Hill-Burton program.
- Because participation by the federal government would decrease 75 to 60, to 45 to 30 percent in the four years following construction of the centers, the cost of operating a center would be met by the traditional financing patterns for the care of the physically ill in a community. The administration of the staffing grants would be in the Public Health Service.

Jones concluded:

> So what we are really advocating, Mr. Chairman, is, in a sense, removing the care of the mentally ill from complete, almost complete, responsibility of the state through tax funds and direct operations in these isolated large state mental institutions, and putting this care back in the community to be financed and supported and operated through the traditional patterns of medical care to which we have become accustomed in this country. This means providing for the mentally ill in precisely the same pattern that we care for the physically ill.
>
> But we think that some grant-in-aid support of the kind envisioned in this proposal will be important to encourage and stimulate communities to develop the comprehensive center that will make possible caring for the emotionally disturbed, the mentally ill, and to assist in preventing mental illness through training of ministers, of social workers, of teachers, of police officers, of juvenile court representation in the community in order that mental health will be promoted.
>
> That is the concept of the operating support for a limited period of years. [Hearings 1963, p. 97]

The history of NIMH and its programmatic accomplishments in research, training, and services were introduced into the record of the House hearings.

To Representative Ancher Nelson's (R-Minn) suggestion that it might be difficult to withdraw staffing support at the end of the proposed four-year period, Jones responded that the decreasing authorities during the four years were designed to prepare state and local communities for the full assumption of staffing costs at the end of the program. Representative Paul Rogers (D-Fla) supported the administration's argument by referring to the current shortage of medical personnel and questioning the wisdom of providing facilities without assuring sources of staff (Ibid., pp.99-107).

It fell to Wilbur Cohen to explain the mental retardation aspects of the bill and to keep the uneasy mental retardation-mental health coalition together. Cohen succeeded by delineating mental retardation and mental illness as separate health problems: mental retardation involved intellectual deficits frequently present at birth or in early childhood; mental illness included disturbances of personality and behavior often manifested in young and older adults after a period of relatively normal development. He argued that separating earmarked, or categorical, funds for mental retardation efforts from the mental health bill would not mean that there would be division in the community about federal funds, but that different groups interested in each of these problems in the local community would give full support and attention to their problem.

The mental retardation bill (H.R. 3689) would provide for establishment of ten regional research centers to investigate the problems of mental retardation and to train persons to work with the mentally retarded, and for construction of facilities for the mentally retarded. There were no staffing provisions in the bill. The description of HEW programs in the mental retardation field was inserted into the record (Ibid., pp. 107-46). In thus meeting the interests of the mental retardation advocates, Cohen helped to keep the coalition together.

The committee members heard Governor Frank G. Clement of Tennessee speak of the governors' support for the CMHC program; he produced written supportive statements of many of the governors, especially from the most populous states (Ibid., pp. 147-68). Dr. V. Terrel Davis, vice-president of the National Association of State Mental Program Directors, testified for his group that the CMHC program was in keeping with the trend to community services. (At their meeting in September 1963, the directors would agree that their main problem was inadequate funds and that the large state hospitals had to be improved to take care of the overcrowding, short-staffing and increasingly complex administration.) In response to the committee's questions on the current percentage of state budgets devoted to mental health and mental retardation, Davis produced tables of estimated per capita expenditures for a ten-year period. In effect, he documented the fiscal efforts of the states. Despite their expenditures, the states required federal financial assistance (Ibid, pp. 215-23).

Dr. Jack R. Ewalt, speaking on behalf of his colleagues on the joint commission and in the organizations they represented, told the subcommittee that he supported the CMHC program, describing it as well-planned and based on existing technology (Ibid., pp. 239-43). Ewalt's testimony was crucial, since it capped the political myth that the joint commission supported a bill directing major federal effort into the community rather than into the state mental hospital system. This was an excellent finesse by the mental health alliance, which also arranged for favorable testimony from the American Psychiatric Association, American Hospital Association, American Public Health Association, the AFL-CIO, pharmaceutical interests and others as well. However, this chorus of approbation arranged by the mental health alliance subsided when the AMA presented its testimony.

... The AMA Objects

A careful listener to the AMA testimony in March—an AMA seemingly in support of the bill—could detect potential disagreement between factions of the organization with respect to the staffing grant provisions. The AMA's board of trustees differed with its Council on Mental Health. The AMA board of trustees took this position:

> Whether the Federal Government should provide a part of the funds for staffing is a question we cannot resolve within the limited time we have had to consider the measure. One viewpoint holds that such Federal financial assistance during the early years will enable the community mental health center to undertake a properly staffed program from the start. Further, that within a short period of time, the influx of patients and the probable transfer of state funds from other institutional facilities will make continued Federal financing support unnecessary. And, finally, that many communities do not have the resources to pay the initial staffing costs needed to insure a successful program. This opinion is conditioned upon the four-year limitation placed on Federal participation.
>
> A second point of view maintains that the Federal participation under the bill should be limited to the construction costs of the community mental health center. It is urged that once a center has been constructed, the community should assume the remaining responsibility. This viewpoint reflects the feeling that once reliance is placed on Federal subsidy for staffing, the role of the Federal Government as provider of funds will not easily be terminated. [Hearings 1963, pp. 339-40]

The psychiatrists of the AMA's Council on Mental Health, on the other hand, had negotiated this single-minded plank in the AMA "Statement of Principles on Mental Health":

> In terms of tax dollars, responsibility for the support and development of community mental health programs must be shared by local, state and Federal agencies. In such programs, the apportionment of funds will vary depending on the wealth and industrial tax base of communities and states involved. [Ibid., p. 335]

Inclusion of a "second point of view" in the board of trustees' statement reflected the fact that, in March 1963, the AMA had not yet made up its mind. Indeed, three months later the AMA house of delegates publicly repudiated the actions of the Council on Mental Health by adopting a motion which disapproved of "the concept of Federal funds for staffing mental health institutions." The delegates also expressed "serious misgivings" about federal grants for bricks-and-mortar for mental health centers (Memorandum 1963). Thus, resoundingly, did the AMA rank-and-file support their leaders maneuvers to protect their monopoly in the medical marketplace, and to counter the "liberal drift" of the Council on Mental Health. The council had served as the AMA beachhead for the mental health alliance. The staffing grant controversy represented a fight by AMA conservatives against federal intervention in doctors' salaries at the state and local level. Part of the wider "socialized medicine" battle, the doctors were fighting for a principle and believed that, if they won, they would block "socialized medicine" for some time to come.

But on the same day as the action of the AMA delegates, Roberts' House subcommittee voted for the bill, including the initial staffing provisions. Representative Harris had indicated his support for initial staffing, a signal to Roberts that the full House committee would do so also. Coupled with Harris' support was the fact that Republican members of Roberts' subcommittee had voted for the bill—some, perhaps, because it was considered together with the noncontroversial, even popular mental retardation bill (Blue Sheet 1963).

This turn of events led the House Republican Policy Committee to enlist the AMA in a stand against the staffing provisions of President Kennedy's measure (Ibid.). The GOP and the AMA were philosophically in agreement on health measures. From a political point of view, the opposition president's standing with Congress was weak; GOP action could deprive him of total success on these domestic measures of special importance to him.

House committee chairman Harris, seeing that opposition to the measure had to be reckoned with, used a technicality to move the administration's bill back to Roberts' subcommittee. Late in June, responding to Roberts' request, Dr. F. J. L. Blasingame formally notified the subcommittee of the AMA's position, which was now unequivocal: "The American Medical Association supports the provision ... which pertains to the construction of facilities. The Association, however, is opposed to the Federal participation in the financing of the cost of initial staffing of community mental health centers" (AMA 1963). Ten days later, Roberts conducted special hearings on the staffing provisions, calling on the administration's top spokesmen to restate their intent. Accordingly, Bo Jones, Surgeon General Terry, and NIMH Director Felix attempted to assure the opposition that federal support for initial staffing was essential to stimulate local responsibility. Too little, too late, additional testimony from supporters was unavailing. Jones told Felix the staffing grants were doomed (Jones 1963). Worse, to insist on their inclusion would jeopardize the chances for passage of the entire mental retardation-mental health bill. This last effort concluded, Roberts' subcommittee promptly dispensed with the technicality and returned the measure to the full committee, where Harris took over its fate.

In Harris' House committee, opposition to the bill generally and the staffing provisions particularly was now a majority position. The committee voted to cut by 70 percent the Senate committee's authorization (from $847 million to $238 million), and entirely eliminated the mental health staffing grants. The GOP-AMA alliance had succeeded: twelve of the fifteen Democrats voted with Chairman Harris, but three voted with the twelve Republican members.

Thus it was that a much shrunken version of the administration bill was reported to the full House in mid-August. Harris realized that any other course would have risked a fight on the floor of the House and cost him, as committee chairman, a good deal of political capital. The White House was of the same mind with respect to the escalating political costs of congressional approval of the bill. Harris' committee had served as the negotiating ground between the mental health leadership and the AMA. As Representative Abner Sibal (R-Conn) put it, the committee had forged a compromise consisting in "the smallest common denominator possible" (Cong. Record 1963, p. 15803). The political decision was to accept half a loaf rather than risk losing all. Federal staffing support was an idea whose time might be near, but was not now.

Final Negotiations

Less willing to relinquish the field to the opposition, especially to organized medicine, three major lobby groups swung into high gear in this, the eleventh hour. The National Association for Mental Health and Gorman's National Committee Against Mental Illness joined the National Association of State Mental Health Program Directors to buoy support for a pro-staffing amendment should one be offered from the House floor. The groups organized a flood of mail to House representatives to give the impression of a rising tide of opinion favorable to mental health legislation. They urged the media to express concern about congressional irresolution and to summon the president to renewed leadership in support of his mental health program. Members of these groups sent telegrams to President Kennedy pressing him to give outspoken leadership and to Senator Lister Hill thanking him for his efforts (Ryan 1963).

Although these intensive lobbying activities failed to snatch victory from the GOP-AMA alliance, they did exact a heavy political toll from organized medicine. On September 10 the House met to debate the bill (formally, the Mental Retardation Facilities and Community Mental Health Centers Construction Act of 1963). Speaking for many, Representative George M. Rhodes (D-Penn) identified AMA politics as the key force blocking grants for staffing:

> The staffing provision has widespread national support and the endorsement of many local groups interested in this problem. . . . The overwhelming weight of professional opinion is [on record] in strong support of the initial staffing funds. . . .
>
>   A political decision later resulted in the AMA's opposition to this provision. This body should not fail to note that the competent professionals—the experts on mental health within the AMA—recommended otherwise. It is unfortunate that the majority of the committee . . . chose to follow the political views of the AMA leadership rather than the professional views of the AMA's own expert body in this field. [Cong. Record 1963, p. 15801]

Many others agreed with Rhodes' making this point a part of the record and thus exposing the AMA to the warranted opprobrium of public health proponents. Such remarks would occur frequently in the next few years in relation to this bill and to other health measures. Powerful as it was, organized medicine could withstand such pressure only so long before it would be obliged to capitulate and compromise with the liberal forces of the future Great Society agenda lying just over the horizon. In retrospect, the GOP-AMA alliance won a Pyrrhic victory when it succeeded in eliminating the staffing provisions from President Kennedy's mental health bill.

During the House debate itself, chairman Harris sounded the federalism theme when he made the point that the majority of his committee had deleted the controversial staffing provision because the committee did not wish to set a new federal precedent (Ibid., p.15788). Although it seemed obvious to all that the need for services at the local level far outweighed the ability of local communities to pay for them, Representative William L. Springer (R-Ill), ranking minority member, echoed President Pierce's argument: it would be impossible for Congress to deny staffing in other programs if the members approved staffing in this bill (Ibid., p.15794).

The House approved the committee's much shrunken version of the president's bill (yeas, 335; nays, 18; not voting, 80), and the bill then went to a House-Senate conference committee for the purpose of reconciling the differences between the two chambers.

The mental health lobby kept up the pressure. Nine House members of the conference committee received telegrams from thirty physicians in twenty states favoring temporary operational support of the centers (NASMHPD 1963a). Members of the National Association of State Mental Health Program Directors were advised by their leadership to notify the House-Senate conferees that the states wanted the initial staffing provision (Davis 1963). New support for staffing came from an unexpected quarter. The Mental Hospital Institute, representing more than 500 direct-care, administrative and other mental hospital personnel, urged the House-Senate conferees to restore some of the provisions for temporary federal operating assistance. The lobbying activity continued at a pitch but to no avail, as events inside the conference indicated.

In the conference on October 1, all of the House Democratic members, led by Harris, said "no staffing" for mental health centers. This was a surprise; the administration thought there might yet be a compromise along lines suggested by Wilbur Cohen (Cohen 1963), and the Senate Republican members (particularly Senator Jacob Javits of New York) wanted a compromise (Warren 1963). The conference deadlocked; another meeting was scheduled a week hence. But there was to be no compromise. As Republican Representative J. Arthur Younger, M.D. (Calif) wrote a constituent on October 4, 1963:

> We will not agree to the staffing provision and if they were to put that
> back in the conference report, the entire bill would be defeated in the
> House. We feel it is far more important to get the construction pro-
> grams underway rather than being concerned with the staffing of the
> clinics at the present time. [Younger 1963]

Indeed, as the administration was well aware, an Arkansas physician—a long-time personal friend and political supporter of
Harris—was behind Harris' position, as other politically conservative physicians were similarly behind the Democrats on the Harris
committee who had voted with the Republicans to defeat the staffing
provision. Dr. Stafford L. Warren, special assistant to the president for
mental retardation, suggested a last negotiating position to the president (Chapter Note 3-3); but Bo Jones advised that the president
should not ask a friend (Harris) that which a friend felt he could not
do (Interview 1972k.).

On October 17 the conferees held the decisive meeting. The
National Association for Mental Health had advised the two conference chairmen that 247 congressmen would support a bill with
staffing (NASMHPD 1963b). But House leaders preferred their own
unofficial polling. They knew that, however recently their colleagues
may agree with constituents, complex last-minute changes in a bill
always require a representative to exercise judgment, including
"changing position." Chairman Harris certainly felt that way, since he
repudiated the NAMH poll in later testimony to the full House (Cong.
Record 1963, p.18968). Virtually all conferees acknowledged the
necessity of initial staffing money for the states, but the majority from
the House side feared to risk the entire bill for the sake of the staffing
provision. Consequently, the Senate-House conferees approved the
measure without initial staffing provisions, and compromised on the
total cost for the approved programs by authorizing $91 million more
than the House-passed bill and $521 million less than the Senate-
passed bill. The final total authorized was $329 million: $179 million
for the retardation programs and $150 million for the construction of
community mental health centers.

When on October 21 Hill submitted to the Senate the report of the
Conference Committee, he stated that it was the intent of the conferees that, in addition to this bill, the Public Health Service use
existing authorities and resources for the establishment and temporary operation of the centers. The Senate agreed to the report (Ibid.,
p.18851). On the same day, Harris reported to the House that the

House conferees had held the line on staffing. Nonetheless, he went on, the conferees had accepted a new concept in dealing with the mentally ill in this country, never before put into operation on a national scale.

> [W]e will have an opportunity to watch this program develop. And if it does appear it cannot get off the ground without additional psychiatrists, psychologists, and nurses trained in this field, I hope to offer a bill later on to accomplish these purposes . . . .
>
> Although since the beginning of the attack on . . . mental illness [it] has been subject to state socialized medicine, this conference bill will utilize and encourage private medicine to make its contribution. [Ibid., p.18969]

The question was taken. The conference bill passed—yeas, 296; nays, 4; not voting, 123.

President Kennedy signed the bill into law—Public Law 88-164—on October 31, 1963 (Appendix B). The mental health leadership had won a great battle. The construction of facilities must necessitate staffing in the near future. Doubtless their opponents in organized medicine knew it too. The mental health alliance had taken the king with a pawn.

Completion of JFK's "Unfinished Business"

The last months of 1963 were heavy with triumph and tragedy. The cause of vastly improved care for the mentally ill in America had become law, and John Kennedy, the president whose moral tenacity this achievement was, had been assassinated in Dallas, Texas. The succeeding president, Lyndon B. Johnson, quickly established that he intended to clean up the essential unfinished domestic business begun by Kennedy. He informed HEW of his intention to take care of the most pressing issues. This was the time, too, when Robert Felix retired as director of the National Institute of Mental Health. Stanley Yolles became director, and he put Bertram Brown in charge of CMHC program administration. Psychiatry's star declined with Felix's departure and the ascendancy of Yolles. In the years ahead the institute's propensity for public health principles was to be less often tempered by medical-model perspectives.

During the presidential election campaign of 1964, President Johnson declared: "We must step up the fight on mental health and mental retardation. I intend to ask for increased funds for research centers, for special teacher training, and for helping coordinate state and local programs" (Johnson 1965a, p.564). Yolles directed the NIMH staff to begin developing the legislative proposal.

Earlier, in a position paper prepared for Yolles' deputy, Dr. Philip Sirotkin, Robert Atwell had assessed the political consequences for the mental health program of having Johnson as president (Atwell 1964). (Atwell had left the Bureau of the Budget, joined the institute, and became the first deputy to Brown.) Atwell recommended that NIMH and the mental health alliance generally act *immediately* to obtain the authority to support the operation of community mental health programs.

Atwell argued that the time for a new initiative for mental health staffing was the fall of 1964, because the next January would see a newly elected president and a new Congress. He predicted that President Johnson would be elected by a substantial majority in November and that the new Congress would be politically more liberal. He also noted that there were other changes in the "congressional complexion," such as weakened ties between Oren Harris, chairman of the House Committee on Interstate and Foreign Commerce, and the American Medical Association.

Atwell went on to speculate that President Johnson would be more aggressive in seeking passage of his legislative programs than was President Kennedy, that Johnson was eager to put his own stamp on those programs. He added another prediction: "The projected decline in defense expenditures together with the probable increase in tax revenues because of economic growth (at least on a cyclical basis) point to some opportunities for increases in social welfare program support" (Atwell 1964, p.2).

Atwell mentioned that HEW Assistant Secretary Wilbur Cohen had raised the subject of mental health staffing subsidies as an item for consideration by Johnson's Task Force on Health Services. Prior to outlining steps to implement the recommendation, Atwell argued that immediate legislative initiative would result in progress in the centers program and counteract efforts to dismember NIMH during the initial post-Felix period.

He suggested that the implementation of the president's legislative program follow some of the basic lines of the strategy of 1962-63: inclusion of the proposal in President Johnson's Task Force on Health Services; inclusion of the proposal in the Democratic party platform (a suggestion which was not acted on); presentation of the proposal to key White House officials and to the Bureau of the

Budget; utilization of mental retardation forces; support of key congressional leaders; mobilization of key professional agencies and individuals; and supporting staff work. He identified the key persons to be contacted. Just as the early planning and proposals in child health and mental retardation had been formulated during the campaign and preinaugural period of the Kennedy administration, Atwell wanted the staffing proposal developed during the Johnson campaign. Atwell argued: "We have everything to gain and nothing to lose through immediate action" (Ibid., p.6). Philip Sirotkin agreed (Interview 1972o.).

Sirotkin discussed the strategy with Yolles, who at first resisted. Gorman had persuaded Yolles that he should not request additional substantive legislation until centers had been constructed. In Gorman's view, NIMH had yet to "tangibilate" the centers, "get the buildings up." Gorman felt that the defeat on the staffing provisions was too recent (Interview 1972j.). Yolles came around to the Atwell-Sirotkin position, however, and ran a bureaucratic end run around his chief, the surgeon general (Interview 1972q.). He reached an understanding with Wilbur Cohen that, when the time was ripe, the administration would introduce the staffing legislation (Interview 1972f.).

NIMH's legislative package proposed wider discretionary power for the institute than that originally proposed in the rejected versions of the 1963 bill. For one thing, NIMH suggested that legislation not be limited to initial staffing or to the support of projects for which the federal government provided construction assistance under the Hill-Burton formula. For another, Yolles, Sirotkin and Atwell backed the concept of bypassing the states by developing control of program approval to the level of local communities. Atwell wanted priority eventually given to programs for the poor. Sirotkin favored this approach, while Yolles wanted a universal approach, covering any income group. The supporting documents included a state-by-state analysis of the status of the centers program and of the inability within existing PHS authority to meet the objectives of the 1963 law. NIMH staff had also developed projections on increased insurance coverage in order to answer the question of how the local communities would be able to finance fully the centers program as the federal funds decreased, then ceased. That the United Auto Workers' contract and the federal employees health benefits program included mental health insurance programs, and that the proposed Medicare program might cover mental health benefits for senior citizens, suggested that other industry, labor, professional and insurance groups would expand their mental health benefits. Yet it was only an outside chance that insurance coverage would grow fast enough to cover the operating costs of the centers. Therefore, the concept of multiple sources of funding—initial federal funds, followed by state, local and insurance monies—was a reasonable political strategem.

Nevertheless, Yolles, Sirotkin, Atwell and other NIMH staff anticipated a future progression to greater federal investment on the local level. As Sirotkin recalled, "We weren't kidding ourselves about this. At the end of eight years, we'd renew" (Interview 1972o.). Yolles and his staff did not broadcast that view within the American Psychiatric Association because the psychiatric profession was divided on whether the federal government should assume a permanent role. Nor did Yolles and his staff share their view with Wilbur Cohen. Cohen's approach was to use decreasing funding, that is, the gradual decrease of the proportion contributed by the federal government. Nevertheless, if continued federal funding was needed in the future, he was likely to support an extension of federal assistance. "I only accepted the declining proportion because it was the only way to get Secretary Celebrezze's approval without extensive internal discussion and delay." Cohen calculated that a decreasing staffing grant approach would give "us more flexibility on how much to fund the program and how it would grow" (Cohen 1975). Both the NIMH strategists and Cohen doubted that Representative Fogarty or Senator Hill feared indefinite federal financing.

In November, President Johnson's historic electoral victory—the largest plurality in the history of the country, nearly 16 million voters, or 61.1 percent of the electorate—swept in a Democratic Congress. Before the expected attrition of public support set in, the president proposed to use the victory for his Great Society health and education bills. Johnson's early approach to Congress coincided with the mental health alliance's strategy. Medicare offered the opportunity to distract the AMA from other medical bills, such as the staffing grant proposal. Moreover, the president proposed only the legislation that had been garnering public support for so long that most members of Congress would vote for it or risk losing in the next election. Johnson's strategy also called for sending bills to Congress when the committee slates were clear enough to permit the legislation to move swiftly through the legislative process, a tactic that foreclosed a buildup of opposition and also took advantage of the enthusiasm of supporters when it was ripest.

Early in December, a new lineup of mental health leadership met to discuss the proposed legislation. The groups represented were the familiar ones—the American Psychiatric Association, NIMH and National Association for Mental Health—and more recent allies, the National Association of State Mental Health Program Directors and the American Psychological Association. Mike Gorman was also present. This group, along with the AFL-CIO, would coordinate their lobbying activities. Some of the old guard were retired; Felix, Ewalt, Braceland and Blain were supportive but no longer dominant. Instead, Yolles, Sirotkin, Atwell and Bert Brown, public-health-minded and less deferential to the states, were now in charge at NIMH.

The legislation proposed by NIMH would not leave the states empty-handed in terms of money but it would diminish even further their control over public mental health care, even as it offered sweeteners to the states and territorial mental health authorities. Not that the state interest group which was once Felix's junior constituency needed to be persuaded on staffing grants. The state mental health program directors, especially those from states with community mental health legislation of their own, viewed the grants as advantageous and supplemental to their states' efforts. County directors, especially in California, desired this new source of financing. At the annual National Advisory Mental Health Council meeting in January 1965, Yolles and Sirotkin also emphasized to them the proposed increase in the Hospital Improvement Program (HIP) and Hospital Improvement of Staffing Program (HIS) budgets.

Moving quickly, the citizen organizations mounted an effective, grassroots letter-writing campaign. Mrs. Winthrop Rockefeller, serving as president of the National Association for Mental Health, mobilized forces in Arkansas close to Representative Harris. Dr. Harold Visotsky, state mental health director of Illinois, was able to reach Representative William Springer. Dr. Walter Barton of the American Psychiatric Association negotiated with the leadership of the AMA: if the AMA would mute their opposition to the staffing grants, the American Psychiatric Association would offer its support as a medical specialty to the AMA at a time when the complexion of AMA organizational membership was shifting from general practitioners to specialists (Interview 1972c.). Wilbur Cohen briefed President Johnson on every aspect of the proposed legislation. Gorman met with the congressional leaders. Atwell's immediate-action strategy paid off: the administration and the key congressional leaders would sponsor a staffing bill.

On January 7, 1965, President Johnson delivered his health message to Congress in which a section entitled "Improved Community Mental Health Services" stated:

> Few communities have the funds to support adequate programs, particularly during the first years.
>
> Communities with the greatest needs are hesitant to build centers without being able to identify the sources of operating funds.
>
> Most of the people in need are children, the aged, or patients with low income.
>
> I, therefore, recommend legislation to authorize a five-year program of grants for the initial-cost personnel to man community mental health centers which offer comprehensive services. [Johnson 1965b]

The theme of compassion—for the children, the aged, the poor— echoed Kennedy's special message, and the service program was of mental health alliance design. Choosing the right moment for proposing it came of President Johnson's political acumen.

On January 19, Representative Oren Harris introduced a bill "to authorize assistance in meeting the initial cost of professional and technical personnel for comprehensive community mental health centers." Senator Lister Hill introduced the same bill in the Senate. James Menger, a member of Harris' committee staff, and Robert Barclay, one of Hill's staff members, were critical expediters of the bills and links to Yolles and Sirotkin (Interview 1972o.). Both Menger and Barclay felt, at that point, that the president could obtain anything he wanted from the Congress (Interview 1972l.,b.).

The AMA Retreats

In February, the American Psychiatric Association gathered 500 experts from various fields to discuss future plans for the new CMHC program. Participants were representative of more than 30,000 citizens in communities throughout the nation who had become involved in the planning process after the 1963 enactment as well as state mental health authorities, state NAMH chapters and state medical societies. Also present: the presidents of both the American Psychiatric Association and the AMA, the secretary of HEW, the vice-president of the National Council of Churches, the president of the American Nurses Association, the governor of Illinois and United

Auto Workers president Walter Reuther. Following exhortations by Mrs. Rockefeller, Wilber Cohen, Mike Gorman and Robert Felix, Dr. Donovan F. Ward, AMA president, rose to defend the organization's stand on the staffing issue; this time, a small but crucial opening appeared:

> The AMA is firmly committed to the proposition that the local community is most responsive to the health needs of its citizens and that it should assume the basic responsibility for their needs. The next level is that of state government and *if its resources prove inadequate then there is the Federal Government.* [Ward 1965, emphasis added]

At the closing banquet, Harris, Fogarty and Hill were seated at the head table. Harris challenged the audience: "I hope we can get this bill passed but I want you to know that it is highly controversial and you'd better get busy and muster all the support you can find for it in every nook and cranny of this land" (Harris 1965). Hill rose to pin the 1963 defeat of the staffing provisions on the vigorous opposition of the AMA. But, he went on, "I say to you, our defeat was only a temporary one. This time we will not be denied" (Hill 1965). By acclamation the conference participants resolved that actions be taken "so as to make possible the achievement of our common national goal of adequate community mental health services for all citizens" (Hearings 1965, p. 205).

Representative Harris conducted hearings on the bill before the full committee early in March. HEW Secretary Celebrezze delegated Yolles to handle the testimony on the staffing provisions. Yolles addressed himself to the issues of the need for staffing, its temporary quality, its form, and NIMH's practical concern about state mental hospitals. His testimony revealed that no center facilities were under construction in March of 1965 because money had only become available in November 1964 and the state plans, mandatory by law, had not come in as yet. No application could be approved until a state plan was approved. Certain communities would not submit plans until they were assured of operating costs. Indeed, it had become clear a few months earlier, during the NIMH-sponsored Appalachia Conference, that the bricks-and-mortar nature of the program gave it relatively low priority in the "have-not" states, which desperately needed the services themselves before new buildings.

On the mechanism of the staffing provisions, Yolles testified that the proposed staffing grants be on the project-grant basis (not on the formula basis) so "that their funds can be administered flexibly, at least in the beginning of the program, and so that those communities that are ready to move forward and extend their services, and also those communities that are in most need, can be assisted" (Ibid., p.52). Project grants, in contradistinction to the formula-grant mechanism, placed administrative authority at the federal rather than the state level. Yolles emphasized the state hospital facility and staff improvement programs to demonstrate NIMH's concern with the patients then in the state mental hospitals. He mentioned that the increasing size of the mental health manpower pool, fed by NIMH funds, would forestall any shift of scarce manpower from state mental hospitals to community programs.

When Yolles had finished, Gorman's drumroll of witnesses started. Lisbeth Bamberger, assistant director of the AFL-CIO Social Security Department, voiced labor's support. Governors John Volpe (Mass), Otto Kerner (Ill) and John N. Dempsey (Conn) stated the governors' desire for the staffing funds. Dr. Isadore Tuerk, commissioner of Maryland's Department of Mental Hygiene, testified for the National Association of State Mental Health Program Directors and provided specific data on the clinical appropriateness and cost savings of the community mental health center. He added a remark about the state role:

> It is our hope that Federal assistance in staffing community mental health centers will stimulate the eventual operation of most centers not by the states, but by local, private, non-profit organizations. The local organizations today cannot afford to initiate and staff a mental health center. The state is—we hope—a temporary intermediary. [Tuerk 1965, p.2]

He stressed the need to attract graduates of professional training programs into the community mental health centers by providing competitive salary levels initially subsidized by the federal government. "Money which communities can gradually supplant once their centers have been catapulted into existence with a heavy transfusion of Federal money" (Ibid., p.6).

Robert Felix testified on behalf of the National Association for Mental Health: "We need the staff before we can operate—and we must begin operating before we can have the funds to finance the necessary staff to make operation possible." Warmly, being among friends, he remarked:

I might say I feel somewhat like Moses in the last chapter of the book of Deuteronomy when Moses went up on Mount Nebo, and was told to look over the land of Canaan, but the Lord said, "You shall not go over thither." I got closer, but I didn't go there; first we didn't get the staffing provision and then I had to retire. [Hearings 1965, p.245]

For its part, the AMA was preoccupied in the Medicare battle, labeling it "socialized medicine." The organization could not reasonably use the label, nor mobilize its constituency, on every health issue before the Congress. In 1965 Medicare, not staffing, was the AMA's key issue. When called upon to testify before the Harris committee, Dr. James Z. Appel, president-elect of AMA, held firm: "There does not appear to be any justification for Federal participation in financing this type of expense, nor is it likely to phase out as stated in the bill, once the Federal Government has assumed this responsibility" (Ibid., p.225). But when his associate, Dr. Robert C. Long, a member of the board of trustees, attempted to reinforce the AMA position, the committee members trapped him. Representative Farnsley, trained in political science, described the lack of funds in poor local communities, in poor states, and in poor counties, plus the lack of sufficient tax bases. Representative Tim Lee Carter, a physician himself and from Appalachia in Kentucky, strongly supported Farnsley.

> *Dr. Long.* Mr. Chairman, I am sorry to be so slow . . . Mr. Farnsley, it finally came through my thick head what you are talking about. It is obvious under the terms of your question, where there is a need, if it cannot be met in one manner, it must be met in another manner. And if it cannot be met on the local level or the county or state level, then obviously, if the need can be met on the Federal level, it must be met on the Federal level. Does that answer it?
>
> *Mr. Farnsley.* That answers it beautifully. [Ibid., pp. 227-28]

The AMA had indeed retreated; the passage of staffing provisions for CMHCs was now assured.

NIMH Wins the Prize

Following the hearings, Yolles and Sirotkin worked closely with the committee staff considering the testimony of the hearings and deciding on the final language of the bill, which was reported out unanimously on April 15, 1965. On May 4, by a vote of 390 to 0, the House passed the measure (H.R. 2985) authorizing federal funds to assist in the initial staffing of community mental health centers.

In the Senate some five weeks later, Hill called his committee into executive session with Yolles in attendance. The Hill committee subsequently reported out the House bill unanimously on June 24, its report generally repeating the House report almost verbatim (Chapter Note 3-4). On June 28, the Senate passed H.R. 2985, "Initial Staffing for Mental Health Centers," on a voice vote without debate. On July 15, the House chafed at the price of the half-billion-dollar, Senate-passed version of the bill and requested a conference, wherein the conferees agreed to an authorization of $224,174,000 for initial staffing over a seven-year period (through 1972).

The Senate approved the conference report on a voice vote on July 26. In the House, Representative William Springer—who had been a key participant in the GOP-AMA victory less than two years before—now spoke in support of the conference bill:

> [In 1963] it was suggested that the Federal Government assist in the initial staffing of these facilities. This was not done at that time. Now that the program is underway and the very real problems begin to emerge, *it becomes clear that in the case of community mental health centers, some staffing assistance is justified and necessary.* [Cong. Record 1965, p.18430; emphasis added]

Springer called for a roll call vote on July 27, and the House adopted the conference report by a record unanimous vote—414 yeas, 0 nays, and 19 not voting.

On August 4, President Johnson signed the Community Mental Health Centers Act Amendments of 1965 into law, remarking upon the contribution of Secretary Celebrezze and the legislative leadership of such "skilled craftsmen in the Congress" as Lister Hill, Oren Harris, and John Fogarty (Johnson 1966). The biblical references of Robert Felix had been apposite. During the span of his career in the Public Health Service, a national community mental health service system had been fashioned into public policy from his "more a dream than a thesis." A man of Felix's wisdom and maturity might well experience a seemly humility with respect to the long history of madness and government. Yet during Felix's lifetime, a kind of miracle was wrought by the American system of representative democracy. Thanks to the revolutions in communication and transportation technologies, a few dozen like-minded people became hundreds, then hundreds of thousands, then millions. In the end it took millions of citizens and their chief executive, the president, to make a new public policy. In so doing Americans' twentieth-century way of thinking about care of their mentally ill replaced the institutional arrangements of an earlier century with new ones featuring modern technologies of health care and service delivery systems.

Indeed, the cup of NIMH ranneth over: the 1965 amendment not only endowed the CMHC program with adequate, albeit short-range, funding, but the amended Kennedy-Johnson law authorized considerable regulatory and rule-making discretion to NIMH. The institute staff, led by the extremely knowledgeable and experienced Yolles and Brown, were well-prepared to write the regulations that would specify what would qualify for federal funds and then to carry out the program.

Notwithstanding these bright prospects, the basic legislation was to be amended seven times during its first ten years. In effect, the program was to become a victim of creeping conditionalism, whereby special interests effectively induced Congress through its laws and the bureaucracy through its regulations to add annually to the burden of an already too broadly mandated federal program freighted and entangled with too many requirements. The numerous changes of fortune encountered by the program during the period 1966-1976, and their consequences, are recounted in the next chapter.

CHAPTER FOUR

Implementation and Transformation of the Community Mental Health Center Program (1966-1976)

Original Nature of a Community Mental Health Center

Irresistible Forces of Transformation
Changes in Leadership and Constituencies
The Phenomena of "Deinstitutionalization"

Fiscal and Clinical Realities

The Role of Community Mental Health Centers
in the Revolution of Care

*We have come to the end of an era. . . . For over 100 years we have
been guided in our efforts by the utopian vision of the "good"
mental institution. . . . [That] illusion is being abandoned . . . and the
majority of mentally ill patients are now being treated as outpatients. . . .
The mental health system has experienced a major shift from almost total
reliance on a system of involuntary incarceration and treatment in
public institutions to a voluntaristic and pluralistic system.*

Gerald L. Klerman, M.D.
1977

Implementation and Transformation of the Community Mental Health Center Program (1966-1976)

Implementation of the community mental health centers legislation was NIMH's foremost mandate after 1963. The institute staff wrote the regulations governing the administration of the basic 1963 Act and its 1965 staffing amendments. They drew on data generated in several community mental health facilities within and outside the United States. The NIMH staff and others traveled throughout the country and abroad to study these facilities. Dr. A. Querido from Holland and Maxwell Jones from Great Britain came to America and spoke of their experiences with emergency care and therapeutic communities. The Milbank Memorial Fund sent superintendents of state hospitals to Great Britain to observe their open mental hospitals. NIMH staff were informed about the community programs in Canada and Colorado; they had also been involved since 1949 with an experimental mental health program in Prince George's County, Maryland. The writers attempted to capture the wisdom of experience in their specifications of what could qualify for federal financial assistance.

The regulation writers also strived to encode the intent of Congress, which in turn had been informed and motivated by the report of the joint commission, then shaped into public policy decisions by the Kennedy legislative initiative which the report evoked. By the time all the political compromises and technical trade-offs were concluded, the recommendations of the joint commission had been molded into a program to develop 2,000 community mental health centers throughout the United States.

A few idealists envisioned that 2,000 monopolistic mental health service centers would come to be established and be responsible to the public as a new type of public utility. This vision was improbable, however, because Congress did not intend that the 2,000 be monopolistic, and because the notion ignored the cultural reality that Americans do not view their health care systems as public utilities. A more practical long-range goal sought by a great many institute staff was to move the treatment of the mentally ill fully into the mainstream of medicine, to build a one-class system of care with guaranteed continuity of care. This represented the break with tradition, the bold new approach consistent with the intent of Presidents Kennedy and Johnson and the Congresses.

Original Nature of a Community Mental Health Center

The regulations defined a CMHC in terms of demographics, organization and, most relevant here, services (Chapter Note 4-1). A CMHC was defined as five essential mental health services. Inpatient, emergency, partial hospitalization (for example, day care), and out-patient services were designed to provide for acute care in the community and thus to reduce the number of those who would otherwise have been admitted to state and county hospitals. The fifth essential service was designed to provide education and consultation for the information of other community agencies and individuals (for example, general practioners, officers of the court, members of the clergy, school teachers). It was intended to reduce the number of those at risk of mental illness and to increase community awareness of sound mental health practices. In addition, the CMHC regulations mandated linkages of information, personnel and patients among the essential services; these linkages incorporated the public health requirement of a *continuum of care*. Several other services were recommended but not mandated. These included pre-admission and post-discharge services for state hospital patients and specialized diagnostic services; also research, evaluation and training. Taken together, the essential and recommended services constituted a proper *services' balance* for a public mental health program.

It is necessary to point out, however, that the regulations mandated—not all of the services noted above—but only the five essential services. The CMHC program itself, as designed by NIMH, was meant to build an alternative to certain but not all of the services heretofore provided almost exclusively by state hospitals. In the beginning, then, CMHC services *plus* those of state hospitals theoretically represented a balanced array, but the CMHC program alone did not. Ewalt, Tarjan and Gorman—all members of the National Advisory Mental Health Council—agreed to this professional-political compromise. The unanticipated consequence of this compromise was the failure of most CMHCs to develop even minimal rehabilitation and aftercare services for the mentally ill being discharged or diverted from state hospitals in ever-increasing numbers after 1963.

In keeping with congressional intent and with the spirit if not the letter of the joint commission, these regulations were designed to stimulate a radical rebalancing of the mental health care system—specifically, to catalyze a massive transfer of resources, both fiscal and human, from the old state hospital system to a new nationwide community system. As the old system was being undone ("deinstitutionalized"), a modest proportion of the CMHC funds could be used to support improvement of care for its patients and retraining in community techniques for its staff. The great bulk of the funds, however, was for building and staffing the new community system. In this way, the generation of social reformers born in the first third of the twentieth century, deeply offended by the custodialism of the state system, utterly repudiated their predecessors' belief in the efficacy of institutional asylums for care of the mentally ill. With the passage of community mental health legislation, they got the chance to "tangibilate" for real, to dismantle and eventually shut down the institutional, mostly state-supported system while they constructed an alternative, (initially) federally assisted community system. The NIMH staff began their implementation task in good heart, for they believed they had both the momentum and the means to effect the radical rebalance within the next generation.

The momentum sprang from twenty years practical experience of demonstrating and evaluating community mental health services; and from a training program that had generated a fifteen- to twenty-fold increase in the number of community mental health service providers; which in turn had made possible a four-fold increase in the number of general hospital psychiatric units in American communities (from about 160 in 1946 to 750 in 1970. [Lipowski 1981]). Community mental health services were a reality, they were already "out there." The federal CMHC program could serve to stimulate their increase and lead their development into a nationwide network of universally available mental health care services. As for the means available to institute staff, they were fiscal and clinical in nature. The fiscal empowerment was, of course, the new law. Although stringently limited in amount and term, the newly authorized federal funds seemed adequate to the pump-priming purpose they were intended to serve. Moreover, other public health assistance programs enacted in 1965 (especially Medicaid) would hasten the demise of state hospitals by enabling them to transfer their elderly and senile patients to nursing homes, where they might hope to receive more appropriate treatment and care in the community mainstream. The clinical means were of two major sorts—a body of promising new psychosocial treatments and an array of new and potent psychotropic drugs.

With the support of federal funds and with demonstrably effective treatments for mental illness in hand, the optimism of the twentieth-century reformers was plausible. In the event, however, it took very little time—far less than it had in the nineteenth century—for the appearance of unmistakable signs that these means were being consistently under-financed and over-sold, as had those of the earlier century. Like its predecessor reform but more swiftly, "What began as a limited-purpose, noble experiment [was] transformed into a general-purpose solution to the [health and] welfare burdens of a society undergoing rapid [change]." (Morrissey et al. 1980. See Chapter Note 4-2). The pace of rending change during the 1966-1976 decade, doubtless because so close to us in time, seems to have been more intense and more ferocious than the historic social turmoil of the Jacksonian era.

Irresistible Forces of Transformation

It was the decade when America was locked in an undeclared land war in Asia whose unpopularity was great enough to force the retirement of the incumbent Democratic president and to fuel so spectacular a display of outrage at his party's national convention in 1968 as to assure its rejection at the polls. The victorious presidential candidate, representing the Republican political party's traditional fiscal and social conservatism, ended the war in Vietnam but lost the confidence of the people and was about to be impeached by the Congress in 1974 when he resigned from office. It was said of these events that they tested the American way of government, which was found to be in good working order. In the case of the Democratic party, its method of choosing delegates was reformed in favor of democratization, and it was ready and able in 1976 to carry its populist candidate to the presidency. (This Democratic president's efforts to renew the nation's moral commitment to humane and effective care of the mentally ill—which faltered badly during the decade—are a subject of the next chapter of this history.)

It was the decade when the use and abuse of drugs both licit and illicit swept into every level of the social strata. Having put their faith in the CMHC concept, the Congress responded in 1968 by adding to the CMHC mandate new programs for special facilities for alcohol and narcotics addiction. The addition of specialized alcohol and narcotics grants to the CMHC law set the stage for expansion of such programs culminating in the establishment of two new categorical health institutes in the mid-1970s, the National Institute on Alcoholism and Alcohol Abuse and the National Institute on Drug Abuse.

It was also a decade of strident activism for political and social justice, of which the democratization of the Democratic party was both cause and effect. This activism produced several notable effects on the CMHC program. Some were evident in the 1970 amendments to the CMHC law wherein the Congress, having concluded that state and local sources of funding were inadequate to pick up the cost of operating CMHCs as federal support declined, authorized additional federal financial support—particularly providing for a higher percentage of federal support for centers located in so-called poverty areas, and for a new program for children's mental health services, which added another categorical population to the growing set of direct grants for special populations (Chapter Note 4-3).

Other effects produced indirect but ultimately profound consequences. These were the changes wrought by congressional amendment of the social security laws—Medicare and Medicaid in 1965 and SSI (supplemental security income) in 1972, and by a series of judicial decisions affirming the civil rights of mentally ill persons and upholding their right to treatment in the least restrictive environment commensurate with their needs. It is notable that Earl Warren was chief justice of the Supreme Court during the years 1953-1969. According to a recent biography, Warren rejected the "neutral principles" of adjudication in favor of the "basic ethical imperatives of the Constitution ... principles of fairness, decency, individuality, and dignity. . . ." (White 1982).

This was also a decade when constituted authority had to respond to the symptoms of the social upheaval—from Watts in 1965, to Detroit in 1967, to Chicago in 1968, to Kent State University in 1970, to a firefight in Los Angeles that ended in the conflagration of the self-styled Symbionese Liberation Army. Manifestly, it was a fateful period of future shock and great expectation to end the nation's second century and begin the history of community mental health centers.

The CMHC law was significantly amended again in 1975, in its eleventh year of implementation. The background for this major reassessment included the fact that in 1972 the Republican administration of President Richard M. Nixon determined that the CMHC program should be phased out because it was a "demonstrated success"; local programs and private funding sources should and could pick up the cost of its continued development. (When the Congress disagreed and appropriated funds to continue the initiation of new CMHCs, the Nixon administration impounded the money. Several court suits resulted, leading to the release of these funds. When Congress passed the 1975 amendments—formally, Title III of the Health Revenue Sharing and Health Services Act of 1975—the Republican successor, President Gerald R. Ford, vetoed the bill on July 26, 1975. The House and Senate both overrode this veto, thereby enacting a new law. Later, Congress had to override another presidential veto on appropriations for the measure in order to get it funded.) In addition, the 1975 reassessment of the CMHC program was influenced by two reports of the General Accounting Office (GAO), which provides studies and evaluations for the Congress. One in 1971 and another in 1974 revealed the extreme complexity of program administration and implementation and pointed out a number of shortfalls which had become evident. These reports set the stage for the revision of the program, especially its management.

In consequence of both partisan political pressure and strong evidence of the need for reassessment, the Congress had conducted a major review of the program in 1973-74, declaring that the law's "patchwork history" made it necessary to provide a more explicit and specific definition of a CMHC. Their 1975 amendments added seven new services to the original definition of essential services, and called for numerous new requirements regarding the organization and operation of a CMHC, the coordination of services with other entities, and the development of an integrated system of care, staffing, governance and quality assurance.

The new definition required each CMHC to provide all stipulated services, expanded from five to twelve in number, as a condition to receiving support. All of these services were to be provided at center or satellite facilities throughout the program area. In addition to the original five essential services, specialized services for children and the elderly; screening services, followup care and transitional services for the chronic patient; alcohol- and drug-abuse services—all were newly mandated.

The 1975 amendments also created grant programs to help CMHCs that were graduating from the basic federal support, including a program of financial distress grants which authorized funds for centers experiencing major fiscal problems. Two other grant mechanisms were established with these amendments, for conversion and for consultation and education. The purpose of conversion grants was to assist existing centers to meet the initial costs of instituting the new services mandated by these selfsame 1975 amendments; these grants were to be available for only two years. Consultation and education grants, however, were to be available on an ongoing basis to continue support for what was thought to be a vital primary-prevention program element for which third-party reimbursement was scarce or unavailable. These grants were available, on an annual basis, for centers beginning their fifth year of operation.

By 1977, 650 CMHCs would be funded, covering 43 percent of the U.S. population and serving 1.9 million individuals that year. The $1.5 billion federal investment generated an additional $2.5 billion in other sources of funds including state, other categorical health and human service dollars, and third-party payments.

(Following enactment of the 1975 amendments, PL 94-63, CMHCs were reauthorized twice more before the CMHC program was subsumed under the Mental Health Systems Act of 1980. Congressional reauthorizations were made in 1977 for one year and in 1978 for two years with minor changes attempting to provide a little more flexibility in the initiation of new programs. See Chapter Note 4-4 for an outline history of comprehensive community mental health programs, 1964-1980.)

Changes in Leadership and Constituencies

The passage of the 1975 amendments over administration opposition signalled the arrival of powerful constituency support for CMHCs and the federal role. Two of the program's most effective proponents were the National Council of CMHCs (NCCMHC), a

Washington-based lobby formed in 1971 under the leadership of Executive Director Jonas Morris and Dr. Donald Weston, its first president, and the National Mental Health Association (NMHA) (formerly the National Association for Mental Health), whose Executive Director Brian O'Connell provided direction to a citizens lobby with chapters in every state of the U.S. This professional-citizen coalition had vigorously lobbied members of Congress in their districts and in Washington for mental health services in the community. NMHA volunteers and volunteers of many other mental health interest groups had donated countless hours in the 1960s to the development of their neighborhood CMHCs and to providing propaganda in communities for the acceptance of the mentally ill.

The civil rights movement and federal poverty programs, which stimulated broad citizen participation, led NIMH to foster a policy of citizen participation through service on CMHC boards. The first CMHC legislation left the functions and responsibilities of these boards undefined and the accountability unfixed. But the 1975 legislation mandated that these boards be composed, where practical, of residents of a service area, no more than one-half of whom were to be health care providers. Each board was to meet at least once a month, establish general policy, appoint the director and approve the annual budget.

CMHC citizen involvement provided some vivid lessons in the dynamics between providers and consumers. Physicians were (generally still are) untrained to take into account the nonmedical needs, capabilities and life-styles of those they treat. Community activists, distrusting the medical model of deviance, wanted a social program rather than a clinically oriented mental health program. They rejected the notion that health program funding was insufficient to meet all the needs of a poverty population in a service area. Such were the circumstances in 1969 when local mental health workers, acting in the name of the community, seized the Lincoln Hospital Mental Health Center in New York and the Temple University Mental Health Center in Philadelphia. The national experience, however, was that citizen involvement was vital to the political support of the program throughout the process of implementation, amendment and renewal. Indeed, the CMHC concept of geopolitical "catchment areas" captured the entitlement mood of the 1960s. NIMH stated that CMHCs were open to all members of society and, as the preamble to the 1975 amendments pointed out, were programs "to which all Americans should enjoy access."

Since the halcyon days of the Washington health syndicate, key congressional legislators had been supportive of mental health. However, presidential support for CMHCs varied sharply: Kennedy and Johnson strongly supported them; Nixon and Ford consistently opposed them. The program's champions in the Congress, therefore, were often in contact with members of the national CMHC lobby who, along with NIMH staff, worked on the language of the 1975 amendments. The results of NIMH evaluation studies of the CMHC program were considered in their formulation; the Office of Program Development and Analysis under James Stockdill, and the Services Division under Dr. Frank Ochberg, provided constituency groups and staff of the Senate and House authorizations and appropriations committees with data and critiques of the programs which pointed out program areas in need of amendment.

The Nixon and Ford administrations, especially the Office of Management and Budget (successor agency to the Bureau of the Budget), began their opposition immediately on taking office in 1969, when implementation of the CMHC law was in its fourth year. By 1970, coincident with the resignations of NIMH Director Stanley Yolles and Dr. Joseph English, administrator of NIMH's parent agency, the Nixon administration was declaring its unequivocal opposition to the continuation of federal support of the CMHC program on the basis that direct federal grants-in-aid for community mental health services ought not to continue, that states and localities should assume total responsibility for these programs. Despite forcing from office the top CMHC leadership, the Nixon and Ford administrations lost these battles with the Congress, but the line between those on opposite sides of the federalism issue was already blurred by this time by the growth of yet another lobby with strong interests in the federal CMHC program—the intergovernmental lobby.

In their implementation of the centers legislation the mental health leadership was involved in the conscious attempt to change the existing intergovernmental relations in the United States. In order to diminish the domination of the public mental health care system by state government and to enhance the role of local communities and the federal government in controlling community services, both the statute and the regulations were designed so that local communities were provided leverage to obtain community mental health grants with or without state concurrence. Frequently, the elected officials both at state and at local government levels perceived that they did not control programs supported by taxpayer dollars and located in their jurisdictions. In response to the introduction of this particular program and similar programs of President Johnson's Great Society agenda, an intergovernmental lobby came into being. It consists of governors, mayors, county supervisors, city managers and other office holders who press the federal government for administrative or legislative advantage for their constituents. They lobby individually or through their organizations, the National Governors Conference, the Council of State Governments, the United States Conference of Mayors, the National League of Cities, the National Association of Counties, the International City Management Association and the National Legislative Conference. Members of this lobby assumed an increasingly more influential role in the continuation and development of the CMHC program, which would culminate in 1980 with their partnership with the federal government in the design of the Mental Health Systems Act.

During this 1966-1976 time period, members of the professional-bureaucratic complex in the federal government encouraged both unions and businesses to expand insurance coverage for mental health. Through such promotion, the fiscal base of the mental health industry grew even as NIMH training funds (as well as those of the Veterans Administration and the armed services) were enabling a rapid expansion in the numbers and types of mental health providers in the United States. One consequence of this course of action was development of the team approach, with local psychiatrists, psychiatric nurses, psychologists, social workers and nonprofessional aides jointly providing mental health services to citizens in the community—a valuable clinical achievement of the CMHC program.

Utilization of nonprofessional mental health workers was also of major significance in community mental health center programming. Such workers were especially valuable as bridges for cultural and ethnic groups to the CMHCs services. In 1976 they accounted for 36 percent of total CMHC staff hours (NIMH 1978, p.36). These new careerists, when acting in responsible staff positions, increased a CMHC's responsiveness, a stated goal of the program. Yet many among these personnel had cause to contest the career opportunity differentials which left them little hope for advancement.

Another consequence, only partly anticipated, was a diminution of psychiatry's domination of mental health issues. Organized psychiatry found itself competing with fast-organizing psychologists, psychiatric nurses and psychiatric social workers as well as new types of aide personnel. While psychiatrists continued to be in full control in the psychiatric units of community hospitals, their control was weaker in the CMHCs and other community health programs. In 1971, 55 percent of center directors were psychiatrists. By 1977 the percentage had decreased to 26. The decrease had been offset by sharp increases in center directors with backgrounds in social work, from 17 to 33 percent, and administration, from 3 to 12 percent (Ibid., p. 41).

Further evidence for the decreasing impact of psychiatrists in CMHCs can be found in comparisons of their presence with that of other mental health professionals. While there has been an increase in the percentage of psychiatrists who work in CMHCs, from 12.2 percent in 1972 to 14.9 percent in 1976, the increase is small compared with the percentage of all mental health professionals who work in CMHCs. During the same time period, this percentage increased from 6.6 to 11.5 percent (Beigel et al. 1979).

Instead of one guild in dominance, the American Psychiatric Association, there were then many guilds, notably the American Psychological Association, the American Nurses Association, the National Association of Social Workers. Their voices were sometimes in agreement, oftentimes not, when they lobbied members of the Congress about mental health services.

The CMHC program also stimulated experimentation with mental health curricula in professional schools. For example, of the 110 academic departments of psychiatry with approved residency programs in the U.S., 74 percent used the CMHC as the setting for rotation of psychiatric residents (Faulkner and Eaton 1979).

All of the changes described above might be collectively construed as major progress in the reformation of public care for the mentally ill, and trend data covering this period (presented in the last section of this chapter) support such an interpretation. Yet these changes are also explanatory of what has become the number-one public mental health problem today, severely and chronically ill patients discharged and diverted from the rapidly deinstitutionalized state mental hospital system (Sharfstein 1979). Before turning to this subject, however, there is one more notable twist to the tale of how NIMH's most controversial program escaped dissolution in the teeth of full-bore efforts by the executive branch to do it in.

To begin, recall the hybrid nature of NIMH and the dual character of its mission. The institute was conceived of medical and public health principles as they apply to mental illness and health. Direction was to come from the top institute staff of Public Health Service officers with the advice and concurrence of the National Advisory Mental Health Council. In the early years when the political economy was robust, the federal treasury full, and the national mental health enterprise flourishing, the tension between the goal of treating mental illness and the goal of preserving mental health was hardly noticeable. By 1964 and increasingly thereafter—against the background of fiscal drains on the treasury and political drains on the public confidence caused by the Vietnam war, of the conquest of space, of the poverty programs of the New Frontier and Great Society, and of three successive failed presidencies—this tension came to the surface as competition for ever-scarcer health care resources and the support of a disillusioned public.

The disillusion stemmed from the failure of the CMHC program vis a vis the concurrent massive migration to communities of patients discharged and diverted from state mental institutions. The joint commission report had called for treatment and care of the chronically mentally disabled in a reformed state hospital system. The HEW recommendations, however, were based on the judgment that prevailing congressional intent disallowed federal funds for institutional reform. Thus, the NIMH professional-bureaucratic complex could conclude that any federally funded mental health care program should consist of centers where services for both treatment of illness and preservation of mental health were offered. But none of these decision-makers anticipated or was willing to address the consequences of passively permitting the deinstitutionalization, instead of actively supporting the reformation, of the state hospital system. The CMHCs' failure vis a vis chronic patients in communities put a heavy strain on the viability of NIMH's hybrid approach to issues of mental illness and health.

Shelving their internal disputes, the institute leadership in the director's office and on the national advisory council managed to preserve the CMHC program throughout eight years of national administrations hostile to it. Stanley Yolles led this effort until he resigned under fire from the Nixon administration in 1970. Yolles left the defense of the embattled program to Bertram Brown. Brown was so adroit in achieving this objective that rumor had it he had attracted the political enmity of John Erlichman, President Nixon's special assistant for domestic affairs. Brown was successful not only in saving the CMHC program (and himself) from political adversaries, but in supporting institute efforts to confront the hard issues generated by federal fiscal constraints and the withdrawal of state responsibility for care and support of chronically disabled patients.

Yet Brown's gift for personalizing the issues and his allegiance to the public health mission he had inherited from Felix and Yolles antagonized those in academia who favored a more medical approach to mental illness. This fact goes a long way toward illuminating why it was that, when the newly appointed HEW secretary of the Carter administration considered replacing Brown because of his "too autonomous" power, a divided NIMH leadership and constituencies acquiesced in Brown's removal in December 1977. Notwithstanding Brown's bureaucratic fate, the institute's basic policy directions—including its CMHC program—were to be continued by the new leaders, who ably interacted with the mental health constituencies during the deliberations of the President's Commission on Mental Health and the negotiations around the Mental Health Systems Act. The continuity of the CMHC program, under four different NIMH directors, deserves special notice.

The Phenomena of "Deinstitutionalization"

The word "deinstitutionalization" came into use sometime after 1955 as a neologism to mean "moving patients out of hospitals" (Clarke 1979). Elderly, chronic patients who had resided for years in state hospitals and might have been expected to end their days there, and other mid-aged and young mental patients who might have become long-term institutional residents were—after 1955—being moved out of hospitals, discharged and diverted to other resident-care and service facilities in communities. The state policies which effected these changes cited numerous medical, fiscal, legal and moral justifications. Certainly society as a whole supported the change, having long since lost faith in the effectiveness of hospital treatment and lately been made aware of other failings. The mental health alliance, the joint commission and finally the federal law itself backed the idea that the pre-1955 public mental care system—that is, the state system—be deinstitutionalized by dismantling the state hospitals while building an alternative, community-based system. State hospital censuses began to decline gradually after 1955, when 559,000 patients were resident. After 1963, when the total was 505,000, the rate of decrease quickened sharply and the number of residents declined to 216,000 in 1974, then to approximately 146,000 in 1979.

Deinstitutionalization as a deliberate public policy has been pursued in earnest by states since 1970. Encouraged by the development and widespread acceptance of the major tranquilizers, which control a number (but not all) of asocial behavioral symptoms, and by increased legal concern for the civil rights of institutionalized mentally ill patients, advocates of community mental health strongly pushed for rapid phase-down of state mental hospitals. Major federal financing initiatives, especially Medicaid, supplemental security income (SSI) and supplemental security disability insurance (SSDI), and Title XX programs have provided an economic base for deinstitutionalization, as most of the individuals discharged and diverted from state hospitals remain economically and socially dependent. Further, the ideology and justification of the CMHC program proclaimed a more humane and cost-effective alternative in the community.

Many stories in the news media have documented this major issue in communities across the country (New York Times 1979, U.S. News 1979, Hartley 1980). The numbers of individuals with chronic mental disorders are harder to pin down. One analysis reviews the prevalence and statistical literature and estimates that no fewer than 1.7 million individuals in 1977 suffered from a chronic mental disorder. Of the group, 900,000 are institutionalized (the great majority in nursing homes) and 800,000 to 1.5 million are living elsewhere in the community. They were with families or on their own in board-and-care homes, single-room-occupancy hotels or literally in the streets, intermittently and/or repeatedly hospitalized for short terms (Goldman et al. 1981). The number of homeless former mental patients in the communities of America is not known, but researchers estimate that about half of the approximately 60,000 homeless individuals in five eastern cities are mentally ill (New York, Boston, Washington, Baltimore, Philadelphia). It is practically impossible for the homeless to secure welfare entitlements, by the way, for no one is eligible without a home address (Baxter and Hopper 1981).

On the upper west side of New York, for example, many former state hospital patients are visible every day, carrying their worldly belongings in paper shopping bags, talking out loud with hallucinated companions, subsisting on a bare minimum. Once discharged from the total institution, the asylum, they often arrive in hostile communities with a "non-system of care" supported by a bewildering array of federal, state and local programs making up a confusing, "patchwork quilt" of services and financing (Sharfstein et al. 1978). Many turn to local charities for shelter and a warm meal and many run afoul of the law and are incarcerated by the criminal justice system. A GAO study estimate puts the number of mentally ill persons in U.S. jails at 28,000-84,000 (GAO 1980). Tens of thousands more are inmates in prisons.

This policy's social costs—the deterioration of the quality of life in America—have surfaced (Arnoff 1975), and CMHCs have come under attack for failing to care for a substantial portion of these chronically disabled individuals (GAO 1977). Indeed, with broad acute-care and prevention mandates and a reliance on third-party insurance funding, CMHCs seemed unwilling or unable to assume the habilitation-rehabilitation, social support and case management services needed by patients with chronic mental disorders. The situation was compounded by the absence of administrative and clinical coordination with state mental hospitals and the refusal of many community governing boards to make services for discharged patients residing in their CMHC service area a high priority. These increasingly pervasive public health and social welfare problems were made worse by a crazy collage of federal financial assistance programs. The 1975 amendments tried to remedy the situation by adding requirements relating to screening for admission to state mental hospitals, aftercare and transitional, halfway house services. Yet these mandates were ordered without sufficient additional federal resources or a cutback on other "essential services" (Sharfstein 1978).

Indeed, after 1975 CMHCs were required to assist courts and other public agencies in screening persons for inpatient treatment and, where appropriate, provide alternatives. This mandate accelerated the diversion of young adult chronic mental patients from state institutions into communities. As a result, a great and growing number of such persons are presenting to CMHC service programs across the country. This new generation of persons disabled by mental illness requires a different approach from that most service providers are able to offer (Bachrach 1982). Many of these individuals living in communities present risk to themselves and others.

Community acceptance of the mentally ill has been less than imagined by the policymakers. The growing number of mentally disabled persons—out of sight formerly—has provoked the social and economic prejudices of community groups rather than their humanitarian ideals, and some communities have screened out patients by restrictive zoning statutes. Moreover, high concentrations of chronic patients lead to rapid therapist burnout. One center director wished openly that some of the chronic patients in his service area be reinstitutionalized. Another was angered by the state hospital's "dumping chronics" in his center, and frustrated by his inability to persuade his board that the center should seek out more affluent clients for needed revenues. One of the center's biggest problems was its inability to collect fees from its patients, 85 percent of whom were of poverty status.

Deinstitutionalization seems to have substituted for the functional disability caused by long-term custodialism other types of disability, as evidenced by the involvement of the criminal justice system and the presence in communities of thousands of homeless, mentally impaired persons without adequate treatment and support. Reviewing the nation's deinstitutionalization experience in 1977, Dr. Gerald L. Klerman identified a number of social and ethical dilemmas. He wrote:

> As a whole, patients in the community are "better but not well," and their limited capacity to lead independent social lives generates complex issues for public welfare, urban zoning, health care agencies and legal institutions. In some areas there are signs of backlash...as the wave of reform and progress associated with a period of economic growth in the 1950s and 1960s now gives way to retrenchment and conservatism. [Klerman 1977]

Fiscal and Clinical Realities

In its preamble to Public Law 94-63 enacting the 1975 amendments, the Congress stated its findings as follows.

> [C]ommunity mental health care is the most effective and humane form of care for a majority of mentally ill individuals; the federally funded community mental health centers have had a major impact on the improvement of mental health care by (a) fostering coordination and cooperation between agencies responsible for mental health care, which in turn has resulted in a decrease of overlapping services and more efficient utilization of available resources, (b) bringing comprehensive community mental health care to all who need care within a specific geographic area regardless of ability to pay, and (c) developing a system of care which insures continuity of care for all patients and thus our national resource to which *all Americans should enjoy access.* [emphasis added]

The confidence expressed here was never matched by budget reality. Funds have always been appropriated at much lower levels than the laws authorized. There have always been many projects recommended for approval but unfunded, and it has often happened that those centers receiving funds received less than they had requested. A large number of areas in need and acceptable programs remained unfunded.

The 1970 amendments had tried to ameliorate this problem in part by targeting the creation of new CMHCs to poverty populations, which lacked the resources enjoyed by other income groups. These other income groups were likely to use insurance coverage or other means to avail themselves of mental health services. By and large the poor did not have these choices. Such a public policy decision can be accepted only as long as middle-income classes perceive some benefit to themselves, either direct or indirect. In the years since 1970, however, no such perception has emerged. The combined efforts of the professional-bureaucratic complex and the intergovernmental lobby had produced a significant expansion in public support of mental health services, especially for mid- and low-income populations. At the same time, expanded insurance coverage enabled more of the middle class to utilize services; by 1980, 40 percent to 60 percent of the population had some insurance coverage for outpatient mental health services. Yet private health insurance plans that include mental health have remained unattainable or unaffordable for much of the mid- and low-income populations and, of course, for all the poor. The insurance industry was put off by the CMHC shift from a medical to a social model in the early 1970s. National health insurance was an issue whose time had come and gone; on the agenda for years, it is still rhetoric, not reality.

As the public became increasingly aware of the differences among mental health care providers and learned that a patient's diagnosis was changeable, that there was a great deal of professional uncertainty about this same patient but agreement that cure was mostly unattainable, then an element of distrust of professional judgment began to take hold in the United States. The social mobility of patients and absence of central recordkeeping added to the possibility that such patients as this might come to the attention of law enforcement or the courts and reveal for the public record a grievous muddle of cause and effect and abandonment of responsibility on all sides.

In no other aspect of the CMHC program was the oversell more egregious, the rhetoric more exalted than in its promised elimination of the need for state hospital services. Hospitals would close, it was claimed, and humane care would prevail; costs would even be reduced if only the CMHC legislation were enacted. Exactly how, and how soon, CMHCs would accomplish this was never explicated, but in so exuberant an atmosphere such sober considerations were set aside. Although the scientific nature of psychiatry was in its formative stage, psychiatrists gave the impression to elected officials that cures were the rule, not the exception. As a result, despite pleas from some courageous leaders within organized psychiatry, inflated expectations went unchallenged and no support developed for review of the effectiveness of various old and new therapies. (At the same time, a very diverse array of psychosocial therapies and growth programs for "the worried well" was being aggressively marketed.) In short, CMHCs were oversold as curative organizational units. Neither the legislation nor the regulations governing implementation addressed what with hindsight appeared to be a most obvious question: where and how would all the patients with chronic mental disability live once diverted or discharged from state mental hospitals? This vagueness about objectives and the use of such affect-laden words as "community," "citizen participation" and the like permitted the program to be seen as the vehicle for meeting a wide assortment of divergent and conflicting needs.

Because CMHCs were creations of a categorical health program, consumers of CMHC services often found that, although they could obtain public health services in both medical institutions and in CMHCs, there were few or no social services in the community to help them meet such basic needs as food, housing and clothing. Yet the little they could obtain, funded through such as the federal SSI, SSDI, and Title XX programs and county and city resources—in aggregate—was significant compared to the period prior to 1965.

In fulfillment of responsibilities of program oversight, the Congress undertook two important initiatives in the mid-1970s. The Senate subcommittee on long-term care of the Special Committee on Aging looked into the role of nursing homes in caring for discharged mental patients, and the General Accounting Office carried out a study for the House (U.S. Senate 1976, GAO 1977). The findings of both investigations documented numerous shortcomings in public mental health care service organization and delivery. The NIMH took the lead in devising a demonstration of how these problems might be approached. Following studies, workshops and national discussions conducted by NIMH from 1975, the institute initiated a pilot demonstration program, targeted toward adult patients discharged from state institutions, which provided planning and service dollars to and through states to develop comprehensive "community support systems" for the chronically mentally ill (Turner and TenHoor 1978). This program initiative reflected the growing agreement that both medical support and social support are necessary for caring for the mentally ill in communities. In a later chapter we address the question of how available fiscal resources can be made to jibe with this new professional consensus.

The Role of Community Mental Health Centers in the Revolution of Care

We began this chapter by noting a similarity in the nineteenth- and twentieth-century reforms of the public mental health care system—namely, both were transformed from limited- to general-purpose programs by prevailing social, political and economic forces. We should note one other cautionary similarity before showing that, in the main, history has not repeated itself. It is that these reforms were far more complex and costly to implement than their proponents were able or willing to foresee.

The federal CMHC program was being implemented at the same time as state policies were resulting in an ever-accelerating release of mentally disabled patients. The bold new CMHC approach had little time and too meager resources to test its mettle before being overtaken, as it were, by the urgent needs of patients with chronic mental illness. (Remember, CMHCs were originally intended more to serve new constituencies in their own communities than large numbers of a great under-constituency of patients discharged "better but not well" from mental institutions into these communities. Consequently, many CMHCs had no formal linkages with state and county mental hospitals which might have prevented former patients from "falling through the cracks" of services discontinuity in the public mental health system. This was the unforeseen consequence of the political-professional compromise on the original five essential services.) However, notwithstanding that many CMHCs failed to meet the needs of chronic patients, the CMHC program was a strong positive force in the most revolutionary period in the history of psychiatric treatment. Unlike the degeneration of purpose suffered by the ninteenth-century reform—from treatment to social control and community protection, with emphasis on custody of the largest number of patients at the lowest cost—the purpose of the CMHC program was fragmented and broadened to include something near all of human misery, in some part because it was proving successful in its narrow, original intention. Despite the countervailing demands, CMHCs as a whole were successful in increasing accessibility to mental health services, in generating additional sources of funds for community programs and in providing some alternative inpatient care facilities.

- By 1977 CMHCs were serving almost 2 million people; about one-third of all services in the specialty mental health sector were provided by the federally initiated CMHCs. Nonwhites were served at a higher rate than whites, youth and aged were served in CMHCs although these groups under-utilize CMHCs as they have under-utilized mental health services generally. Almost two out of five CMHCs were serving rural areas; the CMHC program was successful in redistributing professional personnel and services to populations that previously had none.

- The federal seed-money concept indeed primed the pump of a well of state, local and third-party funds. In 1977, for every federal dollar invested three dollars of state and local dollars were generated. In the first two years of federal support, every federal dollar for the average CMHC was matched by 1.5 nonfederal dollars, and by the seventh or eighth year, at the point of the CMHCs graduating from federal support, the federal dollar was being matched by four nonfederal dollars. As an increasing number of CMHCs graduated from the core federal support they continued to fulfill the intent of the program, although cutbacks occurred, especially in consultation and education services. Two well-publicized CMHC bankruptcies in California and Kentucky created the impression that the financial viability of the federal program was itself in doubt. However, for the vast majority of programs initiated with federal funds, program operations have continued even as the federal funds dwindled or disappeared.

- Mental health centers have been an important factor in reducing the use of state mental hospital facilities in many areas throughout the country by providing a range of alternatives, including community-based inpatient and day treatment. One study showed lowered admission rates to state hospitals in areas with CMHCs than in areas without CMHCs (Windle and Scully 1976).

The successes of the CMHC program were part and parcel of a large-scale revolution in mental health care during the period 1955-1977. These years were marked by great changes in the scope and diversity of mental health services and providers, in the range and effectiveness of psychiatric treatments, and in the number of alternatives to mental institutions, especially private nursing and board-and-care homes, which took in a large number of the patients discharged from large public asylums.

The declining role of the state hospital epitomized the revolution in society's views on the care and treatment of the mentally ill. In 1955 the vast majority of patients seen in the specialty mental health sector were cared for in the public asylum system. In that year the number of residents in state mental hospitals reached a high of 559,000. More than three-quarters of all patient-care episodes in mental health facilities were inpatient, and inpatient care episodes of state mental hospitals comprised nearly half of all U.S. patient-care episodes, both inpatient and outpatient (Chapter Note 4-5). By 1977 the number of residents had fallen to approximately 160,000, and the percentage of total patient-care episodes accounted for by state mental hospitals to 9 percent (Regier and Taube 1981).

Average length of stay of state hospital admissions is one critical change which partially accounts for this massive shift. In 1955 a patient admitted to a state hospital stayed six months. By 1977 a patient's stay averaged three weeks. Admissions increased up to 1971 and remained steady as of 1977. Readmissions accounted for 70 percent of all state hospital admissions. The rate of inpatient care episodes per 100,000 population in state hospitals declined from a high of 502 in 1955 to 266 in 1977 (Witkin 1980).

There were correspondingly dramatic declines in the number of days of inpatient care and in the number of psychiatric beds. Between 1971 and 1977 the total number of inpatient days declined from 153 million to 91 million (40 percent), and the number of beds in inpatient psychiatric settings decreased from 471,800 to 301,011 (35 percent). The decrease in the number of beds was due to a plummet in state mental hospital beds—by 50 percent, from 361,578 to 184,079—that was only partially offset by increases in psychiatric beds in nonfederal general hospitals (from 23,308 to 29,384) and in psychiatric beds in for-profit settings (from 14,412 to 16,637) (Regier and Taube 1981).

Despite these shifts, public facilities in 1971 still accounted for approximately 80 percent of all inpatient days of care, and inflation-adjusted expenditures for state mental hospitals remained stable between 1971 and 1975 (Witkin 1980). Many have cited the inability to shift the financial and personnel resources of state hospitals *with* the patients into community settings as a major impediment blocking humane transition from the institution into the community (Ozarin and Sharfstein 1978).

From 1955 to 1977 there was also a four-fold increase in patient-care episodes in the specialty mental health sector from 1.7 million to 6.9 million episodes. This expansion was entirely due to the number of outpatient services established during this time period, including both those provided in CMHCs and those provided in private office practices (Taube et al. 1978). Patients seen in the private offices of psychiatrists and psychologists numbered about 1.3 million, 20 percent of all patients seen in the specialty mental health sector in 1975 (Regier et al. 1978).

The sweeping shifts in use of facilities and the reversal of dependence on state hospital psychiatric beds in favor of outpatient services were accompanied by a steep increase in the number of mental health professionals, many of whom found employment in the new facilities (especially in CMHCs after 1965) and in private practice. The National Institute of Mental Health provided training grants as a subsidy for this expansion of mental health professional personnel, especially psychiatrists, psychologists and psychiatric social workers. The number of both psychologists and social workers increased 300 percent from 1955; 13,500 members of the American Psychological Association in 1955 became 56,933 by 1980, and 20,000 social workers increased to 83,000. The number of psychiatrists increased 183 percent from 10,600 in 1955 to more than 30,000 by 1980 (Table, p. 27). The direct expenditures for mental illness increased dramatically from $1.2 billion to $19.6 billion in 1977, a greater than 1,500 percent increase during the twenty-two-year period under consideration. (Table).

Filling the gap made by the steep reduction in state hospital beds only partially offset by the increase in outpatient services was the phenomenal growth of the private-nursing-home industry (Goldman et al. 1981). Medicare (Title XVIII) and Medicaid (Title XIX) amend-

Trends in the Specialty Mental Health System, 1955-1977

Item	1955	1977	Change
Patient care episodes[a]			
Inpatient			
State mental hospital	818,000	574,000	30% less
Other	478,000	1,243,000	160% more
Total	1,296,000	1,817,000	40% more
Outpatient			
Federally funded community mental health centers		1,741,000	648% more
Other	379,000	2,835,000	1,107% more
Total	379,000	4,576,000	282% more
Psychiatric beds			
Psychiatric hospitals			
State	623,000	184,000	70% less
VA[b]	56,000	34,000	40% less
Proprietary	16,000	17,000	6% more
Psychiatric units in nonfederal general hospitals	7,000	29,000	314% more
Community mental health centers		15,000	
Direct expenditures for mental illness	$1.2 billion[c]	$19.6 billion[d]	1,533% more

From: Sharfstein 1982.

[a]Source of data, unless otherwise noted, is NIMH Division of Biometry and Epidemiology published and unpublished data.

[b]Includes VA psychiatric hospital beds and beds in psychiatric units of VA general hospitals.

[c]See Fein (1959).

[d]Report of the Research Triangle Institute: "The Cost to Society of Alcohol, Drug Abuse, and Mental Illness," contract 283-79-001, Alcohol, Drug Abuse, and Mental Health Administration, Nov. 1980.

ments to the Social Security Act in 1965 had allowed the burden of the costs of caring for the aged mentally ill to shift from the states to the federal treasury. Between 1954 and 1976 the number of nursing home beds increased over eight times from 170,000 to 1,407,000. Between 1969 and 1973, the number of individuals residing in nursing homes who were 65 and older with a primary diagnosis of mental disorder doubled from 96,000 to 194,000. During this same time period the mentally ill aged in psychiatric hospitals decreased by almost 40 percent (Redick 1974).

The 1977 National Nursing Home Survey of the National Center for Health Statistics found that, of the 1.3 million residents of nursing homes surveyed, approximately 290,000 had a primary diagnosis of mental disorder; 100,000 had a secondary diagnosed mental condition; and 400,000 were found to have "senility without psychosis." This number included a great many under-65 mentally ill individuals shifted to nursing homes supported by Medicaid (the law entitled nursing-home support so long as the homes had not more than 50 percent of their residents with a primary mental disorder [Regier 1978]). It became increasingly clear from several studies and congressional hearings made during this period that the shift in locus from state mental hospital to nursing homes—the result of ostensibly deinstitutionalizing practices—in fact amounted to a "trans-institutionalization" to these community "mini-asylums" (Lamb 1979).

In sum, the revolutionary shifts in psychiatric treatment and society's views on the care and treatment of mental illness inadvertently resulted in a decline in the overall quality of care for some large proportion of public patients. This unacceptable situation galvanized a concerned president to commission a national study—Jimmy Carter's mental health presidential initiative of 1977-78, which is described in the next chapter.

It is important to note that we have focused here on trend data from the specialty mental health care sector—that is, individuals hospitalized in public mental hospitals and psychiatric units in general hospitals and seen in mental health outpatient settings such as CMHCs. Yet the importance of the general health sector, especially the primary care setting, cannot be overlooked. The mental health training of primary care practitioners and the development of linkages between general health care with specialty health care settings are also issues of public health policy because most patients with mental disorders are cared for not in specialty mental health facilities but in general health facilities. In 1975, of the total estimated number of individuals with a mental disorder (32 million), approximately 57 percent (19 million) received services *only* in primary care or outpatient medical settings and general hospital or nursing home settings. About 20 percent of the total (7 million) were seen in the specialty mental health sector (Regier et al. 1978). The significance of this finding was highlighted in the President's Commission on Mental Health Report of 1978 and was underscored in several provisions of the Mental Health Systems Act of 1980.

CHAPTER FIVE

Crossroads:
Recommitment and Reversal
(1977-1982)

The President's Commission on Mental Health
NIMH's Community Support Program

Designing a Legislative Proposal

The Congressional Process
The Senate Mediates a Peace Treaty
The House Attends to the Data
The New Law Is Enacted

A Loss of Will

The Mental Health Systems Act of 1980:
A Case Study on the Limits of Legislative Reform

I *went to the hospital when I was around eight . . . and I stayed there for almost ten years. So I was about 19 when they asked if I wanted to leave the hospital and come back to New York City where I was born . . . . I know that the needs of the mentally ill are great, but I only want to suggest that this is the case because so little is really being done. I don't think it would take very much . . . and it will be a good day . . . when we are no longer described in the newspapers as a major problem facing society . . . I have tried to talk about the housing we need, the chance to work on real jobs, and most of all, a place in the community . . . not based on what's wrong with us, but rather on what we can do to be helpful, to contribute, a place where people believe in our potential . . . .*

Ronald Peterson
From *The Chronic Mental Patient*, 1978

CHAPTER FIVE

Crossroads: Recommitment and Reversal (1977-1982)

When Jimmy Carter was narrowly elected to the presidency in 1976 the CMHC program was a rare survivor of the previous administrations' attempts to close down federal categorical community programs which originated in the Great Society of the 1960s. The enactment of PL 94-63 in July 1975 over a presidential veto climaxed a seven-year struggle for program survival which included appropriation battles and impoundment suits. Efforts to combine the CMHC grant program with other categorical programs and Medicaid were turned back by the Congress as well. By 1976 the program had been authorized for twelve years and represented a federal investment of $1.3 billion and a total investment, including nonfederal sources, of almost $4 billion.

Yet despite its survival and the passage of PL 94-63, community mental health was a program and policy in trouble. By 1976 the entire country was to have been covered by 1,500 CMHCs (an adjustment of the original number of 2,000), but the program was less than halfway there with just over 600 funded. Alternative sources of funds were failing to materialize to the extent hoped for by the early planners. States would not or could not close their mental hospital institutions and move dollars with the patients into the community. Third-party payments discriminated against mental illness, especially in the reimbursements for outpatient and day-care treatment services, the bulk of which were being delivered in CMHCs and in private offices. Programs were beginning to graduate from their eight-year terms of federal seed-money supports. Graduation of the first batch of thirty CMHC programs came in 1976 and included the bankruptcy and collapse of the first program that had been supported by staffing funds. Other signs of distress were mounting. PL 94-63 contained some relief for CMHCs in straitened circumstances through its provisions for so-called distress grants, but it became clear that the fiscal survival issues of previously funded CMHCs were compromising the funding of new CMHCs. From 1976 through 1979 an additional $1 billion of federal financial assistance initiated only 160 new programs, thereby increasing the percentage of the U.S. population covered by CMHCs from 41 to 49 percent. Political survival seemed easier than fiscal survival in the 1970s, especially as the national economy showed signs of "stagflation"—real growth and productivity stagnate while prices inflate.

Further, the CMHC program had been thoroughly evaluated and found wanting in several respects. Chronically mentally disabled patients discharged and diverted from state and county mental hospitals were poorly served. Children and the elderly were underserved. The effectiveness of primary prevention remained in doubt. Ethnic minorities and women condemned cultural insensitivity and other hindrances to accessibility. A new programmatic focus was needed.

The President's Commission on Mental Health

In 1977 some factors similar to those surrounding the passage of the CMHC Act of 1963 were present: White House interest and willingness to initiate, legislatively skillful congressional support and widespread professional agreement on the need for changes. Many of the individuals who had brought about the 1963 Act, however, were gone from the scene. Felix was retired, and Gorman and Lasker had moved on to other health issues. Fogarty and Hill had departed; Representative Henry A. Waxman (D-Calif) and Senator Edward M. Kennedy (D-Mass) chaired the relevant subcommittees.

The White House interest came from the president's wife, Rosalynn Carter, who had been an active member of the National Mental Health Association in Georgia prior to her husband's election to the presidency. She had successfully led a drive to transform that state's mental health system from a nineteenth-century asylum approach to community mental health. Dr. Peter Bourne, a key Carter aide and former deputy campaign director, wanted a platform for Mrs. Carter and suggested to the president that, given her interest and experience, chairing a presidential commission on mental health would be appropriate. When the attorney general advised the president that his wife could only be an honorary chairperson, Carter gave her that role and appointed Dr. Thomas E. Bryant to the chairmanship. Tom Bryant was a close Carter family friend and a former director of health programs in the Johnson administration. He was to assume a role similar to Gorman's in the passage of the 1963 Act.

In one of his first official acts, on February 17, 1977, President Jimmy Carter signed an executive order establishing the President's Commission on Mental Health (PCMH), which was to undertake a one-year study of the mental health needs of the nation and recommend to the president how the nation might best meet these needs (PCMH 1978). The commission was composed of twenty prominent citizens among whom were Florence Mahoney, still an influential advocate of mental health programs, and Dr. George Tarjan. Thirty-five task panels composed of mental health authorities and other interested citizens were to provide analyses and recommendations. Chairman Tom Bryant directed a staff of professional and support personnel; Dr. Gary L. Tischler, professor of psychiatry at Yale University, came down for the year to be the commission's study director. Bryant and Tischler were able to attract many staff from NIMH and its parent agency the Alcohol, Drug Abuse, and Mental Health Administration, who were detailed to the commission for the year of its work. The commission had a small White House budget and some outside private resources. The White House staff through Kathryn Cade, Rosalynn Carter's special projects director, took a keen interest in the commission's work.

During the year of its deliberations the PCMH held public hearings in four cities and reviewed task panel reports and special study contributions. The message was loud and clear that the nation's "de facto system" of mental health care services was sprawling and fragmented and only nominally a system at all (Regier et al. 1978). The quantity and diversity of services and providers had mushroomed since the mid-1960s, making the definitions of mental health, mental illness and appropriate care more complex and controversial than ever before.

It was also very soon clear that the president's commission would not have the time to forge a grand consensus as the joint commission had done during the period 1956-60. The temper of the mid-1970s would not support a stately accretion of expert knowledge and opinion. Americans distrusted such an approach and the new populism of the Carter administration (as reflected in the campaign slogan "Grits and Fritz in '76") followed a different rationale in creating the PCMH. Eleven of the thirty-five task panels were focused on special, heretofore underserved populations, ensuring that the commission's recommendations would address their needs (Chapter Note 5-1). These underserved populations—notably among them the chronically mentally ill and disabled—embraced the most vulnerable, most dependent, most powerless citizens in the land. The president's commission was determined that their interests be addressed along with those of the new constituencies that had emerged since the mid-1950s.

These new constituencies of providers, assurers and consumers of mental health care services pressed for different policies based on different ideologies and self-interests. Some of them had well-organized lobbies in Washington—for example, the National Association of State Mental Health Program Directors under the spirited management of Harry Schnibbe. This lobby and others made up the "mental health liaison group" which served as an unofficial adjunct to the National Advisory Mental Health Council of NIMH and attempted to influence the White House and PCMH throughout the entire process. Although the splintering of interests disallowed formation of a consensus on problem definition and solution, and the hot, sometimes destructive competition for resources often seemed to harry its work, the PCMH process succeeded in being extremely participatory and in producing a four-volume report of great comprehensiveness.

The report of the PCMH was submitted to the president on schedule in April 1978. The report highlighted the scarcity of third-party financing; the need for federal support for indirect services (for example, consultation and education) on an ongoing basis; the inflexibility in initiating new programs; the needs of underserved populations, especially the chronically mentally ill, elderly, children and minorities; the erosion of the national research capacity; and the continuing need for training programs and the responsibility of federally supported trainees to pay for their training by service in programs with few personnel resources. It included over 100 major recommendations and findings on mental health needs, resources, rights, treatments, financing, research, training and prevention; but it did not specify a course of action.

The report was the source document upon which a consensual agreement might be formed, a first step in a series that might unfold during a congressional legislative process. Its strength lay in its independence; it had escaped becoming captive to any single constituency or special-interest lobby. Instead, the report was a fair-minded and cogent critique of current service efforts whose message was encapsulated in the PCMH's call for a "more responsive services system."

The PCMH asserted that a new program was needed to fulfill the "national commitment to community mental health services." This new program should aim at *(a)* increased flexibility in planning for networks of comprehensive services in service areas which had not yet had the opportunity for federal funding; and *(b)* the initiation of new services for children, adolescents and elderly and specialized services for racial and ethnic minorities and for people with chronic mental illness. These aims were somewhat inconsistent in that the comprehensiveness of services delivery could be defeated by the categorization of grant programs.

Further, the PCMH called for a "national priority" to meet the needs of people with chronic mental illness, including formulation of "a national plan for the chronically mentally ill." This planning process should consider *(a)* changes in Medicare, Medicaid, health planning and Title XX (flexible social services appropriations); *(b)* and changes in certain regulations of the Department of Housing and Urban Development and in the supplemental security income program, with the object of improving the shelter and life-support opportunities for individuals with long-term mental disabilities. The agenda was a most ambitious one. Nevertheless, with the support of HEW Secretary Patricia Roberts Harris (who succeeded Califano in mid-1979), staff of NIMH and the Health Care Financing Administration undertook an intensive, year-long effort and succeeded in carrying out such a planning process (Chapter Note 5-2).

The PCMH also called for "performance contracts" with states to achieve the goals of an orderly phase-down of state hospitals where appropriate, and a humane transition of patients from the hospital to a community-based system. The performance contract would establish a "new partnership" between the federal government and the states. In the past, as has been noted, federal policies did not attempt to integrate commitments or program objectives of state-supported programs with the requirements for federal financial assistance.

States were bypassed as CMHC grants were awarded directly to local communities. States had been held accountable, however, by their legislatures and citizenry for performance in the delivery of their own mental health services. The federal CMHC program had established some direct accountability with local CMHCs, but since CMHCs also received fiscal support from states, these lines of accountability often duplicated each other.

Under the performance contract concept the federal government and individual states would enter into an accountability relationship in an effort to integrate both financial assistance and services delivery efforts. The partners would agree in advance on activities to be undertaken and outcomes which the state would commit itself to achieve. "Satisfactory performance" would then be a precondition to continued disbursement of all or a significant portion of the federal mental health funding through the state mental health authority. The performance contract with states was the most creative idea to come out of the commission according to Bryant. Representatives from state government, particularly Dr. James D. Bray and Paul Ahr, had crafted the notion in the commissions' task panel on state mental health issues.

NIMH's Community Support Program

In urging a more focused effort to coordinate general health and mental health services the commission's report took on a particular *systems* cast. In this it was reflecting the new thinking in the field, which sought ways to transform the de facto mental health service system into an intentional system that would articulate with other systems of health and human services where these other systems impinged on the treatment and care of the mentally ill. The new generation of professional leadership had made some conceptual advances in calling attention to functional as distinguished from medical approaches to the mentally ill, especially with respect to the chronically mentally ill. Considerations of duration and extent of disability as well as diagnosis were seen to be equally relevant to any rational and humane approach to the public health problem posed by this population (Allegheny County 1974). Chronic mental illness was seen to be "a form of suffering that transcends diagnostic labeling because, for the most part, diagnoses are dependent on the symptoms present at onset" (Steering Committee 1981, p. 2-100). The practical implication of this shift in focus was recognition of this population's need of life and social supports and opportunities in addition to mental and general health care services. There were already several relevant service programs available in communities; these should be better coordinated to provide the full continuum of needed services.

As noted earlier, Bert Brown had encouraged the development of these new concepts within the institute, beginning in 1975. The pilot project initiated to test a framework and provide a data base on "comprehensive community support systems for severely mentally disabled adults"—NIMH's Community Support Program (CSP)—began with modest funding in 1977 (Turner and TenHoor 1978). In addition to "offering a systems perspective as a basis for planning services," CSP offered "an opportunity . . . to document and . . . compare the costs and benefits of alternative approaches to developing, organizing and funding such systems." This aspect of CSP reflected the institute's concern with cost-benefit and cost-effective analyses of financing services for the mentally ill (Sharfstein et al. 1978). CSP under the energetic leadership of Judith C. Turner was well underway by the time of the release of the commission report the following April.

By that time, too, new leadership had taken hold at NIMH and its parent agency. Dr. Gerald Klerman had been appointed to head the agency in January 1978. Klerman had firsthand experience directing two federally funded community mental health centers (in New Haven and Boston), experience that amply prepared him to direct NIMH's efforts to implement the report of the President's commission. Klerman had recommended to Secretary Califano that Dr. Herbert Pardes succeed Bert Brown as director of NIMH. Pardes came from academic psychiatry, having been chairman of the department of psychiatry at the University of Colorado and the New York Downstate Medical Center. Although his background differed from those of the first three NIMH directors, Pardes was strongly committed to the integration of mental health and general health services and to the public health perspectives of community mental health. He provided important professional-bureaucratic continuity not only in the transition to the Carter administration but also later on, after the Carter presidency, when sharply differing policies were initiated by the executive branch. Indeed, one of the institute's great strengths has been the philosophical consistency of its leadership in responding to the social and political vicissitudes of the past quarter-century.

Designing a Legislative Proposal

Following submission of the PCMH report to President Carter at a ceremony in the White House in the spring of 1978, the president charged HEW Secretary Joseph A. Califano, Jr., to devise a legislative proposal to respond to the recommendations. The secretary directed that this proposal focus exclusively on revising the CMHC Act and categorical mental health services. This decision was made because the secretary's staff had concluded that a piece of legislation which attempted to address the comprehensive range of service, support and shelter needs of the mentally ill would be far more difficult to get through Congress, even though such changes may have been most critical to the provision of opportunities for treatment and life support for the mentally ill. The secretary's direction had at least a reasonable chance of producing a proposal acceptable to the Congress. Further, the department had already proposed other significant social legislation which occupied the attention of Califano and his staff, including hospital cost-containment, welfare reform and civil rights.

Cognizant of the lack of consensus among the numerous constituencies that would be affected by any new legislation, the secretary and the agency leadership considered it strategically necessary to involve several different program elements within the complex and far-reaching department bureaucracy. This instruction took some time to implement, given the recency of Klerman's appointment and the absence of a permanent NIMH director (Pardes assumed the position two months after the PCMH report was released). Consequently, the drafting of new mental health legislation proceeded at a snail's pace. Tom Bryant, who had formed a "public committee" to help implement the commission's recommendations, and Kathryn Cade, of the White House staff, were displeased with this pace and suggested to Rosalynn Carter that she remind the secretary of the need to sustain the PCMH momentum. In response, Califano assigned two of his staff, Bruce Wolfe and Ellen Silverman, to coordinate the bureaucratic actors within HEW to produce a draft bill.

The departmental process included the appointment of a task force involving representatives of all the principal operating components. Klerman led this effort. The task force served as a policy steering committee for a staff work group, which took the legislative proposal through the bureaucratic layers from institute to agency to assistant secretarial levels. The draft legislative proposal went through six major rewrites, incrementally involving the assistant secretaries of health, planning, legislation, and management and budget. Informal consultation was solicited from outside groups, which continued to disagree on the shape of new legislation but were anxious to participate in the drafting of the administration bill. However, the process was mostly an inside effort.

A draft proposal was submitted in March 1979 to the White House and the Office of Management and Budget. Thanks to the White House confidence he enjoyed, Bryant himself reviewed the draft bill. He found it not entirely what the president had in mind. He wrote:

> In general, the current draft is just not exciting, it does not represent the bold new thrust in mental health that many hoped would come with the Carter Commission. Rather it is a sort of "fix-things-up" bill. (It does seek to "fix" a number of things that need repair!) I think the bill can be made far more exciting and attractive.
>
> The major mental health-related problem at the present, so far as public program and dollars are concerned, is the care of the chronically mentally ill—the "deinstitutionalized" population. The federal government's role in caring for this population is unclear. This bill offers the chance to clarify that role and to forge the necessary new partnerships with the states to implement a new national effort in this regard. That opportunity should not be missed. [Bryant 1979]

Bryant returned the draft bill to Klerman's task force for one more rewrite in April. A year had elapsed since the PCMH report. Within two weeks, however, the seventh and final draft of a new bill was submitted to and accepted by the White House.

President Carter submitted the Mental Health Systems Act to the Congress on May 15, 1979. Accompanying the bill was a special message on mental health, the first since President Kennedy's sixteen years previously. In his special message President Carter declared: "I am convinced that...passage of the Mental Health Systems Act will reduce the number of Americans robbed of vital and satisfying lives by mental illness. I ask the Congress to join me in developing a new system of mental health care designed to deal more effectively with our nation's unmet mental health needs" (Appendix A).

The administration's Mental Health Systems Act proposed six major titles, among which was the main community mental health title to provide grant funds directly to communities for the following purposes: to plan and provide services to underserved groups (with great latitude, or flexibility, in the kinds of services and requirements); to develop comprehensive mental health services in areas which had not yet had the opportunity for a CMHC; to link general health and mental health care; to continue currently funded CMHCs; and to provide for ongoing distress-grant funds to old CMHCs for services that did not generate third-party revenues such as prevention, coordination, consultation and education, and outreach (Chapter Note 5-3).

It was to take eighteen months for the Mental Health Systems Act to be enacted. The continuing absence of a broad-based consensus on both the need for and the specifics of new mental health legislation largely accounted for the length of the process. Nevertheless, the time permitted for the steady growth of a coalition of groups representing states, local communities and professionals that backed the emerging new federal policy. Indispensable to the ultimate success was the moral commitment of the president's wife.

Rosalynn Carter's personal attention sustained congressional interest and generated momentum for passage of the legislation throughout the conflict-ridden months of the process. Mrs. Carter prepared the way for the submission of the bill to Congress by appearing on February 6, 1979 before Senator Kennedy's subcommittee. She presented the president's commission report to the Senator and remarked that, although CMHCs had made an enormous contribution, they did not adequately address the country's mental health needs. Giving the first testimony by a chief executive's wife since Eleanor Roosevelt testified in 1940, Mrs. Carter impressed the chairman with her knowledgeability and sincerity. She concluded by proposing a program targeted to aid chronically mentally ill individuals, thereby setting the stage for the special presidential message.

The Congressional Process

The Congress could accept and modify the proposed bill or take an alternative course of action—that is, a simple extension of the CMHC Act. An extension was unattractive because the Congress had already done a two-year simple extension in the fall of 1978. Another short-term extension would add to the uncertainty of federal support in the field and to the CMHCs' difficulty in recruiting and retaining personnel. Nor could a simple extension provide for a larger role for states or encourage state funding of community alternatives. Yet, compelling as was the need for a correction in the course of the CMHC program, every title of the administration bill was known to be controversial.

Senator Kennedy himself was dissatisfied, describing the draft bill as "a rather modest legislative proposal of community support programs based on more coordination, continuity and collaboration. Although a first step, these services alone will not go very far toward dealing with the basic problem .... The emerging question is whether or not, left to their own devices, the states will expand their resource commitment to serve the mentally ill. History has taught us that this has not happened on any broad scale and that the federal government must fill the void." Yet the administration bill "begs the question of expanding resources," he wrote, "[and] backs away from the federal role as defined in the 1963 legislation ...." (Kennedy 1979).

Kennedy introduced the president's bill to the Senate with the expectation that Congress would amend it significantly but not compromise its general objectives. Although he predicted that increased support for the chronically and severely mentally ill was doomed to failure unless there were accompanying improvements in the relevant titles of the Social Security Act, neither the administration nor the Congress offered amendments to that legislation. On May 24 Secretary Califano testified before the Kennedy subcommittee that HEW was "studying ways" to make Medicare, Medicaid and Titles XVIII, XIX and XX more responsive to the needs of the mentally handicapped. The administration was also supporting legislation to increase the Medicare ceiling on reimbursement for outpatient mental health care from $250 to $750 annually and to reduce from 50 to 20 percent the co-payment required by Medicare beneficiaries for mental health care—both recommendations of the president's commission. In addition, the secretary said, the administration's proposed child health insurance program would, if enacted, mandate that states provide mental health services for children who were eligible for Medicaid coverage.

In early summer of 1979 there were several days of hearings in the Senate and House on the administration's bill (Hearings 1979a., b.). In addition to testimony defending the proposal by administration witnesses, favorable testimony was solicited from such interest groups as the National Governors Association, the National Mental Health Association, the National Council of CMHCs, the American Federation of State, County and Municipal Employees, the Mental Health Law Project, the American Psychiatric Association and other professional groups, and other groups representative of elderly, minority and women's interests. Compared to 1963 when four or five groups were concerned in a major way with the initial CMHC legislation, the 1979 hearings elicited testimony from more than twenty groups, many of which were established during the intervening years (Ibid.). Although there was general agreement by these groups on the need for new mental health legislation to implement the PCMH recommendations, there was general disagreement on which recommendations to emphasize as well as on the scope of the proposed legislation. The testimony from virtually every group focused on different aspects of the administration's bill. They also differed from one another on what was necessary to implement their favorite PCMH recommendations.

For example, one key issue was the role of the states under this new legislation. The governors expressed one strong point of view and the CMHC directors another. The administration had proposed a state program for services for chronically mentally ill and severely disturbed children, traditionally a state responsibility. Federal funds, however, would go to local communities for community service. On the other hand, the administration bill also proposed a pilot program for states to manage all the funds under the Act without specifying criteria for states which could qualify for such a pilot. But this attempt at evenhandedness was attacked by both sides of the issue. On one side, states felt it did not go far enough in allowing them to manage all the federal funds. On the other, community programs felt there were too few procedural safeguards for local programs in relation to the pilot state program, and the CMHC directors felt there was a lack of accountability for state responsibilities when states manage federal funds. The community groups also wanted to be eligible to receive support directly for program areas that were reserved for states under the administration's bill. Indeed, the CMHC group and the governors association became involved in vitriolic attacks on each other over the role of state government in the Mental Health Systems Act.

John Wolfe, executive director of the CMHC group, testified to the Senate subcommittee that

> [T]he Systems Act will grant the states an undue amount of authority over CMHCs since most states still struggle with the problems of deinstitutionalization. It isn't wise to give them unlimited and unregulated authority over CMHCs especially in regard to Federal funding and evaluation .... The states have not demonstrated a commitment to-

wards community mental health care [and] to give them control over the CMHC program would be devastating [Hearings 1979a., p. 128]

Speaking to the House subcommittee on health and environment in June 1979, Dr. George Zitnay of Maine and Paul Ahr of Virginia criticized the Systems Act from the states' point of view: "In the torturous course of developing federal legislation through federal agencies, much of the PCMH's intentions suffered from a metamorphosis that made the final product a fragmented, uncoordinated, nonsystem of projects, impossible for the state mental health agencies to support" (Hearings 1979b., p. 229). Evidently, notwithstanding the seven rewrites, the bill was viewed as failing to provide for a satisfactory working relationship among local organizations, state governments and the federal government.

Other controversies erupted as well. The proposed legislation was accused of fragmenting the community mental health system with discrete (categorical) provisions for services for the underserved groups, of lacking sufficient legal protection for patients, and of inadequate attention to job retraining and placement of state hospital employees who would be displaced by policies of discharge and closure. Rob McGarrah of the American Federation of State and County Municipal Employees was particularly critical of the PCMH report for its lack of emphasis on the irreducible population of chronic patients who could not be discharged or diverted to communities, and on the protection of the jobs of public employees displaced by the proposed new mental health policies.

So despite the PCMH process and its report, despite the general agreement on the need for change and the First Lady's sustained interest, the administration's Mental Health Systems Act stood dead in the water in the summer of 1979. This third summer of the Carter administration was marked also by the firing of Secretary Califano and the departure of some of the HEW administration team. Patricia Roberts Harris was appointed to head the department. A new team was needed to work during the forthcoming legislative season at developing compromises with the constituency groups and modifying the Systems Act accordingly. Dr. Steven S. Sharfstein and Lee Dixon of NIMH, Gerald Connor of the HEW Office of Legislation and Anthony Imler of the White House domestic policy staff, with the assistance of Bryant and Cade, formed a new administration team which met periodically under the leadership of Dr. Julius Richmond,

assistant secretary for health and a member of the President's Commission on Mental Health. During the next year and a half, this group
along with Klerman and Pardes developed the administration's ultimately winning strategy. The strategy focused on building a coalition
of mental health interests strong and durable enough to get the
legislation through the rigors of subcommittee review and revision.

The Senate Mediates a Peace Treaty

The Senate subcommittee staff headed by Stuart Shapiro and David
Reimer (for Senator Kennedy and the majority), David Winston and
Cynthia Hilton (for Senator Richard S. Schweiker [R-Penn] and the
minority), led an emotional interaction with representatives of the
key outside constituencies. It began early on when a major rewrite of
the legislation, composed with little outside consultation, passed the
subcommittee in October 1979, and only a last-minute promise by a
feisty, provocative Shapiro to work with the constituency groups
between subcommittee and full committee passage averted a
threatened telegram campaign by all the major groups to oppose the
rewrite. Seven more rewrites were made before the full Committee
on Labor and Human Resources reported the bill out in April 1980.
Each represented an increasingly broader statement of agreement if
not actual consensus among the groups and the administration; more
significantly, these exercises created an increasingly cohesive coalition which advocated passage of the Mental Health Systems Act. Key
participants in this labor-intensive process included Leslie Scallet of
the Mental Health Law Project, Robert Vandivier of the National Mental
Health Association, ably assisted by citizen volunteers Beverly Long
and Hilda Robbins, and John Wolfe and David Sandler of the National
Council of CMHCs. Key among these mental health interest groups
was the one representing state government. The constitutional issues
of federalism gave way to political pragmatism as a leadership group
put together by Ahr and Dr. James Prevost of New York, through its
executive director, Harry Schnibbe, was pivotal in devising a formula
for states to gain greater control over federal funds.

In fact, states were already contributing 29 percent of the CMHC
funding in 1977 compared to the federal share of 25 percent. The
ratio of state and federal share of overall funding of community
programs was two-to-one. The states paid approximately $4 billion
into mental health systems; two-thirds, or almost $3 billion, for
mental institutions; and one-third, or about $1.3 billion, for

community-based programs. Federal programs contributed approx-imately $2 billion: $1 billion from Medicaid and $230 million from the CMHC programs, $400 million from Medicare and the remainder from assorted federal programs like CHAMPUS (Civilian Health and Medical Program of the Uniformed Services) and the VA (NIMH 1978). The state commissioners of mental health lobbied hard to undo those provisions of the 1975 CMHC amendments which ac-corded them too little control over programs which their funds supported. This was part of an overall perception of federal intrusion into state government. During the eighteen-month legislative pro-cess the influence of the commissioners was especially strong in the Senate where the markup process specifically looked to their leadership.

The series of compromises worked out draft by draft, however, resulted in a complex, highly regulatory product, which was rigid in terms of perspective and implementation. This was its major strength and weakness. On the one hand, it represented a hard-won consen-sus of state and local program interests which achieved a com-promise between the goals of comprehensiveness at the local level and flexibility on the use of federal funds to meet the needs of the underserved. On the other hand, to assure these ends to the satisfac-tion of the various constituencies, the bill specified a potential swamp of rules, deadlines, hearings, appeals, requirements and paper, pa-per, paper. It assumed an unrealistically great federal capacity to mediate conflicts between local interests and state mental health authorities. It also provided for a strong state management role tempered with strong accountability mechanisms. It would serve to move states into the dominant role in the delivery of public mental health services while guaranteeing increased federal fiscal support. At the same time, there were very detailed, explicit protections for local programs in the context of state review and management. In a sense, the product was a peace treaty mediated by the Senate be-tween the local CMHCs and the states—provided that the states would develop a system to treat the chronic mental patient in the community, and the Senate bill authorized more money than the administration bill in an effort to make good on this proviso.

The bill which emerged from the full committee in April 1980 was consequently very different from the bill submitted by the adminis-tration. It was developed during the same time period that Edward Kennedy was running against Jimmy Carter for the Democratic party presidential nomination. Although this competition in no way detracted from the close and cordial working relationship between Senate committee members and the president's wife, the flaws which Kennedy found in the Carter bill were addressed in the Senate version, which emphasized continuing the task of covering the country with comprehensive CMHCs—the original goal of President John Kennedy. The Senate version also contained many more requirements for community programs and established a new, complex process of combined local, state and federal planning and management. It included a new title, The Patient's Bill of Rights and Advocacy Program; stronger employee protection, guarantees to be administered by the Department of Labor; a program of services to rape victims; and more requirements for specialized programs for the chronic patient. Compared to the administration bill, the Senate version of the Mental Health Systems Act contained more services, more dollars and more promises.

The House Attends to the Data

In the House, jurisdiction over the CMHC program fell to the Subcommittee on Health and the Environment of the Committee on Interstate and Foreign Commerce, chaired by Representative Henry A. Waxman of California. Waxman wanted to see that underserved populations had access to CMHCs and that the federal government had more flexibililty in administration. Waxman and the ranking Republican member, Dr. Tim Lee Carter from Kentucky, emphasized different aspects of the administration bill. Carter, committed to a coordinated comprehensive approach, feared a proliferation of small service entities and further fragmentation. Because fiscal troubles in federally initiated CMHCs were well known to the House members, the leadership wished to continue the CMHC program basically as it was while adding earmarked funds to meet the needs of chronic patients and thus to shore up the program fiscally. In contrast to the simultaneously proceeding Senate hearings, House members themselves played much more prominent a role in the development of the new legislation. For one thing, much more forceful dissent was presented in the House committee, led by Republican Representatives William E. Dannemeyer of California and Dave Stockman of Michigan and Democrat Phil Gramm of Texas. For another, the administration found a strong advocate for the changes it sought in the CMHC Act in Representative Andrew Maguire of New Jersey, a liberal Democrat who had read the entire president's commission report. (To secure his active advocacy, NIMH expedited review of a distress-grant application to aid a failing center in Mid-Bergen, New Jersey.)

Testimony before the subcommittee in the summer of 1979 to the effect that CMHCs were not meeting the needs of the chronic patient impressed the members and staff. Indeed, the testimony prompted the leadership to schedule two additional days of hearings, one on chronic care and the other on the CMHC program itself. The key staff who developed these hearings and the final subcommittee markup were Dr. George Hardy; Tim Westmoreland, assistant counsel; and Frances Lee de Peyster, for the minority.

The CMHC program oversight hearings, held in February 1980, were an opportunity for NIMH to list the program's accomplishments as well as to describe its pilot federal-state effort in behalf of the underserved population of chronically and seriously disabled persons. The director of the institute's Division of Mental Health Service Programs, Dr. Steven S. Sharfstein, made the following points in testimony to Waxman's subcommittee.

- Since passage of the 1963 legislation, 763 CMHCs have been funded. Fifty percent of the U.S. population, or 111 million people, today live within areas served by these centers.

- In 1979, an estimated 2.4 million people received services at CMHCs.

- CMHCs have redistributed mental health resources to many areas that previously did not have services and personnel. Thirty-seven percent of the centers serve rural areas.

- More than 54 percent of the patients seen in centers have an average annual family income of less than $5,000.

- Local interest in the program continues. As of October, 1979, 67 communities throughout the nation have initiated community mental health center planning activities based on their own assessment of need. [Hearings 1980]

This testimony was received with courteous respect, yet the opposition could not resist taunting the administration witness as follows:

   Mr. Dannemeyer: You are a psychiatrist, are you not?
   Dr. Sharfstein: Yes.
   Mr. Dannemeyer: Is not one of the elements of mental illness the failure of the person to be in touch with reality?

Dr. Sharfstein: Yes.

Mr. Dannemeyer: How would you assess a Congress which year after year exhibits an addiction to spending more money than it takes in, in the way of taxes? How would you describe that in terms of your perspective as a psychiatrist and in terms of mental illness?

Dr. Sharfstein: I feel that I am competent to diagnose patients but in terms of a group process such as the Congress, to venture an opinion would exceed my competence. [Ibid., p. 27]

The exchange occasioned much good-natured laughter. Dannemeyer's complaint echoed that of Iowa Republican Representative Gwynne, made in 1946 during debate on the passage of the first mental health act. Gwynne had declared, "It seems to me the conduct of this Congress in constantly adding to the national debt and in constantly building up bureaucracy is driving more people crazy than this bill will ever cure" (Reichenbach 1977, p. 36). In the end, the House subcommittee basically accepted the administration's reasoning and its bill. Their version was more modest than the Senate's, which set the stage for knotty negotiations between the two chambers in conference.

Three major issues stood in the way of a final compromise on the Mental Health Systems Act, and they were resolved by the conferees in a steamy, hectic three-hour session in Senator Kennedy's office. The conference committee itself was chaired by the retiring Republican, Representative Carter, as an honor to him for his service to health and public policy.

The first issue concerned the regulations on employee protection in the Senate bill which were to be promulgated by the Department of Labor. This was the main point for the American Federation of State and County Municipal Employees (AFSCME) union. In a letter dated March 19, 1980 to Stuart Eisenstat of the White House staff, Jerry Wurf, the international president of AFSCME, stated that the administration bill "utterly fails" in numerous areas and that AFSCME must oppose it. Kennedy, mindful of the million-member union and the primary elections, acceded to all of AFSCME's demands in the bill that came from his subcommittee, but Waxman was adamantly in opposition to the Senate version's process of protecting state employees from displacement. A compromise was put together which gave the lead for joint development of these regulations to the Department of Health and Human Services and the Department of Labor.

A second major issue was the patient's bill of rights in the Senate bill, an issue which had aroused debate and controversy on the floor of the Senate before its passage. Senator Robert Morgan of North Carolina had led a successful floor fight to make the patient's bill of rights a statement of principle—"a sense of the Congress"—which states could choose to adopt rather than federal law. Morgan threatened to filibuster the bill unless his substitute was accepted. Senator Kennedy was obliged to yield, much to the chagrin of Leslie Scallet and other legal advocates and the majority of the mental health advocacy groups (including the National Mental Health Association, the National Association of State Mental Health Program Directors, the National Council of Community Mental Health Centers, the Association for the Advancement of Psychology, the National Association of Social Workers, and the author of this section of the bill, the Mental Health Law Project) (Mental Health Association 1980). Supporting Senator Morgan's position was the American Psychiatric Association and its extremely effective spokesman, Jay Cutler. Even in its diluted form the patient's bill of rights provoked a good deal of controversy during the House-Senate conference, though it was eventually accepted by House Democrats and Republicans alike.

A third controversy of more concern to the administration than to either House or Senate was the House amendment which provided for additional physician bonuses in the Public Health Service comparable to the military pay bill recently signed by the president. The Office of Management and Budget led the fight to try to get this stricken from the legislation and even went so far as to suggest that the president might veto the Systems Act because of this "budget-busting" quality. It seemed unlikely that the president would veto his wife's major bill! The PHS amendment made it into the final Systems Act.

The New Law Is Enacted

So it was that—although the lack of consensus, the temper of the times which created congressional inertia in legislation of this type, the timing of its submission and competing administration priorities did not bode well for passage—the Systems Act became law. Granted that hundreds had worked diligently since the start of President Carter's administration to produce this mid-course correction of the federal mental health commitment, one person must be singled out for special recognition. Rosalynn Carter supported this legislation to give life to the recommendations of the PCMH. In coordination with Tom Bryant and Kathryn Cade, her activities on behalf of the legislation were vital to its passage throughout the often contentious enactment process. At critical junctures, she created congressional priority for the legislation, pressed the interest groups to join together to support it, even telephoned individual members of Congress to push for the bill. She called Henry Waxman and Tim Lee Carter often. Mrs. Carter's appearance before the Senate subcommittee in February 1979 had favorably impressed that controlling party to the events—certainly the senator from Massachusetts, the president's rival for Democratic leadership as well as one whose family was strongly identified with the cause of caring for the mentally ill and retarded. Senator Kennedy had been personally and politically charmed. The enactment of the Mental Health Systems Act thus revealed a new facet of the presidency: a knowledgeable and committed First Lady can act effectively as the president's surrogate during a legislative process.

The Act had been introduced by the president in May 1979; a version passed the Senate (93 to 3) on July 24, 1980, and another the House (277 to 15) on August 22, 1980. The conference report was filed on September 22, 1980 at midnight, just in time for passage before the election recess. President Jimmy Carter signed the Act, Public Law 96-398, on October 7, 1980 at a ceremony in the Woodburn CMHC in northern Virginia. Edward Kennedy and his sister, Eunice Shriver, shared the platform and listened as the president expressed the nation's indebtedness to the Kennedy family for their concern with the human problems of mental illness and mental retardation. Representative Waxman and Health and Human Services (HHS) Secretary Patricia Harris were also present as were representatives of all the groups which had labored over the provisions and formed a coalition to get the Act passed. Although the general election which was to take place in a month's time led, in the summer of 1981, to its repeal, a review of the contents of the Mental Health Systems Act is in order.

Public Law 96-398 was a complex and somewhat mysterious statement of conflicting views on community services for the mentally ill. It was landmark legislation which continued a significant federal leadership role in the improvement of community-based services, even as the CMHC program was to be phased out of federal funding. More than a corrective for the CMHC program, it developed new opportunities and directions for federal support and defined a new partnership with states.

The Mental Health Systems Act encoded expressions of both discouragement and hope about what we as a society might strive for in the treatment, rehabilitation and social support of individuals who by reason of illness cannot sustain themselves unaided within normal community life. The main themes of this Act were: (*a*) priority for community mental health and related support services for the most vulnerable groups, including individuals with chronic mental illness, severely mentally disturbed children and adolescents and the elderly; (*b*) restructuring of federal, state and local roles in the review and management of federally initiated services; (*c*) emphasis on planning and accountability for services developed with public funds, including a mandated "performance contract" with every program as a condition of federal funding; (*d*) opportunities for closer linkages between mental health and general health care settings and for programs designed to prevent mental illness; and (*e*) emphasis on patients' rights, including programs to increase advocacy services for the mentally ill. In total, a four-year program and almost $800 million of "new dollars" was authorized in addition to continuation costs of funded CMHCs. (Appendix B). The following paragraphs describe how these contrary motives affected the major features of the final product.

The seventeen-year federally initiated Community Mental Health Centers program, extensively evaluated from many different perspectives, had its detractors as well as its proponents. The PCMH task panel on CMHC assessment reflected these diverse judgments, and the PCMH report recommended a "new program" of community mental health services. In the Congress itself CMHCs were lauded by some, berated by others: the idea of community mental health was given high rhetorical praise, while the implementation of the federal CMHC program was scored for numerous perceived shortcomings. The Systems Act incorporated this ambivalence about CMHCs.

On the one hand, the CMHC program was continued with opportunities for new grants for the approximately 650 mental health service areas of the country that had not yet been the recipient of a federal CMHC grant. The requirements for designating and funding CMHCs were made more flexible but more exacting accountability for performance was added. On the other hand, perhaps in recognition of centers' fiscal incapacity to provide both mental health and related support services, the Act made available to existing CMHCs funding opportunities for new programs aimed specifically at highly vulnerable populations in need of mental health and related support services—the chronically mentally ill, severely mentally disturbed children and adolescents and the elderly—the groups which CMHCs had been criticized for underserving.

All additional grant dollars were meant to "supplement, not supplant" existing programs. The very availability of the specialized grant dollars for the categorically needy represented an attempt to rectify the too-broad nature of the CMHC mission. Yet the Systems Act continued that broad mission as well as the strategy of a seed-money approach, even though seed money made little sense for those centers which served a population without adequate private or public insurance for mental illness and without adequate state fiscal support. The CMHC program had brought to the awareness of public policymakers the range and cost of current needs of priority groups. Raised but unmet expectations, however, could lead to program disillusionment and proposals for defunding. As the PCMH report put it, "The Community Mental Health Centers program is at a crossroads." Yet the Act did not resolve the fiscal and priority issues around the gap between supply and demand.

The Mental Health Systems Act was a creature of the times in its fiscal conservatism and regulatory expansion. Although its 1963 progenitor looked very different in these respects upon initiation, requirements added to it and appropriations withheld from it made the Systems Act the logical next step. For, as funding failed to keep pace with the costs of mandated services, there had been a progression of expanding federal regulatory review of local and state mental health programs, particularly as these programs related to "deinstitutionalization." Protests against this regulatory emphasis were certainly made by local programs and states, yet the pressing need for reform spurred a decision to use a combination of positive and negative reinforcements thought to be critical to accomplishing reform. More rules and less money to improve the nation's system of mental health care amounts to wishful thinking which could lead to further disenchantment with community mental health as a federal program.

The Systems Act incorporated two contradictory perspectives. The first, aimed at local mental health programs and states, stressed aggressive followup care of persons discharged or diverted from state mental hospitals and the prevention of over-concentration of patients in any single neighborhood. The objectives of knowing where the patients are, providing "case management" services, and detailing and updating "treatment plans" reemphasized the protective role of the state and the doctor's responsibilities even for patients no longer hospitalized. At the same time, the Act promoted a strong bill of patients' rights which emphasized freedom from the state and doctors, especially as patients moved into "least-restrictive" settings.

As the social consensus of the early 1980s turns away from funding the support services and shelter needed for patients returned to the community, the disruptive characteristics of the mentally ill have provoked community rejection and could lead to demands for reinstitutionalization. The 1980s are likely to be the decade in which these key issues are played out and advocates for all views can point to the Mental Health Systems Act for support and justification of their position.

The primary mission of community mental health has been disputed since the beginning; the Systems Act forcefully restated each of three missions without resolving priorities. The first mission in the Act involved the provision in the community of clinical, psychiatric and other mental health services to the mentally ill, with "special attention" to the chronically mentally ill. Adequate clinical care is essential—including the basic inpatient, emergency, outpatient, and day-treatment services.

Next, the Act recognized that patients no longer in the total institution need adequate support services and shelter to maintain stability or improvement. These services are often supported through social and welfare assistance programs whose byzantine bureaucracies require beneficiaries to negotiate a maze of rules, which put the chronically mentally ill at extreme disadvantage. Thus, "case management" emerged as a crucial integrative element. Who supervises the "case manager"? Are individuals who have had major mental illness and suffer from mental disabilities requiring rehabilitation and community support services to be referred to as patients or clients? The medical and social missions of mental health agencies were not clarified by the Systems Act and would have led to further confusion and competition for limited dollars among critical interlocking priorities.

The third community mental health mission was prevention. Data on the effectiveness of consultation and education are sparse. Moreover, there are conflicting judgments about the relative priority of preventing risk factors for mental illness on one hand and, on the other, of early detection and intervention. Overlooking such difficulties, the Systems Act reiterated the prevention mandate and sought to strengthen it by establishing a categorical grant program in prevention as well as an office of prevention within the National Institute of Mental Health.

Limited dollars require that the broad clinical, social and prevention objectives of community mental health programs be assigned priorities at the state and local levels. Congressional leadership has been unable to make these politically hazardous decisions. In the absence of priority-ranking of its missions, community mental health will always be seen by some as failing to keep its promises.

Lastly we must note the contrariness of the legislation in providing for both categorical pluralism and systems-building. The Act provided for ten new categorical programs, each with its own authorization requiring a congressional appropriation to become a reality. Each program was justified on the basis of special need, past neglect and current under-service. Yet the Act also specified a complicated process of systems coordination through the preparation of state mental health service plans, state review and management of federal dollars, federal oversight in relation to states, "performance contracts," evidence of linkages and coordination among a wide array of health and human service agencies, and feedback among all participating agencies.

The quixoticism of PL 96-398 became moot with the election of the Republican challenger Ronald Reagan a month after its enactment. One can note of its numerous supporters—from the executive branch to the Congress to the professional and citizen groups—that at least they tried. To paraphrase Robert Felix's words in recollection of both the strengths and foibles of his own generation of reformers, they stuck to the task and did their best under difficult circumstances because they "gave a damn about people" (Interview, 1972i.).

A Loss of Will

After January 29, 1981, it was up to the new president to implement PL 96-398 and he chose not to do so. Quite the contrary, President Ronald W. Reagan commenced immediately to cut the federal budget and institute a "new federalism." His administration recommended to Congress a 25 percent cut in the level of funding and then conversion of the entire federal mental health services program into a single, so-called block grant to the states with few restrictions. The president's resounding election victory was cited as justification for reversing the prevailing view of the appropriate role of government in the lives of citizens.

The new president's leadership on these issues easily overwhelmed the mental health constituencies that had backed enactment of the Mental Health Systems Act. In the spring of 1981 the House staff met with Representative Waxman to decide upon the most needed services. They concluded that block funding through the states should be targeted to CMHCs, which should then be expected to treat the most needy, especially the chronically ill. It was left to each state, however, to determine the funding for a particular CMHC within its jurisdiction. In other words, it was each state's option (and not a condition of federal funding) to leverage this fiscal tool in order to direct CMHCs to serve the most severely mentally ill. The new HHS Secretary was Richard Schweiker. Two years earlier, while a senator on the Kennedy subcommittee, he had declared it "necessary to improve federal efforts to aid deinstitutionalized patients and the chronically mentally ill." Asked his position on the House approach in the spring of 1981, Secretary Schweiker said he would leave the approach to the deinstitutionalization of patients to the states (Hearings 1981).

Almost twenty years of federal policy was expunged within a few days of furious budget activity in the summer of 1981, when the will to sustain the effort to improve care for the mentally ill was lost in a powerful political backlash. On August 13, 1981 President Reagan signed into law the Omnibus Budget Reconciliation Act, which provided a block of funds to the states for "alcohol and drug abuse and mental health services," and substantially repealed the Mental Health Systems Act (excepting the patients' bill of rights, the payback requirements and the Public Health Service pay bill). The federal government was entirely removed from the direction of the program and became a mere conduit of funds to the states. Using these dollars, states could contract with public and private agencies for the provision of services for the chronically mentally ill. The type of accommodation between the states and local CMHCs would vary depending on state and local leadership. Moreover, the amount of funding for this block grant was far short of what had been expected through the Mental Health Systems Act. Preserving even existing services became doubtful. NIMH was targeted for steep reductions in positions and resources as a result of this bold initiative (Table).

Changes in Support for Community Mental Health, 1980–1983

(in millions of dollars)

	Actual	Carter Recommendation		PCMH Recommendation	Reagan Budgets		Reagan Recommendation
	1980	1981	1982	1983	1981	1982	1983
Research	143.5	152.1	177.1	207.1	148.4	137.3	149.9
Training	90.4	93.8	93.0	105.3	81.3	57.6	14.4
Services	293.8	324.3	339.1*	450.0*	272.2	203.0**	206.0**
Program Support	35.1	38.7	41.3	65.0	38.2	28.1	31.4
Total NIMH	562.8	608.9	650.5	827.4	540.1	223.0	195.7
Positions NIMH	(1,121)	(1,121)	(1,121)	N.A.	(1,120)	(744)	(747)

*MH Systems Act.

**Block grant portion for mental health.

Many states now face decreasing tax revenues; yet their costly state hospitals operate with a questionable capacity to absorb any increase in the number of severely mentally ill patients they treat. Indeed many public hospitals are losing the approval of the Joint Commission on the Accreditation of Hospitals and have suffered a decline in bed capacity and a loss of staff. Meanwhile, cutbacks in social security disability payments, food stamps, and other income support programs create additional stresses on the chronic patient in the community. At the same time, many CMHCs are increasingly unable to become fiscally self-sustaining because the population they serve is unable to pay out-of-pocket and does not have health insurance coverage for treatment of mental illness. Although all this adds up to strong incentives for state and local government and CMHCs to cooperate, their future success seems doubtful in this current period of declining resources and capacity. The prognosis for the 1980s will be the subject of our final chapter.

The Mental Health Systems Act of 1980: A Case Study on the Limits of Legislative Reform

In order to maintain and continue the community mental health initiative, federal leadership was forced to become more rhetorical in promoting, and less practical in demonstrating, program performance. Essential to the political success of the community mental health legislative initiative, its modifications and renewal, was that CMHCs were promoted as vehicles of prevention as well as a kind of aid station for all human misery. In the late 1960s, the addition of social-change goals to CMHC programs led them into areas which were nonmedical and controversial. Community mental health was promoted as a vehicle of social welfare—in terms of one of the goals of the Declaration of Independence, a vehicle for furthering "the pursuit of happiness." The prevention aspects of CMHCs, and the later appearance of self-actualization "treatment" goals, diverted the program from the foremost of its original intentions: To treat and rehabilitate the seriously and chronically ill. The mental health leadership went along with this in order to gain middle-class political support for the program. They won that support by making the program's services universally relevant and universally available. In so doing, they dealt a blow to the archaic two-class mental health care system which deeply offended both their professional standards and their moral sensibilities. Services would be the same for the few and the many.

Before long, however, when fiscal resources through the categorical funds began to shrink, the funding of CMHCs was pushed toward a third-party insurance mode. But the insurance strategy incorrectly assumed mental illness to be identical to other medical illnesses; therefore, insurance funds have been unavailable to pay for the total care of a chronic patient, which involves long-term rehabilitation and life support. The need for social service subsidies to sustain the long-term patient in a variety of nonhospital settings was the big issue for the President's Commission on Mental Health and the Mental Health Systems Act of 1980.

Further, as promises on the scope and humane direction of community mental health exceeded the capacity of the resources allotted to it, expectations of the Congress and other important overseeing groups were disappointed. These shortfalls were made known through evaluation processes such as those of the General Accounting Office. More rules were formulated, more inflexibility resulted. The NIMH pilot Community Support Program did demonstrate bureaucratic leadership and presaged the president's commission and the Mental Health Systems Act. But in order to make it through the congressional gauntlet, the Mental Health Systems Act of 1980 had to give a little something to everyone and as a result became unusually complex and, as it happened, politically vulnerable legislation.

In repealing the Systems Act, the Omnibus Budget Reconciliation Act of 1981 scuttled a worthy attempt to resolve the problems and conflicts which have emerged in almost two decades of federal leadership in community mental health. But as one views the Act itself and reviews the process of enactment, it is clear that many outstanding issues were not resolved. Whether or not consciously left for future federal policymakers to settle, these issues now mostly reside at the state and local community levels. There lies the success or failure of community mental health and systems integration: in decisions made about incentives for program development, fiscal or regulatory; about the balance of rights and freedom vs health and protection; about the clinical, social welfare and prevention goals of the program.

The President's Commission on Mental Health recommended a new program for community mental health services partly in response to criticism of past efforts. In the congressional process, the idea of CMHCs was praised but its implementation was scored. The Systems Act authorized a continuation of the CMHC program for the approximately 650 mental health service areas which had not yet received a grant. They were expected to be comprehensive programs and to be accountable for their performance. On the other hand, the Mental Health Systems Act introduced a variety of new categorical programs aimed at underserved and highly vulnerable populations—the chronically mentally ill, severely disturbed children and adolescents, and the elderly. CMHCs previously funded were considered to be unresponsive to the needs of these groups and funds were expected to go to current programs to improve their responsiveness. Clearly, this implied a major failure of the CMHC program as these priority populations should have been basic to their service mission.

The regulatory emphasis of the Act abetted its demise at the hands of the Reagan administration, which willingly responded to protests from states and local programs about the size and scope of the federal presence in the delivery of services. Yet it was in order to contend with the relatively small budget of the Act that rules were made for state mental health agencies, local community programs and mental health professional trainees, and requirements issued for reporting on the funds spent. Disenchantment with rules and regulations is an important lesson for the federal leadership of the future.

Further, as we have described, the Mental Health Systems Act contained within its substance contradictory perspectives. It emphasized aggressive followup care of persons discharged or diverted from inpatient settings to prevent the blight of the "psychiatric ghetto"; it aimed to do so by providing for case management services and detailed, up-to-date treatment plans—all of which reflected the protective role of the state. At the same time the Act promoted a bill of rights for patients which emphasized freedom from the state and doctors, especially as patients move into least-restrictive settings. The goals of the civil rights and community mental health movement were once congruent, but in the move away from institutions their objectives diverged. Also as noted earlier, the priorities of the mission of community mental health remained confused within the limited dollars provided by the Act itself.

Throughout the Act it was recognized that the mental health system was fragmented. Through a statewide planning process and interaction with health planning agencies, it was hoped that an integrated effort would take place at the local level. Yet the Act added ten new categorical programs, each with a constituency which expressed itself during the enactment process. Thus the complexities of systems coordination became a government burden and the tension between system requirements and a fragmenting, multiple-category service program was built into the Act itself. The block-grant approach of the Reagan administration has bucked the problems to the states, where these public policy issues will be debated over the next decade.

CHAPTER SIX

The Choice Is Ours

The Leadership Factor

The Case of Louis

A Brief Primer on Mental Illness and Health
Acute Illness/Medical Model
Chronic Disability/Rehabilitation Model
Social Maladjustment/Behavioral Model
Personal Unhappiness/Self-Actualization Model

The Four Models, Public Policy and Everyday Practice

The Professional Consensus About the Needs
of the Chronically Mentally Ill

The Future of Community Mental Health—"... We Are
Talking About Each Other"

It was just a ... logical division of labor among a group of people who really had the basics of everything [but most of all who shared] a concern for the problems of the human estate .... We just gave a damn about people.

Robert Felix, M.D.
Remarks regarding the President's
Interagency Committee on Mental
Health

CHAPTER SIX

The Choice Is Ours

In telling the story of government's involvement with services for the mentally ill, we have focused on a special kind of moral leadership exercised by public health physicians, mental health professionals, elected politicians, administrators and concerned citizens. Understanding how this leadership managed a developing political momentum and the networking necessary to implement and protect a major new health policy is an important lesson for the leaders of tomorrow. Creative leadership in the forging of a political, social and scientific consensus on mental illness and its treatment first opened the opportunity for new health policies to emerge. The perseverance of this leadership, its capacity to interact with a broad constituency of active concern, its energy in building a program despite political, fiscal, administrative and social obstacles were extraordinary. What motivated these leaders? As Robert Felix, the first NIMH director, put it—"We gave a damn about people."

The Leadership Factor

The mental health leaders evolved a vision of what was needed. Although less than clear about the steps to enliven the vision, they were able to establish and participate in a network of influential national leaders from all walks of life and, within the constraints of our incremental political system, to foster revolutionary changes in the treatment of the mentally ill. They were masters of the use of incentives to mobilize politically effective alignments of interest. They recruited their own successors. They were builders.

They built the National Institute of Mental Health, which was primarily a research-oriented public health agency. In close connection with research and training, they coaxed into being a "technology" of psychiatric treatments and community mental health centers. The NIMH itself became influential in states and local communities through its political alliances, in both parties, with members of Congress, presidents and presidential families. This leadership persuaded our society to direct federal fiscal resources to the care and treatment of the mentally ill. Even in the face of hostile administrations, they were able to sustain the program until 1981.

It should be noted that the disciplined moral leadership of NIMH and its friends would not have succeeded except for presidential politics. The Kennedy administration and the Kennedy family were critical in promoting the first federal initiative, and the election of 1964 was interpreted as a broad mandate to expand health and social programs for U.S. citizens. The Johnson landslide brought the 1963 legislation to fruition with the 1965 staffing grant amendments. In 1976 another presidential family was concerned and involved with the plight of the mentally ill, and worked to bring about the Mental Health Systems Act of 1980. But then presidential politics shifted radically and the Reagan victory of 1980 led to the repeal of the Systems Act and the devolution of the federal role. One need not speculate for long to realize that a Goldwater election in 1964 would probably have left the 1963 legislation as moot as the 1980 Systems Act is today. In brief, the leadership of a federal agency with broad support and constituencies in the Congress requires some additional priority and momentum from the highest office in the land. Presidential leadership, moral and political, is essential to articulate, formulate and sustain public policy decisions.

The Reagan administration, in which conservative-to-reactionary perspectives dominate policymaking, has withdrawn executive branch support of federal involvement in community mental health. As a result, the strategic assumptions of the 1960s mental health leadership have now become invalid: The federal role of guiding and funding improvements in the treatment of mental illness was *not* beyond political recall; the Community Mental Health Center program, even with timely modifications, was *not* to continue forever. Now the direction of fiscal and program development has shifted from Washington to the states. But the states face an inadequate tax base, taxpayer revolts, and the decline in resources characteristic of a stagnant economy. As of the writing of this book, it is unclear whether states have the capacity and willingness to assume the lead role for community mental health.

Further, as the "safety net" of social welfare supports has been shredded by cutbacks in social security disability payments, food stamps, housing subsidies, and Medicaid, the seriously and chronically mentally ill are being increasingly abandoned in the community. These social welfare cuts, as distinguished from the cuts in funds for treatment and rehabilitation, are particularly devastating to our chronically ill population. Hundreds of thousands of these sick people have been abandoned to fend for themselves in our communities. They are left to stay out of harm's way in such modern alms houses as single-room-occupancy hotels, but there are signs that a large proportion fail and are re-incarcerated in our criminal justice system. With few sensationalized exceptions, they are socially invisible—though they can be seen well enough hallucinating in our fast-food emporia, passing by in our streets and parks, and sleeping on top of sidewalk grates. Moreover, these individuals are not a viable political constituency, and the cost-effectiveness of treating them is marginal at best. This is true especially in depressed economic times when large numbers of nonimpaired persons are out of work.

In terms of cycles of reform, we have come back to Dorothea Dix's plea: these people are ill, they don't belong in jails or scrabbling at the grim margins of twentieth-century "outdoor relief." We have grown too knowledgeable to accuse them of being shiftless; have we become so mean-spirited as to penalize them for their illness?

The Case of Louis

Louis, aged 34, has never held a steady job. He is continuously agitated, a man in motion, a fact made more noticeable by his size. Although his weight fluctuates by 50 pounds during the course of the year, his average weight is about 350 pounds. Most days he can be seen wandering along Broadway in upper Manhattan, constantly darting his glance left and right, occasionally blurting out words or gesturing in a pantomime of debate. Alternately angry and appeasing in these parodies of conversation, he is totally absorbed even as he seems distracted by other sounds and movements. Convinced that his thoughts are broadcast electronically, he avoids all shop windows where audiovisual equipment is on display. As he moves along he seems to walk forty paces forward and then abruptly ten paces back—his ritual to avert an unnameable calamity to everybody in the near vicinity.

If asked, Louis would tell you that the Communists are programming his thoughts and motions and surely would take over the White House unless he personally intervenes. The night before, risking the possibility that the KGB is tapping his telephone voice, he placed collect calls to the Air Force, the Secret Service and the FBI in Washington in an effort to pass along his ominous warnings. He is wearing a filthy, tattered raincoat, a food-stained sport shirt with two buttons missing, trousers held up by suspenders, and a run-down pair of shoes. He has not bathed in several weeks, and his approach is announced by his strong body odor.

Born out of wedlock, Louis at age two was given up by his mother when she could no longer cope with him alone in New York on welfare with her own history of psychiatric illness. Adopted by a childless couple at age three, he was raised by his surrogate parents until age twelve, when problems with truancy, petty thievery, and running away from home became too much for them. They placed him in a state facility for boys; tests administered there showed Louis to be of superior intelligence.

His first psychotic episode occurred at age eighteen, three months after enlisting in the U.S. Army. He received a general discharge after signing a statement that his problems predated his joining the military. Despite attempts over the years to establish that his chronic mental disorder was connected to his military service, Louis has never been able to claim VA benefits. Nevertheless, it was during his Army service that he began to develop complex delusional symptoms which periodically thereafter created enough trouble in his life to lead to fifteen hospitalizations in sixteen years, many in VA hospitals despite the contention that his condition predated his military service. His delusional jumbled thoughts, autistic connections, bizarre behavior and irrational fears are muted somewhat by the major tranquillizing medications prescribed for him, which he takes intermittently and irregularly. All of these symptoms and signs indicate that he is suffering from chronic schizophrenia.

Louis has been living in a cramped and shabby hotel room. His financial support comes from SSI payments and Medicaid benefits. Most of his days are spent at the library looking at pictures or wandering the city streets. He is acquainted with others in the same situation, and occasionally meets and converses with one or another of them on a bench in the small park at Broadway and W. 70th St. On Tuesdays he goes to a local psychosocial rehabilitation center for group psychotherapy. A social worker there has been trying for months to place Louis in a sheltered workshop, but so far there has been no room for someone as impaired as he. Getting a job is his single aspiration, for he recalls his Army days as the only time he ever felt he belonged.

On any day in recent years, one could find abroad in American communities tens of thousands of people more or less as impaired and bereft of opportunity as Louis. The hidden hand of government, which had nothing to do with the onset and progression of their illnesses, has a great deal to do with their opportunities for treatment, decent shelter, rehabilitation, some kind of meaningful life.

Epidemiological studies on mental disorders indicate that the incidence of major psychiatric disease has not changed in the last fifty years. Although advances in biological psychiatry and social psychology have begun to unravel the mysteries of mental illness, knowledge of cause and cure remains rudimentary. The helping professions concentrate on symptomatic relief and control over clear dangers from or directed to the patient. Decisions are guided by social values and available resources rather than scientific understanding. Although there has been a tremendous growth in treatment and rehabilitation opportunities for the mentally ill over the past two decades, political values have supported hardly more than a starvation level of resources to follow-through on society's responsibility to care for this dependent population. Before the mid-1960s, most people like Louis were incarcerated, more or less for their lifetimes, in public mental asylums. Today it is estimated that at least one million persons with chronic mental illness are living in the community. A brief primer on the practices of contemporary clinical psychiatry will help explain why this reversal occurred.

A Brief Primer on Mental Illness and Health

The last twenty years of government efforts to develop a nationwide service system of treatment for the mentally ill and mental health care generated a new cross-disciplinary field called community psychiatry. Practitioners employ definitions of mental health and mental illness that differ from the definitions used by their colleagues of earlier generations who practiced asylum psychiatry, especially with respect to opportunities for patients who suffer chronic mental illness. A community perspective attempts to distinguish among mental illness, chronic mental disability, social maladjustment and personal unhappiness. These distinctions become blurred in actual practice but they are useful in framing an understanding of our current mental health service system.

Four models of patients/clients may be said to dominate the scene although they by no means constitute a complete picture of this extremely complex field, where paradigms abound for the poorly understood phenomena representing normal and abnormal psychology. The latest version of the *Comprehensive Textbook of Psychiatry* runs some 3,665 pages. The practitioners of mental health care spend years attempting to master the descriptive and theoretical material of their specialty practices. This primer is intended merely to introduce the lay reader to the real world of patients and practice.

The point of view is one honed from the experience of a clinical psychiatrist who has found the following eclectic, multiple-explanatory approach to be useful in the various practice settings of community mental health. The approach relies on the *Diagnostic and Statistical Manual of Mental Disorders, Third Edition (DSM-III)*, published in 1980 after years of preparation (American Psychiatric Association). *DSM-III* is a descriptive and diagnostic classification scheme of all mental disorders. Its focus on descriptions is a departure from the earlier psychodynamic emphases, which assume a mental health-to-mental illness developmental continuum in the history of the individual. Until recently, the dynamic view dominated the mental health field in both psychiatry and psychology. The descriptive approach embodied in *DSM-III* complements rather than competes with the older explanation. *DSM-III* takes a more clinical and public health approach by pointing to discontinuities between health and illness and "risk factors" as distinguished from the signs and symptoms of mental illness. The character of *DSM-III* is illustrated in the following sketches of the four widely used models.

Acute Illness/Medical Model

The medical model holds that mental health problems and frank madness are no different from somatic health problems and disease. A doctor must diagnose the disease, and a biological cause is assumed although few have been fully explained. A process of differential diagnosis is undertaken by the physician in an effort to rule out competing diagnoses. Diagnosis leads to treatment decisions and a more or less predictable prognosis ensues. Treatments to ameliorate definable symptoms are most often somatic, such as using the drug lithium for bipolar affective disorder, antipsychotic drugs for schizophrenia, electroconvulsive therapy for suicidal depression.

Hospitals are the main institutional derivatives of the medical model, with medical responsibility clearly defined. Patients regard themselves as sick. The sick "role" confers certain duties on the patient (sufferer) to obey the doctor's orders and take the medications the doctor prescribes. Patients accept the doctor's authority without question. They are not to be held responsible for being ill. This model is most compatible with health insurance and with peer review accountability systems.

Chronic Disability/Rehabilitation Model

In this model mental illness is a disability and is often long-term. People become dysfunctional in early life and remain so for many years despite treatment efforts. Causes are not germane, chronicity is; goals are modest. Self-care, resocialization and enhancement of vocational functioning and independent-living skills are the goals of therapeutic intervention. Shelter is paramount. If sheltered in the community, these disabled persons must have community support systems to help them in self-maintenance. So-called tertiary prevention is also emphasized, that is, prevention of further residual disability. "Normalization" and "least-restrictive environments" are other terms in this approach; they refer to assisting patients to live under the most normal circumstances, in settings least restrictive of their freedom, commensurate with their health. Protection of mentally disabled people from exploitation, abuse and discrimination are other aspects.

This book has pointed up the relevancy of this model for the 1980s. The deinstitutionalization of the state hospital system has brought it to the forefront. Twenty years of experience with community mental health has led to an expansion of this conceptualization. It is the model applicable to Louis and tens of thousands of other persons with chronic mental illness. It is key in the question of government's role and society's moral choice about care for the mentally ill.

Social Maladjustment/Behavioral Model

Many people in our society are disruptive of the social order. Whether hallucinating in the streets, frequently antagonizing coworkers, or consistently unable to carry out their everyday tasks, their behavior is unacceptable and considered deviant. A behavioral model sees such behavior as bad rather than sick or stunted. The cause of this bad behavior may be biological (XYY chromosome) or sociological (poverty) or due to learning bad habits. Allied with the criminal justice ideology and system, this moral model is the underpinning of civil commitment statutes. Treatments emphasize positive and negative sanctions to inculcate appropriate behavior. These reinforcements can be in the form of token economies on inpatient units, which use small, concrete rewards and punishments to shape patient behavior, or electrical shocks for modification of homosexual behavior. The social control goals of state mental hospitals, the ward attendants and the locked doors are aspects of this model. Custody and asylum are key; health insurance has no relevance.

Deinstitutionalization has provoked a backlash in many communities and has led to a call for more social control. The failure of community mental health to deal with infringements of the social order is forcing local jails and prisons to take custody of many former long-time state hospital patients as well as younger adult chronic patients who have had little or no hospital treatment.

Personal Unhappiness/Self-Actualization Model

In this model the person is truly a client and not considered sick. The causes of mental health problems stem from the difficulty individuals experience in reaching their full potential. The difficulty can be due to external constraints such as a poorly performing economy or discrimination and/or to internal impediments such as the crippling influences of unloving parents. The universe of mental health problems is enormously expanded with the acceptance of this self-actualization, or growth, model. Problems leading to personal unhappiness that range from identity crises to underemployment are considered part of the mental health enterprise. Such problems can also be conceptualized as risk factors for the development of socially maladjusted behavior or even frank mental illness.

A variety of "therapies" (to broaden the meaning of the medical term here) are proposed as effective. Even encouragement of social action can be seen as desirable therapy—for example, action to promote a full employment policy or to eliminate race, sex and age discrimination. On a more directly personal level, a great array of individual and group psychotherapies, based on various schools of thought, are offered up as solutions. Included are such stylish growth programs for the upwardly mobile individual as est, bioenergetics, rolfing, primal scream and Transcendental Meditation.

Goals in this model are expressed in terms of personal happiness. It is the responsibility of the client to change; the therapist acts as a guide, instructor or trainer. Rarely can health insurance be justified as a third-party payer. The question, "Is it medically necessary and appropriate?" is answered in the negative. The public policy and governmental response to mental health issues related to this model are also more problematic, although the original design of the Community Mental Health Center program partially incorporated this model and promoted these interventions in an attempt to prevent major mental illness.

The Four Models, Public Policy and Everyday Practice

There is much confusion today both in public policy toward the mentally ill and in community treatment programs around the country because, in practice, these four models are often entwined. A practitioner, a CMHC administrator or a government planner may use aspects of each model serially or simultaneously. For example, when a hallucinating patient enters a CMHC the goals of treatment, containment and rehabilitation intermingle. The patient may be placed on a drug protocol and given psychotherapy on an inpatient unit; the door of the inpatient unit may be kept locked; a rehabilitation counselor may be introduced in the context of discharge planning to a long-term sheltered workshop. Sometimes these various procedures and goals conflict with one another. The treatment of the individual may have to take a lower priority to the needs of the neighborhood or the family in removing a disruptive person. In other instances, practitioners or agencies may use the single-treatment approach for all individuals who come to them. Every patient receives drug therapy or inside-oriented psychotherapy because this is what the staff is able to provide; a flexible treatment approach is irrelevant.

Amid the confusion, two things are clear. One, that every individual with a mental health problem would benefit most from a treatment approach designed specifically to meet his or her needs. And two, that very few facilities which provide mental health care are able to offer such individualized approaches because the structure of our system and the opportunities for treatment, shelter and rehabilitation are highly dependent on financing. If that financing is skewed toward the acute illness/medical model and inpatient care, the other therapeutic and rehabilitation programs may atrophy and be inadequate in any specific situation. If all chronic schizophrenics in a CMHC are offered only chemotherapy, other therapeutic and functional needs remain unsatisfied.

As if the situation were not already complex enough, there are at least two other complications. The first is that services within each model of care services can be delivered both within and outside the specialty mental health system. For example, with the social control or behavioral model, individuals may be seen either in the mental health or criminal justice system. Similarly, in both the acute illness and chronic disability models, drug treatment may occur in general health care settings, psychotherapy may take place in family counseling clinics, vocational rehabilitation in a sheltered workshop operated under the auspices of a voluntary agency in the community. The second complication is overlap and confusion within the mental health care system itself. The practitioner or administrator may think therapy is being provided when containment only is offered. Myths about mental illness and its treatment are hard to dispel; traces linger even among professionals. Thus, midway into the twentieth century, asylum approaches were still considered to be treatment, not custody.

Indeed, for 100 years asylum psychiatry dominated public mental health care. The prototypic state mental hospital was a world unto itself, a complex organization of front wards, back wards, open and locked wards, voluntary and involuntary patients, civil and criminal units, geriatric and medical-surgical units, specialized services for children, research, and ancillary support services. In the late 1950s and early 1960s when the decisions were made to deinstitutionalize the public system by dispersing the old and diverting new, potentially long-term patients, it became necessary to develop an alternate, decentralized system that would gradually assume all of the multiple functions of the state hospital. The spectrum of community-based services has had to include all the functions formerly provided by the total institution plus some new services such as case management, income maintenance, and training in the skills of daily living. Acquiring the services of each function is a complicated problem in negotiation for the discharged patient—as it would be for anyone—because services are financed by literally scores of different local, state, federal and private charitable programs with reams of different eligibility criteria. The need for someone to help decipher the patchwork of resource opportunities has evolved into a totally new role for government workers.

Approximately half of the almost 2 million chronically mentally ill Americans live in residential treatment and care facilities. Most are in nursing homes; about 150,000 are in the public mental hospitals. The other half, as noted above, reside in the community, some with family, some in supervised settings such as halfway houses, and others in a variety of independent living arrangements and board-and-care homes (Goldman et al. 1981). In addition to health and mental health care, rehabilitation services—especially in the form of community psychosocial "clubs" for expsychiatric hospital patients, established under volunteer auspices or through private and public agencies such as CMHCs—are essential aspects of patient care in the community. Yet community services are generally incomplete, fragmented and uncoordinated because a diversified multi-agency provider network—rather than a total, rational system—is only as much as society has been willing to support financially and politically. The patients discharged into unprepared and often hostile communities personally confront our society's ambivalence about the level of social welfare that should be provided to the destitute and disabled.

The decisions to move patients from the asylum into the community came as a result of a broad medical and legal consensus that most mentally ill people could live in the community, even during acute episodes of illness, *provided* they had access to a range of medical, mental health, life-support and rehabilitation services when they needed them. This proviso is key because these individuals may be from time to time totally dependent on others for support of their life and human dignity. The resource decisions required to meet their needs entail both professional and political considerations. As for the former, it is now recognized that a flexible mix of rehabilitative and medical approaches can be successful in overcoming the disabling consequences of chronic mental illness. It is proving to be very difficult, however, to combine psychological, medical, social and rehabilitation services in the community. The complexity of the task of combining services can be glimpsed by considering the main lines of the professional consensus about the needs of the population of chronically mentally ill persons.

The Professional Consensus About the Needs of the Chronically Mentally Ill

Four clusters of services, incorporating aspects of the four models described earlier, are needed by chronically mentally ill persons at different times. They are acute treatment services, rehabilitation services, sustaining services and residential treatment services. *Acute treatment services* are necessary to provide rapid intervention and stabilization in periods of acute psychotic decompensation. This is crucial for persons experiencing their first episode of psychotic illness because appropriate early treatment can help prevent occurrence of the disabling consequences of a psychotic episode. These services are provided in numerous hospital and CMHC settings as well as in such nonhospital emergency settings as have emerged in family and foster care homes and hostels. Any of these diverse settings can serve to meet the short-term needs for treatment, protection and support during acute episodes of illness.

For persons with a history of multiple psychotic episodes, an acute episode can be appropriately thought of as a relapse in the chronic course of a major psychiatric illness. These chronically mentally ill patients therefore need, in addition to acute treatment services, the services and opportunities available in the three other clusters noted above. There can be no doubt about the chronically disabling character of schizophrenia, for example, which was demonstrated in 1967 by Schooler and her coworkers. These researchers did a one-year followup study of 299 schizophrenic patients discharged after short-term drug therapy. They found that 176 expatients (59 percent) did not need to be rehospitalized while 123 (41 percent) had been rehospitalized; of these, 78 were subsequently discharged a second time during the study year. Of the 254 expatients residing in the community a year following the initial discharge, only 33 of them (11 percent) could be described as functioning at a level equal to the average person in the community. Nor is it disputed that most persons with schizophrenia should continue medication after an acute episode has abated. In 1974, Hogarty and coworkers studied 374 schizophrenic patients in the community and demonstrated that patients on long-term antipsychotic medication did better than patients on placebo. In twenty-four months, 80 percent of those patients on placebo relapsed as compared to 48 percent of those who were taking active medications. In sum, it is well-established that persons with chronic mental illness need long-term medical followup care to monitor and adjust medications.

It is also now widely acknowledged that adequate post-hospital followup care must include psychosocial and vocational *rehabilitation services*. These are designed to promote as normal a level of functioning as possible in individuals with severe mental illness. Such services are geared toward self-maintenance in the community in such areas as housing, employment and social interaction. Opportunities for fostering psychosocial and vocational potential are ideally based in "clubs" where individuals are considered members, not patients, which allows for acceptance and positive expectations. The social support system in which each person has a meaningful role is the key element in any of these programs. Some also provide a range of residential opportunities and supportive employment—for example, Fountain House in New York City and Horizon House in Philadelphia. All such rehabilitation services aim at maximum independence for persons with chronic mental illness and are clearly conceptualized as long-term care alternatives to custodial asylum. The funding of these rehabilitation services and opportunities has been a difficult problem for many local organizations that wish to offer them, including churches, charity groups, clinics, hospitals and CMHCs. The cost-effectiveness of these alternatives to the traditional asylum is yet to be clearly established but several studies from the University of Wisconsin demonstrate that important new benefits are gained (Stein and Test 1980, Weisbrod 1980).

Sustaining services are needed to assist in maintaining a minimum or modest level of functioning for the disabled person in the community. Quality of life must be attended to, including social support, decent shelter and, as appropriate, protective support such as guardianship and foster care. Such services are essential in a total program of mental health care if the long-term patient is to survive with dignity in the community.

Lastly, some small proportion of the chronically mentally ill need twenty-four-hour *residential treatment services* because they are unable to care for themselves even with strong community support. Services for these populations are provided primarily in state mental hospitals and private-sector nursing homes.

An array of services and opportunities, spelled out in the Table below, indicates the range of needs that must be met in caring for this population. It is important to bear in mind that the array refers to the collective needs of approximately two million people; individual needs are widely diverse and vary over time. These needs can be met by programs based in specially organized settings such as CMHCs and hospitals, depending on the experience of local communities and current institutional arrangements. Note that integrative services are included in the array; they are considered essential to help disabled persons negotiate for their rights and entitlements. Expert professional and paraprofessional personnel who can take the special rigors of working with severely mentally disabled people are obviously vital to quality mental health care. For the chronically mentally ill, as for all of us, sustaining human relationships are key; for the chronically mentally ill person, such relationships are probably the most important element in preventing relapses and avoiding costly hospitalizations.

Clearly, the clinical consensus evolved over the course of our story. But a way has yet to be found to staff, organize and deliver this array of services through multiple networks of public and private agencies. This takes political support. But as our story has also shown, the political consensus lost focus in the face of a growing cast of constituencies, each with its own individual demands. Meanwhile, the program's original intent—to help our least fortunate citizens—sinks in a mire of mandates, priorities, rules and regulations.

The President's Commission on Mental Health was itself weighed down by similar forces. The program's last-minute lifeline, the Mental Health Systems Act of 1980, failed and fell easy prey to the Omnibus Budget Reconciliation Act.

So where lies the future of community mental health? Can a new grand consensus be forged from the old? Obviously, the experience of three decades offers many lessons. The challenge is to learn from them.

The Future of Community Mental Health—"We Are Talking About Each Other"

In the past quarter-century the national mental health enterprise has expanded and diversified its portfolio and produced many dividends. Without specific centralized planning, the federal government promoted opportunities for community-based settings and innovations of treatment and support.

These activities sparked and fueled a revolution in access to care and a reversal in the proportion of hospital inpatient to outpatient care episodes. Three-quarters of all patient-care episodes in 1955 took place in inpatient settings; by 1977, a little over one-quarter of all episodes were in inpatient settings. A great pluralism of new public and private settings emerged. Today's expanded service system allows a considerable degree of consumer choice in practitioner and practice settings for mental health care as well as some cost-

Comprehensive Array of Services and Opportunities for Chronically Mentally Ill Persons

Basic Needs/Opportunities

Shelter
- Protected (with health, rehabilitative and/or social services provided on site)
  Hospital
  Nursing home
  Intermediate care facility
  Crisis facility

- Semi-independent (linked to service)
  Family home
  Group home
  Cooperative apartment
  Foster care home
  Emergency housing facility
  Other board and care home
  Independent apartment/home (access to services)

Food, clothing, and household management
- Fully provided meals
- Food purchase/preparation assistance
- Access to food stamps
- Homemaker service

Income/financial support
- Access to entitlements
- Employment

Meaningful activities
- Work opportunities
- Recreation
- Religious/spiritual
- Human/social interaction

Mobility/transportation

Special Needs/Opportunities

Treatment services
- General medical services
  Physician assessment & care
  Nursing assessment & care
  Dentist assessment & care
  Physical/occupational therapy
  Speech/hearing therapy
  Nutrition counseling
  Medication counseling
  Home health services

- Mental health services
  Acute treatment services
  Crisis stabilization
  Diagnosis & assessment
  Medication monitoring
  Self-medication training
  Psychotherapies
  Hospitalization: Acute and long-term care

Habilitation and rehabilitation
- Social/recreational skills development
- Life skills development
- Leisure time activities

Vocational
- Prevocational assessment counseling
- Sheltered work opportunities
- Transitional employment
- Job development and placement

Social services
- Family support
- Community support assistance
- Housing and milieu management
- Legal services
- Entitlement assistance

Integrative services
- Client identification & outreach
- Individual assessment & service planning
- Case service & resource management
- Advocacy & community organization
- Community information
- Education & support

From: Steering Committee 1981

efficiencies due to competition. In addition, the greater integration of mental health care in general health settings and programs yields evidence that greater cost-effectiveness accrues to both as a result.

These revolutionary changes have been thorough. Today's mental health care system bears little resemblance to the system it replaced—asylum psychiatry for the many and the 1930s-to-1950s psychoanalytic approach for the few outpatients. From 1955 to 1977 the number of patient-care episodes in specialty mental health facilities almost quadrupled from 1.7 million episodes to 6.4 million episodes, and the rate per 100,000 population tripled. In 1955, about half of all care episodes occurred in state and county mental hospitals. By 1977 the largest proportion of total episodes occurred in federally funded CMHCs and free-standing outpatient clinics, with each accounting for around 28 percent of total episodes. Psychiatric units in general hospitals and CMHCs have accounted for the greatest growth in the facility sector of the specialty mental health care system.

Yet, although the number of state and county mental hospitals decreased only 2 percent from 1955 to 1977, the number of beds in these hospitals decreased about 70 percent. The difficulty in closing the hospitals and shifting resources from the fixed costs of large public institutions to the variable costs of community care has been a major obstacle to the funding of community care.

These changes would not have happened except for an expanding array of public and private third-party financial support sources, including federal "seed money" for CMHCs and alcohol and drug treatment programs. Other major sources of funds include Medicaid, private health insurance and federally subsidized third-party insurance such as the federal employees health benefits program. Major medical coverage under private insurance today includes full care for short-term inpatient stays in general hospital settings. Short-term psychiatric units in general hospitals have expanded in number. SSI support and food stamps have been essential in enabling patients to live in community settings.

Amid these changes there continues to be tremendous variation across communities in opportunities for treatment and rehabilitation, depending in large part on patients' social class and local community traditions. Service opportunities and income supports vary widely among communities and from state to state. The poor mentally ill fare quite differently from one another in California and Mississippi, Arkansas and Maine. Almost 800 federally initiated

CMHCs now cover 54 percent of the country. The importance of state hospitals has declined but they remain a significant factor in relation to the population of severely disabled people who require care and support twenty-four hours a day, seven days a week, fifty-two weeks a year. The numbers of chronically mentally ill in communities have increased dramatically and the integration of mental health care for such patients with the general health and social service systems also varies widely across the country. The best opportunities occur in those areas which provide an organized community mental health system utilizing inpatient units of general hospitals, expanded outpatient units, day treatment, close interaction with rehabilitation centers and psychosocial clubs, and supervised shelter. Sustaining such high-quality care is problematic under current conditions of fiscal constraint.

Whether to let lapse the pivotal role of the federal government in sustaining these improvements is the question. One must wonder whether President Pierce's judgment, however correct in his 1854 veto message to the Congress, can continue to hold sway today. The current effort to roll back thirty-five years of progressive social policy, as Senator Patrick Moynihan (D-NY) has characterized the Reagan administration's strategy, tests whether we as a society will countenance a moral retreat to 1854 and forego the gains of our own time.

Despite the shortcomings of the federal program, local communities continued to apply for federal funds to provide community care for their mentally ill. Block grants and shrunken budgets represent a public policy retreat from the goals for community mental health as expressed most recently by the Mental Health Systems Act of 1980. There is a glaring disparity between what could and should be done and what is being done. Leadership from the old and new coalitions of citizens, professionals, and politicians must find the way forward again.

It is a myth that chronically mentally ill persons can pull themselves up by their own bootstraps. It is a myth that volunteerism will replace federal leadership. Why is it that we have turned our back to the facts, that we are buying the myths? To Rosalynn Carter, it was because "we forget we are talking about each other." What we do in the next decade will say something about our society and its capacity to sustain a certain moral vision. For our part we call for renewal of will. What is needed now is to give a damn about people.

Seventy-ninth Congress of the United States of America

At the Second Session

Begun and held at the City of Washington on Monday, the fourteenth
day of January, one thousand nine hundred and forty-six

AN ACT

To amend the Public Health Service Act to provide for research relating to psychiatric disorders and to aid in the development of more
effective methods of prevention, diagnosis, and treament of such
disorders, and for other purposes.

*Be it enacted by the Senate and House of Representatives of the
United States of America in Congress assembled*, That this Act may
be cited as the "National Mental Health Act".

PURPOSE

SEC. 2. The purpose of this Act is the improvement of the mental
health of the people of the United States through the conducting of
researches, investigations, experiments, and demonstrations relating
to the cause, diagnosis, and treatment of psychiatric disorders; assisting and fostering such research activities by public and private agencies, and promoting the coordination of all such researches and activities and the useful application of their results; training personnel in
matters relating to mental health; and developing, and assisting
States in the use of, the most effective methods of prevention, diagnosis, and treatment of psychiatric disorders.

Speaker of the House of Representatives

President of the Senate pro tempore.

Approved July 3, 1946

Harry Truman

**The National Mental Health Act of 1946
as signed by President Harry S. Truman**

There is no single piece of health legislation approved
during my term that is to me a source of greater pride than
the National Mental Health Act of 1946.

Laws, however, are just the framework for action, which,
without the concern of persons like those attending this Silver
Anniversary Conference, would accomplish little. The
mental health profession has made the most of the legislation which we provided on July 3, 1946.

I trust the next twenty-five years will witness a further-
ance of governmental and private partnership, which is so
necessary to solution of great public problems.

Harry S. Truman

**Statement by former president Harry S. Truman on the twenty-fifth
anniversary of the signing of the National Mental Health Act of 1946**

APPENDIX A

Presidential Message on Mental
Illness and Mental Retardation
John F. Kennedy
February 5, 1963

Presidential Message on Mental
Health Systems
Jimmy Carter
May 15, 1979

MENTAL ILLNESS AND MENTAL RETARDATION

MESSAGE

FROM

THE PRESIDENT OF THE UNITED STATES

RELATIVE TO

MENTAL ILLNESS AND MENTAL RETARDATION

FEBRUARY 5, 1963.—Referred to the Committee on Interstate and Foreign Commerce and ordered to be printed

To the Congress of the United States:

It is my intention to send shortly to the Congress a message pertaining to this Nation's most urgent needs in the area of health improvement. But two health problems—because they are of such critical size and tragic impact, and because their susceptibility to public action is so much greater than the attention they have received—are deserving of a wholly new national approach and a separate message to the Congress. These twin problems are mental illness and mental retardation.

From the earliest days of the Public Health Service to the latest research of the National Institutes of Health, the Federal Government has recognized its responsibilities to assist, stimulate, and channel public energies in attacking health problems. Infectious epidemics are now largely under control. Most of the major diseases of the body are beginning to give ground in man's increasing struggle to find their cause and cure. But the public understanding, treatment, and prevention of mental disabilities have not made comparable progress since the earliest days of modern history.

Yet mental illness and mental retardation are among our most critical health problems. They occur more frequently, affect more people, require more prolonged treatment, cause more suffering by

85011

163

the families of the afflicted, waste more of our human resources, and constitute more financial drain upon both the Public Treasury and the personal finances of the individual families than any other single condition.

There are now about 800,000 such patients in this Nation's institutions—600,000 for mental illness and over 200,000 for mental retardation. Every year nearly 1,500,000 people receive treatment in institutions for the mentally ill and mentally retarded. Most of them are confined and compressed within an antiquated, vastly overcrowded, chain of custodial State institutions. The average amount expended on their care is only $4 a day—too little to do much good for the individual, but too much if measured in terms of efficient use of our mental health dollars. In some States the average is less than $2 a day.

The total cost to the taxpayers is over $2.4 billion a year in direct public outlays for services—about $1.8 billion for mental illness and $600 million for mental retardation. Indirect public outlays, in welfare costs and in the waste of human resources, are even higher. But the anguish suffered both by those afflicted and by their families transcends financial statistics—particularly in view of the fact that both mental illness and mental retardation strike so often in childhood, leading in most cases to a lifetime of disablement for the patient and a lifetime of hardship for his family.

This situation has been tolerated far too long. It has troubled our national conscience—but only as a problem unpleasant to mention, easy to postpone, and despairing of solution. The Federal Government, despite the nationwide impact of the problem, has largely left the solutions up to the States. The States have depended on custodial hospitals and homes. Many such hospitals and homes have been shamefully understaffed, overcrowded, unpleasant institutions from which death too often provided the only firm hope of release.

The time has come for a bold new approach. New medical, scientific, and social tools and insights are now available. A series of comprehensive studies initiated by the Congress, the executive branch, and interested private groups have been completed and all point in the same direction.

Governments at every level—Federal, State, and local—private foundations and individual citizens must all face up to their responsibilities in this area. Our attack must be focused on three major objectives:

First, we must seek out the causes of mental illness and of mental retardation and eradicate them. Here, more than in any other area, "an ounce of prevention is worth more than a pound of cure." For prevention is far more desirable for all concerned. It is far more economical and it is far more likely to be successful. Prevention will require both selected specific programs directed especially at known causes, and the general strengthening of our fundamental community, social welfare, and educational programs which can do much to eliminate or correct the harsh environmental conditions which often are associated with mental retardation and mental illness. The proposals contained in my earlier message to the Congress on education and those which will be contained in a later message I will send on the Nation's health will also help achieve this objective.

Second, we must strengthen the underlying resources of knowledge and, above all, of skilled manpower which are necessary to mount and sustain our attack on mental disability for many years to come. Personnel from many of the same professions serve both the mentally ill and the mentally retarded. We must increase our existing training programs and launch new ones, for our efforts cannot succeed unless we increase by severalfold in the next decade the number of professional and subprofessional personnel who work in these fields. My proposals on the health professions and aid for higher education are essential to this goal, and both the proposed youth employment program and a national service corps can be of immense help. We must also expand our research efforts if we are to learn more about how to prevent and treat the crippling or malfunction of the mind.

Third, we must strengthen and improve the programs and facilities serving the mentally ill and the mentally retarded. The emphasis should be upon timely and intensive diagnosis, treatment, training, and rehabilitation so that the mentally afflicted can be cured or their functions restored to the extent possible. Services to both the mentally ill and to the mentally retarded must be community based and provide a range of services to meet community needs.

It is with these objectives in mind that I am proposing a new approach to mental illness and to mental retardation. This approach is designed, in large measure, to use Federal resources to stimulate State, local, and private action. When carried out, reliance on the cold mercy of custodial isolation will be supplanted by the open warmth of community concern and capability. Emphasis on prevention, treatment, and rehabilitation will be substituted for a desultory interest in confining patients in an institution to wither away.

In an effort to hold domestic expenditures down in a period of tax reduction, I have postponed new programs and reduced added expenditures in all areas when that could be done. But we cannot afford to postpone any longer a reversal in our approach to mental affliction. For too long the shabby treatment of the many millions of the mentally disabled in custodial institutions and many millions more now in communities needing help has been justified on grounds of inadequate funds, further studies, and future promises. We can procrastinate no more. The national mental health program and the national program to combat mental retardation herein proposed warrant prompt congressional attention.

I. A NATIONAL PROGRAM FOR MENTAL HEALTH

I propose a national mental health program to assist in the inauguration of a wholly new emphasis and approach to care for the mentally ill. This approach relies primarily upon the new knowledge and new drugs acquired and developed in recent years which make it possible for most of the mentally ill to be successfully and quickly treated in their own communities and returned to a useful place in society.

These breakthroughs have rendered obsolete the traditional methods of treatment which imposed upon the mentally ill a social quarantine, a prolonged or permanent confinement in huge, unhappy mental hospitals where they were out of sight and forgotten. I am not unappreciative of the efforts undertaken by many States to improve conditions in these hospitals, or the dedicated work of many hospital staff members. But their task has been staggering and the results too often dismal, as the comprehensive study by the Joint Commission on

Mental Illness and Health pointed out in 1961. Some States have at times been forced to crowd five, ten, or even fifteen thousand people into one large understaffed institution. Imposed largely for reasons of economy, such practices were costly in human terms, as well as in a real economic sense. The following statistics are illustrative:

Nearly one-fifth of the 279 State mental institutions are fire and health hazards; three-fourths of them were opened prior to World War I.

Nearly half of the 530,000 patients in our State mental hospitals are in institutions with over 3,000 patients, where individual care and consideration are almost impossible.

Many of these institutions have less than half the professional staff required—with less than 1 psychiatrist for every 360 patients.

Forty-five percent of their inmates have been hospitalized continuously for 10 years or more.

But there are hopeful signs. In recent years the increasing trend toward higher and higher concentrations in these institutions has been reversed—by the use of new drugs, by the increasing public awareness of the nature of mental illness, and by a trend toward the provision of community facilities, including psychiatric beds in general hospitals, day care centers, and outpatient psychiatric clinics. Community general hospitals in 1961 treated and discharged as cured more than 200,000 psychiatric patients.

I am convinced that, if we apply our medical knowledge and social insights fully, all but a small portion of the mentally ill can eventually achieve a wholesome and constructive social adjustment. It has been demonstrated that two out of three schizophrenics—our largest category of mentally ill—can be treated and released within 6 months, but under the conditions that prevail today the average stay for schizophrenia is 11 years. In 11 States, by the use of modern techniques, 7 out of every 10 schizophrenia patients admitted were discharged within 9 months. In one instance, where a State hospital deliberately sought an alternative to hospitalization in those patients about to be admitted, it was able to treat successfully in the community 50 percent of them. It is clear that a concerted national attack on mental disorders is now both possible and practical.

If we launch a broad new mental health program now, it will be possible within a decade or two to reduce the number of patients now under custodial care by 50 percent or more. Many more mentally ill can be helped to remain in their own homes without hardship to themselves or their families. Those who are hospitalized can be helped to return to their own communities. All but a small proportion can be restored to useful life. We can spare them and their families much of the misery which mental illness now entails. We can save public funds and we can conserve our manpower resources.

1. Comprehensive community mental health centers

Central to a new mental health program is comprehensive community care. Merely pouring Federal funds into a continuation of the outmoded type of institutional care which now prevails would make little difference. We need a new type of health facility, one which will return mental health care to the main stream of American medicine, and at the same time upgrade mental health services. I recommend, therefore, that the Congress (1) authorize grants to the States for the construction of comprehensive community mental health centers, beginning in fiscal year 1965, with the Federal Government providing 45 to 75 percent of the project cost; (2) authorize short-term project grants for the initial staffing costs of comprehensive community mental health centers, with the Federal Government providing up to 75 percent of the cost in the early months, on a gradually declining basis, terminating such support for a project within slightly over 4 years; and (3) to facilitate the preparation of community plans for these new facilities as a necessary preliminary to any construction or staffing assistance, appropriate $4.2 million for planning grants under the National Institute of Mental Health. These planning funds, which would be in addition to a similar amount appropriated for fiscal year 1963, have been included in my proposed 1964 budget.

While the essential concept of the comprehensive community mental health center is new, the separate elements which would be combined in it are presently found in many communities: diagnostic and evaluation services, emergency psychiatric units, outpatient services, inpatient services, day and night care, foster home care, rehabilitation, consultative services to other community agencies, and mental health information and education.

These centers will focus community resources and provide better community facilities for all aspects of mental health care. Prevention as well as treatment will be a major activity. Located in the patient's own environment and community, the center would make possible a better understanding of his needs, a more cordial atmosphere for his recovery, and a continuum of treatment. As his needs change, the patient could move without delay or difficulty to different services—from diagnosis, to cure, to rehabilitation—without need to transfer to different institutions located in different communities.

A comprehensive community mental health center in receipt of Federal aid may be sponsored through a variety of local organizational arrangements. Construction can follow the successful Hill-Burton pattern, under which the Federal Government matches public or voluntary nonprofit funds. Ideally, the center could be located at an appropriate community general hospital, many of which already have psychiatric units. In such instances, additional services and facilities could be added—either all at once or in several stages—to fill out the comprehensive program. In some instances, an existing outpatient psychiatric clinic might form the nucleus of such a center, its work expanded and integrated with other services in the community. Centers could also function effectively under a variety of other auspices: as affiliates of State mental hospitals, under State or local governments, or under voluntary nonprofit sponsorship.

Private physicians, including general practitioners, psychiatrists, and other medical specialists, would all be able to participate directly and cooperatively in the work of the center. For the first time, a large proportion of our private practitioners will have the opportunity to treat their patients in a mental health facility served by an auxiliary professional staff that is directly and quickly available for outpatient and inpatient care.

While these centers will be primarily designed to serve the mental health needs of the community, the mentally retarded should not be excluded from these centers if emotional problems exist. They should also offer the services of special therapists and consultation services to parents, school systems, health departments, and other public and private agencies concerned with mental retardation.

The services provided by these centers should be financed in the same way as other medical and hospital costs. At one time, this was not feasible in the case of mental illness, where prognosis almost invariably called for long and often permanent courses of treatment. But tranquilizers and new therapeutic methods now permit mental illness to be treated successfully in a very high proportion of cases within relatively short periods of time—weeks or months, rather than years.

Consequently, individual fees for services, individual and group insurance, other third-party payments, voluntary and private contributions, and State and local aid can now better bear the continuing burden of these costs to the individual patient after these services are established. Long-range Federal subsidies for operating costs are neither necessary nor desirable. Nevertheless, because this is a new and expensive undertaking for most communities, temporary Federal aid to help them meet the initial burden of establishing and placing centers in operation is desirable. Such assistance would be stimulatory in purpose, granted on a declining basis and terminated in a few years.

The success of this pattern of local and private financing will depend in large part upon the development of appropriate arrangements for health insurance, particularly in the private sector of our economy. Recent studies have indicated that mental health care—particularly the cost of diagnosis and short-term therapy, which would be major components of service in the new centers—is insurable at a moderate cost.

I have directed the Secretary of Health, Education, and Welfare to explore steps for encouraging and stimulating the expansion of private voluntary health insurance to include mental health care. I have also initiated a review of existing Federal programs, such as the health benefits program for Federal personnel, to determine whether further measures may be necessary and desirable to increase their provisions for mental health care.

These comprehensive community mental health centers should become operational at the earliest feasible date. I recommend that we make a major demonstration effort in the early years of the program to be expanded to all major communities as the necessary manpower and facilities become available.

It is to be hoped that within a few years the combination of increased mental health insurance coverage, added State and local support, and the redirection of State resources from State mental institutions will help achieve our goal of having community-centered mental health services readily accessible to all.

2. *Improved care in State mental institutions*

Until the community mental health center program develops fully, it is imperative that the quality of care in existing State mental institutions be improved. By strengthening their therapeutic services, by becoming open institutions serving their local communities, many such institutions can perform a valuable transitional role. The Federal Government can assist materially by encouraging State mental institutions to undertake intensive demonstration and pilot projects, to improve the quality of care, and to provide inservice training for personnel manning these institutions.

This should be done through special grants for demonstration projects for inpatient care and inservice training. I recommend that $10 million be appropriated for such purposes.

3. Research and manpower

Although we embark on a major national action program for mental health, there is still much more we need to know. We must not relax our effort to push back the frontiers of knowledge in basic and applied research into the mental processes, in therapy, and in other phases of research with a bearing upon mental illness. More needs to be done also to translate research findings into improved practices. I recommend an expansion of clinical, laboratory, and field research in mental illness and mental health.

Availability of trained manpower is a major factor in the determination of how fast we can expand our research and expand our new action program in the mental health field. At present manpower shortages exist in virtually all of the key professional and auxiliary personnel categories—psychiatrists, clinical psychologists, social workers, and psychiatric nurses. To achieve success, the current supply of professional manpower in these fields must be sharply increased—from about 45,000 in 1960 to approximately 85,000 by 1970. To help move toward this goal I recommend the appropriation of $66 million for training of personnel, an increase of $17 million over the current fiscal year.

I have, in addition, directed that the Manpower Development and Training Act be used to assist in the training of psychiatric aids and other auxiliary personnel for employment in mental institutions and community centers.

Success of these specialized training programs, however, requires that they be undergirded by basic training programs. It is essential to the success of our new national mental health program that Congress enact legislation authorizing aid to train more physicians and related health personnel. I will discuss this measure at greater length in the message on health which I will send to the Congress shortly.

II. A NATIONAL PROGRAM TO COMBAT MENTAL RETARDATION

Mental retardation stems from many causes. It can result from mongolism, birth injury or infection, or any of a host of conditions that cause a faulty or arrested development of intelligence to such an extent that the individual's ability to learn and to adapt to the demands of society is impaired. Once the damage is done, lifetime incapacity is likely. With early detection, suitable care and training, however, a significant improvement is social ability and in personal adjustment and achievement can be achieved.

The care and treatment of mental retardation, and research into its causes and cure, have—as in the case of mental illness—been too long neglected. Mental retardation ranks as a major national health, social and economic problem. It strikes our most precious asset—our children. It disables 10 times as many people as diabetes, 20 times as many as tuberculosis, 25 times as many as muscular dystrophy, and 600 times as many as infantile paralysis. About 400,000 children are so retarded they require constant care or supervision; more than 200,000 of these are in residential institutions. There are between 5 and 6 million mentally retarded children and adults—an estimated 3 percent of the population. Yet, despite these grim statistics, and despite an admirable effort by private voluntary associations, until a decade ago not a single State health department offered any special community services for the mentally retarded or their families.

States and local communities spend $300 million a year for residential treatment of the mentally retarded, and another $250 million for special education, welfare, rehabilitation, and other benefits and services. The Federal Government will this year obligate $37 million for research, training and special services for the retarded and about three times as much for their income maintenance. But these efforts are fragmented and inadequate.

Mental retardation strikes children without regard for class, creed, or economic level. Each year sees an estimated 126,000 new cases. But it hits more often—and harder—at the underprivileged and the poor; and most often of all—and most severely—in city tenements and rural slums where there are heavy concentrations of families with poor education and low income.

There are very significant variations in the impact of the incidence of mental retardation. Draft rejections for mental deficiency during World War II were 14 times as heavy in States with low incomes as in others. In some slum areas 10 to 30 percent of the school-age children are mentally retarded, while in the very same cities more prosperous neighborhoods have only 1 or 2 percent retarded.

There is every reason to believe that we stand on the threshold of major advances in this field. Medical knowledge can now identify precise causes of retardation in 15 to 25 percent of the cases. This itself is a major advance. Those identified are usually cases in which there are severe organic injuries or gross brain damage from disease. Severe cases of mental retardation of this type are naturally more evenly spread throughout the population than mild retardation; but even here poor families suffer disproportionately. In most of the mild cases, although specific physical and neurological defects are usually not diagnosable with present biomedical techniques, research is rapidly adding to our knowledge of specific causes: German measles during the first 3 months of pregnancy, Rh blood factor incompatibility in newborn infants, lead poisoning of infants, faulty body chemistry in such diseases as phenylketonuria and galactosemia, and many others.

Many of the specific causes of mental retardation are still obscure. Socioeconomic and medical evidence gathered by a panel which I appointed in 1961, however, shows a major causative role for adverse social, economic, and cultural factors. Families who are deprived of the basic necessities of life, opportunity, and motivation have a high proportion of the Nation's retarded children. Unfavorable health factors clearly play a major role. Lack of prenatal and postnatal health care, in particular, leads to the birth of brain-damaged children or to an inadequate physical and neurological development. Areas of high infant mortality are often the same areas with a high incidence of mental retardation. Studies have shown that women lacking prenatal care have a much higher likelihood of having mentally retarded children. Deprivation of a child's opportunities for learning slows development in slum and distressed areas.   Genetic, hereditary, and other biomedical factors also play a major part in the causes of mental retardation.

The American people, acting through their Government where necessary, have an obligation to prevent mental retardation, whenever possible, and to ameliorate it when it is present.   I am, therefore, recommending action on a comprehensive program to attack this affliction.   The only feasible program with a hope for success must not only aim at the specific causes and the control of mental retardation but seek solutions to the broader problems of our society with which mental retardation is so intimately related.

The panel which I appointed reported that, with present knowledge, at least half and hopefully more than half, of all mental retardation cases can be prevented through this kind of "broad spectrum" attack—aimed at both the specific causes which medical science has identified, and at the broader adverse social, economic, and cultural conditions with which incidence of mental retardation is so heavily correlated. At the same time research must go ahead in all these categories, calling upon the best efforts of many types of scientists, from the geneticist to the sociologist.

The fact that mental retardation ordinarily exists from birth or early childhood, the highly specialized medical, psychological, and educational evaluations which are required, and the complex and unique social, educational, and vocational lifetime needs of the retarded individual, all require that there be developed a comprehensive approach to this specific problem.

1. Prevention

Prevention should be given the highest priority in this effort.   Our general health, education, welfare, and urban renewal programs will make a major contribution in overcoming adverse social and economic conditions.   More adequate medical care, nutrition, housing, and educational opportunities can reduce mental retardation to the low incidence which has been achieved in some other nations.   The recommendations for strengthening American education which I have made to the Congress in my message on education will contribute toward this objective as will the proposals contained in my forthcoming health message.

New programs for comprehensive maternity and infant care and for the improvement of our educational services are also needed. Particular attention should be directed toward the development of such services for slum and distressed areas.   Among expectant mothers who do not receive prenatal care, more than 20 percent of all births are premature—two or three times the rate of prematurity among those who do receive adequate care.   Premature infants have two or three times as many physical defects and 50 percent more illnesses than full-term infants.   The smallest premature babies are 10 times more likely to be mentally retarded.

All of these statistics point to the direct relationship between lack of prenatal care and mental retardation.   Poverty and medical indigency are at the root of most of this problem.   An estimated 35 percent of the mothers in cities over 100,000 population are medically indigent.   In 138 large cities of the country an estimated 455,000 women each year lack resources to pay for adequate health care during pregnancy and following birth. Between 20 and 60 percent of the mothers receiving care in public hospitals in some large cities receive inadequate or no prenatal care—and mental retardation is more prevalent in these areas.

Our existing State and Federal child health programs, though playing a useful and necessary role, do not provide the needed comprehensive care for this high-risk group. To enable the States and localities to move ahead more rapidly in combating mental retardation and other childhood disabilities through the new therapeutic measures being developed by medical science, I am recommending:

(a) A new 5-year program of project grants to stimulate State and local health departments to plan, initiate, and develop comprehensive maternity and child health care service programs, helping primarily families in this high-risk group who are otherwise unable to pay for needed medical care. These grants would be used to provide medical care, hospital care, and additional nursing services, and to expand the number of prenatal clinics. Prenatal and post partum care would be more accessible to mothers. I recommend that the initial appropriation for this purpose be $5 million, allocated on a project basis, rising to an annual appropriation of $30 million by the third year.

(b) Doubling the existing $25 million annual authorization for Federal grants for maternal and child health, a significant portion of which will be used for the mentally retarded.

(c) Doubling over a period of 7 years the present $25 million annual authorization for Federal grants for crippled children's services.

Cultural and educational deprivation resulting in mental retardation can also be prevented. Studies have demonstrated that large numbers of children in urban and rural slums, including preschool children, lack the stimulus necessary for proper development in their intelligence. Even when there is no organic impairment, prolonged neglect and a lack of stimulus and opportunity for learning can result in the failure of young minds to develop. Other studies have shown that, if proper opportunities for learning are provided early enough, many of these deprived children can and will learn and achieve as much as children from more favored neighborhoods. This self-perpetuating intellectual blight should not be allowed to continue.

In my recent message on education, I recommended that at least 10 percent of the proposed aid for elementary and secondary education be committed by the States to special project grants designed to stimulate and make possible the improvement of educational opportunities particularly in slum and distressed areas, both urban and rural. I again urge special consideration by the Congress for this proposal. It will not only help improve educational quality and provide equal opportunity in areas which need assistance; it will also serve humanity by helping prevent mental retardation among the children in such culturally deprived areas.

2. Community services

As in the case of mental illnesses, there is also a desperate need for community facilities and services for the mentally retarded. We must move from the outmoded use of distant custodial institutions to the concept of community-centered agencies that will provide a coördinated range of timely diagnostic, health, educational, training, rehabilitation, employment, welfare, and legal protection services. For those retarded children or adults who cannot be maintained at home by their own families, a new pattern of institutional services is needed.

The key to the development of this comprehensive new approach toward services for the mentally retarded is twofold. First, there must be public understanding and community planning to meet all problems. Second, there must be made available a continuum of services covering the entire range of needs. States and communities need to appraise their needs and resources, review current programs, and undertake preliminary actions leading to comprehensive State and community approaches to these objectives. To stimulate public awareness and the development of comprehensive plans, I recommend legislation to establish a program of special project grants to the States for financing State reviews of needs and programs in the field of mental retardation.

A total of $2 million is recommended for this purpose. Grants will be awarded on a selective basis to State agencies presenting acceptable proposals for this broad interdisciplinary planning activity. The purpose of these grants is to provide for every State an opportunity to begin to develop a comprehensive, integrated program to meet all the needs of the retarded. Additional support for planning health-related facilities and services will be available from the expanding planning grant program for the Public Health Service which I will recommend in my forthcoming message on health.

To assist the States and local communities to construct the facilities which these surveys justify and plan, I recommend that the Congress authorize matching grants for the construction of public and other nonprofit facilities, including centers for the comprehensive treatment, training, and care of the mentally retarded. Every community should be encouraged to include provision for meeting the health requirements of retarded individuals in planning its broader health services and facilities.

Because care of the mentally retarded has traditionally been isolated from centers of medical and nursing education, it is particularly important to develop facilities which will increase the role of highly qualified universities in the improvement and provision of services and the training of specialized personnel. Among the various types of facilities for which grants would be authorized, the legislation I am proposing will permit grants of Federal funds for the construction of facilities for (1) inpatient clinical units as an integral part of university-associated hospitals in which specialists on mental retardation would serve; (2) outpatient diagnostic, evaluation, and treatment clinics associated with such hospitals, including facilities for special training; and (3) satellite clinics in outlying cities and counties for provision of services to the retarded through existing State and local community programs, including those financed by the Children's Bureau, in which universities will participate. Grants of $5 million a year will be provided for these purposes within the total authorizations for facilities in 1965 and this will be increased to $10 million in subsequent years.

Such clinical and teaching facilities will provide superior care for the retarded and will also augment teaching and training facilities for specialists in mental retardation, including physicians, nurses, psychologists, social workers, and speech and other therapists. Funds for operation of such facilities would come from State, local, and private sources. Other existing or proposed programs of the Children's Bureau, of the Public Health Service, of the Office of Education, and of the Department of Labor can provide additional resources for demonstration purposes and for training personnel.

A full-scale attack on mental retardation also requires an expansion of special education, training, and rehabilitation services. Largely due to the lack of qualified teachers, college instructors, directors, and supervisors, only about one-fourth of the 1,250,000 retarded children of school age now have access to special education. During the past 4 years, with Federal support, there has been some improvement in the training of leadership personnel. However, teachers of handicapped children, including the mentally retarded, are still woefully insufficient in number and training. As I pointed out in the message on education, legislation is needed to increase the output of college instructors and classroom teachers for handicapped children.

I am asking the Office of Education to place a new emphasis on research in the learning process, expedite the application of research findings to teaching methods for the mentally retarded, support studies on improvement of curriculums, develop teaching aids, and stimulate the training of special teachers.

Vocational training, youth employment, and vocational rehabilitation programs can all help release the untapped potentialities of mentally retarded individuals. This requires expansion and improvement of our vocational education programs, as already recommended; and, in a subsequent message, I will present proposals for needed youth employment programs.

Currently rehabilitation services can only be provided to disabled individuals for whom, at the outset, a vocational potential can be definitely established. This requirement frequently excludes the mentally retarded from the vocational rehabilitation program. I recommend legislation to permit rehabilitation services to be provided to a mentally retarded person for up to 18 months, to determine whether he has sufficient potential to be rehabilitated vocationally. I also recommend legislation establishing a new program to help public and private nonprofit organizations to construct, equip, and staff rehabilitation facilities and workshops, making particular provision for the mentally retarded.

State institutions for the mentally retarded are badly underfinanced, understaffed, and overcrowded. The standard of care is in most instances so grossly deficient as to shock the conscience of all who see them.

I recommend the appropriation under existing law of project grants to State institutions for the mentally retarded, with an initial appropriation of $5 million to be increased in subsequent years to a level of at least $10 million. Such grants would be awarded, upon presentation of a plan meeting criteria established by the Secretary of Health, Education, and Welfare, to State institutions undertaking to upgrade the quality of residential services through demonstration, research, and pilot projects designed to improve the quality of care in such institutions and to provide impetus to inservice training and the education of professional personnel.

3. Research

Our single greatest challenge in this area is still the discovery of the causes and treatment of mental retardation. To do this we must expand our resources for the pursuit and application of scientific knowledge related to this problem. This will require the training of medical, behavioral, and other professional specialists to staff a growing effort. The new National Institute of Child Health and Human Development which was authorized by the 87th Congress is already embarked on this task.

To provide an additional focus for research into the complex mysteries of mental retardation, I recommend legislation to authorize the establishment of centers for research in human development, including the training of scientific personnel. Funds for 3 such centers are included in the 1964 budget; ultimately 10 centers for clinical, laboratory, behavioral, and social science research should be established. The importance of these problems justifies the talents of our best minds. No single discipline or science holds the answer. These centers must, therefore, be established on an interdisciplinary basis.

Similarly, in order to foster the further development of new techniques for the improvement of child health, I am also recommending new research authority to the Children's Bureau for research in maternal and child health and crippled children's services.

But, once again, the shortage of professional manpower seriously compromises both research and service efforts. The insufficient numbers of medical and nursing training centers now available too often lack a clinical focus on the problems of mental retardation comparable to the psychiatric teaching services relating to care of the mentally ill.

*   *   *

We as a Nation have long neglected the mentally ill and the mentally retarded. This neglect must end, if our Nation is to live up to its own standards of compassion and dignity and achieve the maximum use of its manpower.

This tradition of neglect must be replaced by forceful and far-reaching programs carried out at all levels of government, by private individuals and by State and local agencies in every part of the Union.

We must act—

to bestow the full benefits of our society on those who suffer from metal disabilities;

to prevent the occurrence of mental illness and mental retardation wherever and whenever possible;

to provide for early diagnosis and continuous and comprehensive care, in the community, of those suffering from these disorders;

to stimulate improvements in the level of care given the mentally disabled in our State and private institutions, and to reorient those programs to a community-centered approach;

to reduce, over a number of years, and by hundreds of thousands, the persons confined to these institutions;

to retain in and return to the community the mentally ill and mentally retarded, and there to restore and revitalize their lives through better health programs and strengthened educational and rehabilitation services; and to reinforce the will and capacity of our communities to meet these problems, in order that the communities, in turn, can reinforce the will and capacity of individuals and individual families.

We must promote—to the best of our ability and by all possible and appropriate means—the mental and physical health of all our citizens.

To achieve these important ends, I urge that the Congress favorably act upon the foregoing recommendations.

JOHN F. KENNEDY.

THE WHITE HOUSE, *February 5, 1963.*

MENTAL HEALTH SYSTEMS

MESSAGE

FROM

THE PRESIDENT OF THE UNITED STATES

TRANSMITTING

A DRAFT OF PROPOSED LEGISLATION TO IMPROVE THE PRO-
VISIONS OF MENTAL HEALTH SERVICES AND OTHERWISE
PROMOTE MENTAL HEALTH THROUGHOUT THE UNITED
STATES; AND FOR OTHER PURPOSES

May 15, 1979.—Message and accompanying papers referred to the Committee on Interstate and Foreign Commerce and ordered to be printed

---

U.S. GOVERNMENT PRINTING OFFICE

39–011 O   WASHINGTON : 1979

To the Congress of the United States:

I am today submitting to Congress the Mental Health Systems Act. This proposed legislation establishes a new partnership between the federal government and the states in the planning and provision of mental health services. It seeks to assure that the chronically mentally ill no longer face the cruel alternative of unnecessary institutionalization or inadequate care in the community. It provides local communities with more flexible federal support for mental health services and places a new emphasis on the prevention of mental illness.

I am deeply committed to reducing the tragic toll which mental illness exacts from our citizens and our country. Less than one month after entering office I signed an Executive Order creating the President's Commission on Mental Health with Rosalynn Carter as Honorary Chairperson. I directed the Commission to undertake an intensive study of the mental health needs of our nation and to recommend appropriate ways of meeting these needs.

During our years in Georgia, both Rosalynn and I became keenly aware of the unmet needs of people in our state who suffered from mental and emotional disabilities. Those with chronic mental illness were too often locked away in isolated institutions far from family and friends. Children and adults with signs of developing mental and emotional problems did not have access to early detection and prevention programs. Community-based care was beginning to develop but was constantly stripped of its full potential by inflexible program models designed for the "average" community, rather than for the particular needs of a given locale or state. Special populations such as the elderly, children, and racial and ethnic minorities were not receiving care designed to meet their special needs. For those who required hospitalization there were almost no alternatives to large state mental hospitals. Aftercare was almost non-existent for patients released from those hospitals who returned to their home communities.

While I am proud of what we accomplished in Georgia to begin to solve these problems, my concern that similar problems exist throughout the nation prompted me to establish the Commission and to ask it to report back to me in one year with its findings and recommendations. The excellent final report of the Commission presented to me last April made clear that the past 30 years had seen tremendous achievement on behalf of our mentally ill population. Not only had there been a dramatic shift of emphasis from inpatient care to community-based care, but great strides had been made in mental health-related research, and thousands of mental health personnel had been trained. However, the report also contained unmistakable evidence that there are unmet needs in every region of our country.

Some of the key Commission findings dramatically illustrated the challenges this nation faces in meeting the needs of the mentally ill:

—According to the most recent estimates, between ten and fifteen percent of the population—20–32 million Americans—need some form of mental health services at any one time.

—Substantial numbers of Americans do not have access to mental health care of high quality and at reasonable cost. For many, this is because of where they live; for others, it is because of who they are—their race, age, or sex; for still others, it is because of their particular disability or economic circumstance.

—There are approximately 1.5 million chronically mentally disabled adults in mental hospitals, nursing homes and other residential facilities. Many of these individuals could lead better lives in less restrictive settings if mental health and supporting services were available in their communities. The problem is that for them—and for the hundreds of thousands of patients who have been returned to their communities from large institutions over the past few years—such support services are seldom readily available. As a result, evidence indicates that half the people released from large state mental hospitals are readmitted within a year of discharge.

—There is insufficient emphasis at federal, state, and local levels on prevention and early detection of mental disorders. Infants and children would especially benefit from expanded prevention efforts, since early intervention with problems in physical, emotional and cognitive development can prevent more serious mental and emotional problems in the future.

—Conflicting policy objectives in various Federal health and mental health programs and between federal and state programs often lead to confusion, fragmentation of services, and a lack of contunity of care for those with mental and emotional problems. In addition, diverse federal planning requirements and poorly developed planning capabilities at the state and local levels have perpetuated the lack of integrated planning necessary to build a nationwide network of accessible public and private mental health services.

—The lack of flexibility in Federal funding of community-based services has prevented some communities from providing services to their underserved populations. Although over 700 Community Mental Health Centers provide services to almost 3 million patients annually, this model of organizing services cannot fit the needs of all people and all communities. Therefore, varying approaches to developing comprehensive community mental health services should be encouraged.

—About two-thirds of all mentally ill persons being treated in this country every year are receiving care in the general health care system. Nevertheless, cooperative working arrangements between general health care settings and community mental health programs are rare.

—Over the past several years, there has been a marked increase in the number of professional and paraprofessional mental health practitioners. However, rural areas, small towns, and poor urban areas still have only a fraction of the personnel they need. Many mental health facilities have a shortage of trained personnel. The mental health professions still have too few minority members, and there is a shortage of specialists trained to work with children, adolescents, and the elderly.

—Since 1969, our national mental health research capacity has undergone substantial erosion and our investment in mental health research is now so low that the development of new knowledge is jeopardized.

To deal with these and other problems in the mental health arena, the Commission developed a series of recommendations for bold new action to improve our nation's mental health. Many of these recommendations served as a blueprint for the proposed Mental Health Systems Act.

The proposed Act charts a new course for mental health care which promises comprehensiveness, flexibility and innovation. For the first time in the history of federal involvement with mental health care, a true performance-based partnership would be created between the federal and state governments. Special emphasis is placed on the chronically mentally ill. Recognizing that this population has long been the most neglected of any mentally ill group, the proposed Act provides support to states which are phasing down large state hospitals, upgrading the quality of services in remaining institutions, and providing quality alternatives to institutionalization. I believe that these provisions of the Act will encourage the development of a comprehensive, integrated system of care designed to best serve the needs of chronically mentally ill adults and children.

Another innovation is the proposed Act's emphasis on prevention. States and localities are awarded grants to develop preventive and mental health promotion programs through public and professional education and demonstration projects. Such programs, I believe, will lay the foundation for the future in mental health care as we learn how to prevent mental illness before it occurs.

The proposed legislation gives a new and much needed flexibility to community mental health programs. It authorizes funds for one or more mental health services without requiring that a comprehensive package be developed as a prerequisite for financial assistance. This new flexibility will enable communities to provide services to their most underserved populations—whether the chronically mentally ill, children, the elderly, racial and ethnic minorities, the poor, rural residents, or other groups—and build toward a comprehensive system of care for the entire community over time. In addition, by providing financial incentives for closer coordination between ambulatory health care providers and mental health care providers, the Act takes an important step toward assuring that appropriate mental health care is available for all who need help.

The Act also guarantees increased availability of mental health personnel in underserved areas by requiring that mental health professionals who receive federal support for training work in an area with a shortage of mental health personnel for a period equal to the length of the support.

It is, of course, impossible for any one piece of legislation to meet all the mental health needs of the nation. The Federal Government has already sought to implement many of the recommendations of the Commission in other ways:

—To increase the development of new knowledge about mental illness, the 1980 budget provides additional funding for research into disabling mental illness, and for determining ways to improve the delivery of mental health care.

—To increase the availability of mental health services for the elderly, changes have been proposed increasing the Medicare reimbursement ceiling for outpatient mental health services and decreasing the beneficiary's co-payment requirement. Also, the Child Health Assurance Program will mandate that states provide mental health services for Medicaid-eligible children.

—To assist the chronically mentally ill to function effectively outside of institutions, the Departments of Health, Education, and Welfare and Housing and Urban Development have initiated a joint demonstration project which provides both housing and support services.

—To promote protection of the rights of the mentally ill, the Administration is funding demonstration projects which deliver advocacy services to the mentally ill and is studying existing advocacy programs to determine the appropriate role for the Federal Government in this area.

I am convinced that these actions and the passage of the Mental Health Systems Act will reduce the number of Americans robbed of vital and satisfying lives by mental illness. I ask the Congress to join with me in developing a new system of mental health care designed to deal more effectively with our nation's unmet mental health needs.

JIMMY CARTER.

THE WHITE HOUSE, *May 15, 1979.*

APPENDIX B

Mental Retardation Facilities
and Community Mental Health
Centers Construction Act of 1963

Mental Health Systems Act of 1980

*President Dwight D. Eisenhower signs
the Mental Health Study Act of 1955*

*President John F. Kennedy signs the Mental
Retardation Facilities and Community Mental
Health Centers Construction Act of 1963*

An Act

To provide assistance in combating mental retardation through grants for construction of research centers and grants for facilities for the mentally retarded and assistance in improving mental health through grants for construction of community mental health centers, and for other purposes.

Be it enacted by the Senate and House of Representatives of the United States of America in Congress assembled, That this Act may be cited as the "Mental Retardation Facilities and Community Mental Health Centers Construction Act of 1963".

Mental Retardation Facilities and Community Mental Health Centers Construction Act of 1963.

TITLE I—CONSTRUCTION OF RESEARCH CENTERS AND FACILITIES FOR THE MENTALLY RETARDED

SHORT TITLE

SEC. 100. This title may be cited as the "Mental Retardation Facilities Construction Act".

PART A—GRANTS FOR CONSTRUCTION OF CENTERS FOR RESEARCH ON MENTAL RETARDATION AND RELATED ASPECTS OF HUMAN DEVELMENT

.C. 101. Title VII of the Public Health Service Act is amended by ing at the end thereof the following new part:

70 Stat. 717;
Ante, p. 164.
42 USC 292-
2921.

"PART D—CENTERS FOR RESEARCH ON MENTAL RETARDATION AND RELATED ASPECTS OF HUMAN DEVELOPMENT

"AUTHORIZATION OF APPROPRIATIONS

"SEC. 761. There are authorized to be appropriated $6,000,000 for the fiscal year ending June 30, 1964, $8,000,000 for the fiscal year ending June 30, 1965, and $6,000,000 each for the fiscal year ending June 30, 1966, and the fiscal year ending June 30, 1967, for project grants to assist in meeting the costs of construction of facilities for research, or research and related purposes, relating to human development, whether biological, medical, social, or behavioral, which may assist in finding the causes, and means of prevention, of mental retardation, or in finding means of ameliorating the effects of mental retardation. Sums so appropriated shall remain available until expended for payments with respect to projects or which applications have been filed under this part before July 1, 1967, and approved by the Surgeon General thereunder before July 1, 1968.

"APPLICATIONS

"SEC. 762. (a) Applications for grants under this part with respect to any facility may be approved by the Surgeon General only if—

"(1) the applicant is a public or nonprofit institution which the Surgeon General determines is competent to engage in the type of research for which the facility is to be constructed; and
"(2) the application contains or is supported by reasonable assurances that (A) for not less than twenty years after completion of construction, the facility will be used for the research, or research and related purposes, for which it was constructed; (B) sufficient funds will be available for meeting the non-Federal share of the cost of constructing the facility; (C) sufficient funds

will be available, when the construction is completed, for effective use of the facility for the research, or research and related purposes, for which it was constructed; and (D) all laborers and mechanics employed by contractors or subcontractors in the performance of work on construction of the center will be paid wages at rates not less than those prevailing on similar construction in the locality as determined by the Secretary of Labor in accordance with the Davis-Bacon Act, as amended (40 U.S.C.

49 Stat. 1011.

276a—276a–5); and the Secretary of Labor shall have, with respect to the labor standards specified in this clause (D) the authority and functions set forth in Reorganization Plan

64 Stat. 1267.

Numbered 14 of 1950 (15 F.R. 3176; 5 U.S.C. 133z–15), and section 2 of the Act of June 13, 1934, as amended (40 U.S.C.

63 Stat. 108.

276c).

"(b) In acting on applications for grants, the Surgeon General shall take into consideration the relative effectiveness of the proposed facilities in expanding the Nation's capacity for research and related purposes in the field of mental retardation and related aspects of human development, and such other factors as he, after consultation with the national advisory council or councils concerned with the field or fields of research involved, may by regulation prescribe in order to assure that the facilities constructed with such grants, severally and together, will best serve the purpose of advancing scientific knowledge pertaining to mental retardation and related aspects of human development.

"AMOUNT OF GRANTS; PAYMENTS

"SEC. 763. (a) The total of the grants with respect to any project for the construction of a facility under this part may not exceed 75 per centum of the necessary cost of construction of the center as determined by the Surgeon General.

"(b) Payments of grants under this part shall be made in advance or by way of reimbursement, in such installments consistent with construction progress, and on such conditions as the Surgeon General may determine.

"(c) No grant may be made after January 1, 1964, under any provision of this Act other than this part, for any of the four fiscal years in the period beginning July 1, 1963, and ending June 30, 1967, for construction of any facility described in this part, unless the Surgeon General determines that funds are not available under this part to make a grant for the construction of such facility.

"RECAPTURE OF PAYMENTS

"SEC. 764. If, within twenty years after completion of any construction for which funds have been paid under this part—

"(1) the applicant or other owner of the facility shall cease to be a public or nonprofit institution, or

"(2) the facility shall cease to be used for the research purposes, or research and related purposes, for which it was constructed, unless the Surgeon General determines, in accordance with regulations, that there is good cause for releasing the applicant or other owner from the obligation to do so,

the United States shall be entitled to recover from the applicant or other owner of the facility the amount bearing the same ratio to the then value (as determined by agreement of the parties or by action brought in the United States district court for the district in which such facility is situated) of the facility, as the amount of the Federal participation bore to the cost of construction of such facility.

"NONINTERFERENCE WITH ADMINISTRATION OF INSTITUTIONS

"SEC. 765. Except as otherwise specifically provided in this part, nothing contained in this part shall be construed as authorizing any department, agency, officer, or employee of the United States to exercise any direction, supervision, or control over, or impose any requirement or condition with respect to, the research or related purposes conducted by, and the personnel or administration of, any institution.

"DEFINITIONS

"SEC. 766. As used in this part—
   "(1) the terms 'construction' and 'cost of construction' include (A) the construction of new buildings and the expansion, remodeling, and alteration of existing buildings, including architects' fees, but not including the cost of acquisition of land or off-site improvements, and (B) equipping new buildings and existing buildings, whether or not expanded, remodeled, or altered;
   "(2) the term 'nonprofit institution' means an institution owned and operated by one or more corporations or associations no part of the net earnings of which inures, or may lawfully inure, to the benefit of any private shareholder or individual."

PART B.—PROJECT GRANTS FOR CONSTRUCTION OF UNIVERSITY-AFFILIATED FACILITIES FOR THE MENTALLY RETARDED

AUTHORIZATION OF APPROPRIATIONS

SEC. 121. For the purpose of assisting in the construction of clinical facilities providing, as nearly as practicable, a full range of inpatient and outpatient services for the mentally retarded and facilities which will aid in demonstrating provision of specialized services for the diagnosis and treatment, education, training, or care of the mentally retarded or in the clinical training of physicians and other specialized personnel needed for research, diagnosis and treatment, education, training, or care of the mentally retarded, there are authorized to be appropriated $5,000,000 for the fiscal year ending June 30, 1964, $7,500,000 for the fiscal year ending June 30, 1965, and $10,000,000 each for the fiscal year ending June 30, 1966, and the fiscal year ending June 30, 1967. The sums so appropriated shall be used for project grants for construction of public and other nonprofit facilities for the mentally retarded which are associated with a college or university.

APPLICATIONS

SEC. 122. Applications for grants under this part with respect to any facility may be approved by the Secretary only if the application contains or is supported by reasonable assurances that—
   (1) the facility will be associated, to the extent prescribed in regulations of the Secretary, with a college or university hospital (including affiliated hospitals), or with such other part of a college or university as the Secretary may find appropriate in the light of the purposes of this part;
   (2) the plans and specifications are in accord with regulations prescribed by the Secretary under section 133(3);
   (3) title to the site for the project is or will be vested in one or more of the agencies or institutions filing the application or in a public or other nonprofit agency or institution which is to operate the facility;

(4) adequate financial support will be available for construction of the project and for its maintenance and operation when completed; and

(5) all laborers and mechanics employed by contractors or subcontractors in the performance of work on construction of the project will be paid wages at rates not less than those prevailing on similar construction in the locality as determined by the Secretary of Labor in accordance with the Davis-Bacon Act, as amended (40 U.S.C. 276a—276a-5); and the Secretary of Labor shall have with respect to the labor standards specified in this paragraph the authority and functions set forth in Reorganization Plan Numbered 14 of 1950 (15 F.R. 3176; 5 U.S.C. 133z-15) and section 2 of the Act of June 13, 1934, as amended (40 U.S.C. 276c).

49 Stat. 1011.

64 Stat. 1267.

63 Stat. 108.

AMOUNT OF GRANTS; PAYMENTS

SEC. 123. (a) The total of the grants with respect to any project for the construction of a facility under this part may not exceed 75 per centum of the necessary cost of construction thereof as determined by the Secretary.

(b) Payments of grants under this part shall be made in advance or by way of reimbursement, in such installments consistent with construction progress, and on such conditions as the Secretary may determine.

RECOVERY

SEC. 124. If any facility with respect to which funds have been paid under this part shall, at any time within twenty years after the completion of construction—

(1) be sold or transferred to any person, agency, or organization which is not qualified to file an application under this part, or

(2) cease to be a public or other nonprofit facility for the mentally retarded, unless the Secretary determines, in accordance with regulations, that there is good cause for releasing the applicant or other owner from the obligation to continue such facility as a public or other nonprofit facility for the mentally retarded,

the United States shall be entitled to recover from either the transferor or the transferee (or, in the case of a facility which has ceased to be a public or other nonprofit facility for the mentally retarded, from the owners thereof) an amount bearing the same ratio to the then value (as determined by the agreement of the parties or by action brought in the district court of the United States for the district in which the facility is situated) of so much of the facility as constituted an approved project or projects, as the amount of the Federal participation bore to the cost of the construction of such project or projects.

NONDUPLICATION OF GRANTS

58 Stat. 682.
42 USC 201 note.

SEC. 125. No grant may be made after January 1, 1964, under any provision of the Public Health Service Act, for any of the four fiscal years in the period beginning July 1, 1963, and ending June 30, 1967, for construction of any facility for the mentally retarded described in this part, unless the Secretary determines that funds are not available under this part to make a grant for the construction of such facility.

77 STAT. 286.

PART C—GRANTS FOR CONSTRUCTION OF FACILITIES FOR THE MENTALLY
RETARDED

AUTHORIZATION OF APPROPRIATIONS

SEC. 131. There are authorized to be appropriated, for grants
for construction of public and other nonprofit facilities for the
mentally retarded, $10,000,000 for the fiscal year ending June 30,
1965, $12,500,000 for the fiscal year ending June 30, 1966, $15,000,000
for the fiscal year ending June 30, 1967, and $30,000,000 for the fiscal
year ending June 30, 1968.

ALLOTMENTS TO STATES

SEC. 132. (a) For each fiscal year, the Secretary shall, in accordance with regulations, make allotments from the sums appropriated
under section 131 to the several States on the basis of (1) the
population, (2) the extent of the need for facilities for the mentally
retarded, and (3) the financial need of the respective States; except
that no such allotment to any State, other than the Virgin Islands,
American Samoa, and Guam, for any fiscal year may be less than
$100,000. Sums so allotted to a State for a fiscal year for con-
struction and remaining unobligated at the end of such year shall
remain available to such State for such purpose for the next
fiscal year (and for such year only), in addition to the sums allotted,
to such State for such next fiscal year.

(b) In accordance with regulations of the Secretary, any State
may file with him a request that a specified portion of its allotment
under this part be added to the allotment of another State under this
part for the purpose of meeting a portion of the Federal share of the
cost of a project for the construction of a facility for the mentally
retarded in such other State. If it is found by the Secretary that
construction of the facility with respect to which the request is
made would meet needs of the State making the request and that use
of the specified portion of such State's allotment, as requested
by it, would assist in carrying out the purposes of this part, such
portion of such State's allotment shall be added to the allotment
of the other State under this part, to be used for the purpose referred
to above.

(c) Upon the request of any State that a specified portion of its
allotment under this part be added to the allotment of such State
under title II, and upon (1) the simultaneous certification to the
Secretary by the State agency designated as provided in the State
plan approved under this part to the effect that it has afforded
a reasonable opportunity to make applications for the portion so
specified and there have been no approvable applications for such portion, or (2) a showing satisfactory to the Secretary that the need for
the community mental health centers in such State is substantially
greater than for the facilities for the mentally retarded, the Secretary shall, subject to such limitations as he may by regulations
prescribe, promptly adjust the allotments of such State in accordance with such request and shall notify such State agency and
the State agency designated under the State plan approved under
title II, and thereafter the allotments as so adjusted shall be deemed
the State's allotments for purposes of this part and title II.

REGULATIONS

60 Stat. 1048.
42 USC 291k.

SEC. 133. Within six months after enactment of this Act, the Secretary shall, after consultation with the Federal Hospital Council (established by section 633 of the Public Health Service Act and hereinafter in this part referred to as the "Council"), by general regulations applicable uniformly to all the States, prescribe—

(1) the kinds of services needed to provide adequate services for mentally retarded persons residing in a State;

(2) the general manner in which the State agency (designated as provided in the State plan approved under this part) shall determine the priority of projects based on the relative need of different areas, giving special consideration to facilities which will provide comprehensive services for a particular community or communities;

(3) general standards of construction and equipment for facilities of different classes and in different types of location; and

(4) that the State plan shall provide for adequate facilities for the mentally retarded for persons residing in the State, and shall provide for adequate facilities for the mentally retarded to furnish needed services for persons unable to pay therefor. Such regulations may require that before approval of an application for a facility or addition to a facility is recommended by a State agency, assurance shall be received by the State from the applicant that there will be made available in such facility or addition a reasonable volume of services to persons unable to pay therefor, but an exception shall be made if such a requirement is not feasible from a financial viewpoint.

STATE PLANS

SEC. 134. (a) After such regulations have been issued, any State desiring to take advantage of this part shall submit a State plan for carrying out its purposes. Such State plan must—

(1) designate a single State agency as the sole agency for the administration of the plan, or designate such agency as the sole agency for supervising the administration of the plan;

(2) contain satisfactory evidence that the State agency designated in accordance with paragraph (1) hereof will have authority to carry out such plan in conformity with this part;

(3) provide for the designation of a State advisory council which shall include representatives of State agencies concerned with planning, operation, or utilization of facilities for the mentally retarded and of nongovernment organizations or groups concerned with education, employment, rehabilitation, welfare, and health, and including representatives of consumers of the services provided by such facilities;

(4) set forth a program for construction of facilities for the mentally retarded (A) which is based on a statewide inventory of existing facilities and survey of need; (B) which conforms with the regulations prescribed under section 133(1); and (C) which meets the requirements for furnishing needed services to persons unable to pay therefor, included in regulations prescribed under section 133(4);

(5) set forth the relative need, determined in accordance with the regulations prescribed under section 133(2), for the several projects included in such programs, and provide for the construction, insofar as financial resources available therefor and for

190

maintenance and operation make possible, in the order of such relative need;

(6) provide such methods of administration of the State plan, including methods relating to the establishment and maintenance of personnel standards on a merit basis (except that the Secretary shall exercise no authority with respect to the selection, tenure of office, or compensation of any individual employed in accordance with such methods), as are found by the Secretary to be necessary for the proper and efficient operation of the plan;

(7) provide minimum standards (to be fixed in the discretion of the State) for the maintenance and operation of facilities which receive Federal aid under this part;

(8) provide for affording to every applicant for a construction project an opportunity for hearing before the State agency;

(9) provide that the State agency will make such reports in such form and containing such information as the Secretary may from time to time reasonably require, and will keep such records and afford such access thereto as the Secretary may find necessary to assure the correctness and verification of such reports; and

(10) provide that the State agency will from time to time, but not less often than annually, review its State plan and submit to the Secretary any modifications thereof which it considers necessary.

(b) The Secretary shall approve any State plan and any modification thereof which complies with the provisions of subsection (a). The Secretary shall not finally disapprove a State plan except after reasonable notice and opportunity for a hearing to the State.

APPROVAL OF PROJECTS

SEC. 135. (a) For each project for construction pursuant to a State plan approved under this part, there shall be submitted to the Secretary through the State agency an application by the State or a political subdivision thereof or by a public or other nonprofit agency. If two or more such agencies join in the construction of the project, the application may be filed by one or more of such agencies. Such application shall set forth—

(1) a description of the site for such project;

(2) plans and specifications therefor in accordance with the regulations prescribed by the Secretary under section 133(3);

(3) reasonable assurance that title to such site is or will be vested in one or more of the agencies filing the application or in a public or other nonprofit agency which is to operate the facility;

(4) reasonable assurance that adequate financial support will be available for the construction of the project and for its maintenance and operation when completed;

(5) reasonable assurance that all laborers and mechanics employed by contractors or subcontractors in the performance of work on construction of the project will be paid wages at rates not less than those prevailing on similar construction in the locality as determined by the Secretary of Labor in accordance with the Davis-Bacon Act, as amended (40 U.S.C. 276a—276a–5); and the Secretary of Labor shall have with respect to the labor standards specified in this paragraph the authority and functions set forth in Reorganization Plan Numbered 14 of 1950 (15 F.R. 3176; 5 U.S.C. 133z–15) and section 2 of the Act of June 13, 1934, as amended (40 U.S.C. 276c); and   49 Stat. 1011.
64 Stat. 1267.
63 Stat. 108.

(6) a certification by the State agency of the Federal share for the project.

The Secretary shall approve such application if sufficient funds to pay the Federal share of the cost of construction of such project are available from the allotment to the State, and if the Secretary finds (A) that the application contains such reasonable assurance as to title, financial support, and payment of prevailing rates of wages and overtime pay; (B) that the plans and specifications are in accord with the regulations prescribed pursuant to section 133; (C) that the application is in conformity with the State plan approved under section 134 and contains an assurance that in the operation of the facility there will be compliance with the applicable requirements of the State plan and of the regulations prescribed under section 133(4) for furnishing needed facilities for persons unable to pay therefor, and with State standards for operation and maintenance; and (D) that the application has been approved and recommended by the State agency and is entitled to priority over other projects within the State in accordance with the regulations prescribed pursuant to section 133(2). No application shall be disapproved by the Secretary until he has afforded the State agency an opportunity for a hearing.

(b) Amendment of any approved application shall be subject to approval in the same manner as an original application.

WITHHOLDING OF PAYMENTS

SEC. 136. Whenever the Secretary after reasonable notice and opportunity for hearing to the State agency designated as provided in section 134(a)(1), finds—

(1) that the State agency is not complying substantially with the provisions required by section 134 to be included in its State plan or with regulations under this part;

(2) that any assurance required to be given in an application filed under section 135 is not being or cannot be carried out;

(3) that there is a substantial failure to carry out plans and specifications approved by the Secretary under section 135; or

(4) that adequate State funds are not being provided annually for the direct administration of the State plan,

the Secretary may forthwith notify the State agency that—

(5) no further payments will be made to the State from allotments under this part; or

(6) no further payments will be made from allotments under this part for any project or projects designated by the Secretary as being affected by the action or inaction referred to in paragraph (1), (2), (3), or (4) of this section,

as the Secretary may determine to be appropriate under the circumstances; and, except with regard to any project for which the application has already been approved and which is not directly affected, further payments from such allotments may be withheld, in whole or in part, until there is no longer any failure to comply (or to carry out the assurance or plans and specifications or to provide adequate State funds, as the case may be) or, if such compliance (or other action) is impossible, until the State repays or arranges for the repayment of Federal moneys to which the recipient was not entitled.

NONDUPLICATION OF GRANTS

58 Stat. 682.
42 USC 201 note.

SEC. 137. No grant may be made after January 1, 1964, under any provision of the Public Health Service Act, for any of the four fiscal years in the period beginning July 1, 1964, and ending June 30, 1968, for construction of any facility for the mentally retarded described in this part, unless the Secretary determines that funds are not available under this part to make a grant for the construction of such facility.

TITLE II—CONSTRUCTION OF COMMUNITY MENTAL HEALTH CENTERS

SHORT TITLE

SEC. 200. This title may be cited as the "Community Mental Health Centers Act". Citation of title.

AUTHORIZATION OF APPROPRIATIONS

SEC. 201. There are authorized to be appropriated, for grants for construction of public and other nonprofit community mental health centers, $35,000,000 for the fiscal year ending June 30, 1965, $50,000,000 for the fiscal year ending June 30, 1966, and $65,000,000 for the fiscal year ending June 30, 1967.

ALLOTMENTS TO STATES

SEC. 202. (a) For each fiscal year, the Secretary shall, in accordance with regulations, make allotments from the sums appropriated under section 201 to the several States on the basis of (1) the population, (2) the extent of the need for community mental health centers, and (3) the financial need of the respective States; except that no such allotment to any State, other than the Virgin Islands, American Samoa, and Guam, for any fiscal year may be less than $100,000. Sums so allotted to a State for a fiscal year and remaining unobligated at the end of such year shall remain available to such State for such purpose for the next fiscal year (and for such year only), in addition to the sums allotted for such State for such next fiscal year.

(b) In accordance with regulations of the Secretary, any State may file with him a request that a specified portion of its allotment under this title be added to the allotment of another State under this title for the purpose of meeting a portion of the Federal share of the cost of a project for the construction of a community mental health center in such other State. If it is found by the Secretary that construction of the center with respect to which the request is made would meet needs of the State making the request and that use of the specified portion of such State's allotment, as requested by it, would assist in carrying out the purposes of this title, such portion of such State's allotment shall be added to the allotment of the other State under this title to be used for the purpose referred to above.

(c) Upon the request of any State that a specified portion of its allotment under this title be added to the allotment of such State under part C of title I and upon (1) the simultaneous certification to the Secretary by the State agency designated as provided in the State plan approved under this title to the effect that it has afforded a reasonable opportunity to make applications for the portion so specified and there have been no approvable applications for such portion or (2) a showing satisfactory to the Secretary that the need for facilities for the mentally retarded in such State is substantially greater than for community mental health centers, the Secretary shall, subject to such limitations as he may by regulation prescribe, promptly adjust the allotments of such State in accordance with such request and shall notify such State agency and the State agency designated under the State plan approved under part C of title I, and thereafter the allotments as so adjusted shall be deemed the State's allotments for purposes of this title and part C of title I.

REGULATIONS

Sec. 203. Within six months after enactment of this Act, the Secretary shall, after consultation with the Federal Hospital Council (established by section 633 of the Public Health Service Act) and the National Advisory Mental Health Council (established by section 217 of the Public Health Service Act), by general regulations applicable uniformly to all the States, prescribe—

60 Stat. 1048.
42 USC 291k.
64 Stat. 446.
42 USC 218.

(1) the kinds of community mental health services needed to provide adequate mental health services for persons residing in a State;

(2) the general manner in which the State agency (designated as provided in the State plan approved under this title) shall determine the priority of projects based on the relative need of different areas, giving special consideration to projects on the basis of the extent to which the centers to be constructed thereby will, alone or in conjunction with other facilities owned or operated by the applicant or affiliated or associated with the applicant, provide comprehensive mental health services (as determined by the Secretary in accordance with regulations) for mentally ill persons in a particular community or communities or which will be part of or closely associated with a general hospital;

(3) general standards of construction and equipment for centers of different classes and in different types of location; and

(4) that the State plan shall provide for adequate community mental health centers for people residing in the State, and shall provide for adequate community mental health centers to furnish needed services for persons unable to pay therefor. Such regulations may require that before approval of an application for a center or addition to a center is recommended by a State agency, assurance shall be received by the State from the applicant that there will be made available in such center or addition a reasonable volume of services to persons unable to pay therefor, but an exception shall be made if such a requirement is not feasible from a financial viewpoint.

STATE PLANS

Sec. 204. (a) After such regulations have been issued, any State desiring to take advantage of this title shall submit a State plan for carrying out its purposes. Such State plan must—

(1) designate a single State agency as the sole agency for the administration of the plan, or designate such agency as the sole agency for supervising the administration of the plan;

(2) contain satisfactory evidence that the State agency designated in accordance with paragraph (1) hereof will have authority to carry out such plan in conformity with this title;

(3) provide for the designation of a State advisory council which shall include representatives of nongovernment organizations or groups, and of State agencies, concerned with planning, operation, or utilization of community mental health centers or other mental health facilities, including representatives of consumers of the services provided by such centers and facilities who are familiar with the need for such services, to consult with the State agency in carrying out such plan;

(4) set forth a program for construction of community mental health centers (A) which is based on a statewide inventory of

existing facilities and survey of need; (B) which conforms with the regulations prescribed by the Secretary under section 203(1); and (C) which meets the requirements for furnishing needed services to persons unable to pay therefor, included in regulations prescribed under section 203(4);

(5) set forth the relative need, determined in accordance with the regulations prescribed under section 203(2), for the several projects included in such programs, and provide for the construction, insofar as financial resources available therefor and for maintenance and operation make possible, in the order of such relative need;

(6) provide such methods of administration of the State plan, including methods relating to the establishment and maintenance of personnel standards on a merit basis (except that the Secretary shall exercise no authority with respect to the selection, tenure of office, or compensation of any individual employed in accordance with such methods), as are found by the Secretary to be necessary for the proper and efficient operation of the plan;

(7) provide minimum standards (to be fixed in the discretion of the State) for the maintenance and operation of centers which receive Federal aid under this title;

(8) provide for affording to every applicant for a construction project an opportunity for hearing before the State agency;

(9) provide that the State agency will make such reports in such form and containing such information as the Secretary may from time to time reasonably require, and will keep such records and afford such access thereto as the Secretary may find necessary to assure the correctness and verification of such reports; and

(10) provide that the State agency will from time to time, but not less often than annually, review its State plan and submit to the Secretary any modifications thereof which it considers necessary.

(b) The Secretary shall approve any State plan and any modification thereof which complies with the provisions of subsection (a). The Secretary shall not finally disapprove a State plan except after reasonable notice and opportunity for a hearing to the State.

APPROVAL OF PROJECTS

Sec. 205. (a) For each project for construction pursuant to a State plan approved under this title, there shall be submitted to the Secretary through the State agency an application by the State or a political subdivision thereof or by a public or other nonprofit agency. If two or more such agencies join in the construction of the project, the application may be filed by one or more of such agencies. Such application shall set forth—

(1) a description of the site for such project;

(2) plans and specifications therefor in accordance with the regulations prescribed by the Secretary under section 203(3);

(3) reasonable assurance that title to such site is or will be vested in one or more of the agencies filing the application or in a public or other nonprofit agency which is to operate the community mental health center;

(4) reasonable assurance that adequate financial support will be available for the construction of the project and for its maintenance and operation when completed;

(5) reasonable assurance that all laborers and mechanics employed by contractors or subcontractors in the performance of work on construction of the project will be paid wages at rates not less than those prevailing on similar construction in the

49 Stat. 1011.

64 Stat. 1267.
63 Stat. 108.

locality as determined by the Secretary of Labor in accordance with the Davis-Bacon Act, as amended (40 U.S.C. 276a— 276a–5); and the Secretary of Labor shall have with respect to the labor standards specified in this paragraph the authority and functions set forth in Reorganization Plan Numbered 14 of 1950 (15 F.R. 3176; 5 U.S.C. 133z–15) and section 2 of the Act of June 13, 1934, as amended (40 U.S.C. 276c); and

(6) a certification by the State agency of the Federal share for the project.

The Secretary shall approve such application if sufficient funds to pay the Federal share of the cost of construction of such project are available from the allotment to the State, and if the Secretary finds (A) that the application contains such reasonable assurance as to title, financial support, and payment of prevailing rates of wages and overtime pay; (B) that the plans and specifications are in accord with the regulations prescribed pursuant to section 203; (C) that the application is in conformity with the State plan approved under section 204 and contains an assurance that in the operation of the center there will be compliance with the applicable requirements of the State plan and of the regulations prescribed under section 203(4) for furnishing needed services for persons unable to pay therefor, and with State standards for operation and maintenance; (D) that the services to be provided by the center, alone or in conjunction with other facilities owned or operated by the applicant or affiliated or associated with the applicant, will be part of a program providing, principally for persons residing in a particular community or communities in or near which such center is to be situated, at least those essential elements of comprehensive mental health services for mentally ill persons which are prescribed by the Secretary in accordance with regulations; and (E) that the application has been approved and recommended by the State agency and is entitled to priority over other projects within the State in accordance with the regulations prescribed pursuant to section 203(2). No application shall be disapproved by the Secretary until he has afforded the State agency an opportunity for a hearing.

(b) Amendment of any approved application shall be subject to approval in the same manner as an original application.

WITHHOLDING OF PAYMENTS

SEC. 206. Whenever the Secretary, after reasonable notice and opportunity for hearing to the State agency designated as provided in section 204(a)(1), finds—

(1) that the State agency is not complying substantially with the provisions required by section 204 to be included in its State plan, or with regulations under this title;

(2) that any assurance required to be given in an application filed under section 205 is not being or cannot be carried out;

(3) that there is a substantial failure to carry out plans and specifications approved by the Secretary under section 205; or

(4) that adequate State funds are not being provided annually for the direct administration of the State plan, the Secretary may forthwith notify the State agency that—

(5) no further payments will be made to the State from allotments under this title; or

(6) no further payments will be made from allotments under this title for any project or projects designated by the Secretary as being affected by the action or inaction referred to in paragraph (1), (2), (3), or (4) of this section,

as the Secretary may determine to be appropriate under the circumstances; and, except with regard to any project for which the application has already been approved and which is not directly affected, further payments from such allotments may be withheld, in whole or in part, until there is no longer any failure to comply (or to carry out the assurance or plans and specifications or to provide adequate State funds, as the case may be) or, if such compliance (or other action) is impossible, until the State repays or arranges for the repayment of Federal moneys to which the recipient was not entitled.

NONDUPLICATION OF GRANTS

SEC. 207. No grant may be made after January 1, 1964, under any provision of the Public Health Service Act, for any of the three fiscal years in the period beginning July 1, 1964, and ending June 30, 1967, for construction of any facility described in this title, unless the Secretary determines that funds are not available under this title to make a grant for the construction of such facility.

58 Stat. 682.
42 USC 201
note.

TITLE III—TRAINING OF TEACHERS OF MENTALLY RETARDED AND OTHER HANDICAPPED CHILDREN

TRAINING OF TEACHERS OF HANDICAPPED CHILDREN

SEC. 301. (a) (1) The second sentence of the first section of the Act of September 6, 1958 (Public Law 85–926), is amended by striking out "Such grants" and inserting in lieu thereof "Grants under this section" and by striking out "fellowships" and inserting in lieu thereof "fellowships or traineeships".

72 Stat. 1777.
20 USC 611.

(2) Such section is further amended by inserting before the second sentence thereof, the following new sentence: "He is also authorized to make grants to public or other nonprofit institutions of higher learning to assist them in providing professional or advanced training for personnel engaged or preparing to engage in employment as teachers of handicapped children, as supervisors of such teachers, or as speech correctionists or other specialists providing special services for education of such children, or engaged or preparing to engage in research in fields related to education of such children."

(3) The first sentence of such section is amended by striking out "mentally retarded children" and inserting in lieu thereof "mentally retarded, hard of hearing, deaf, speech impaired, visually handicapped, seriously emotionally disturbed, crippled, or other health impaired children who by reason thereof require special education (hereinafter in this Act referred to as 'handicapped children')". Section 2 of such Act is amended by striking out "mentally retarded children" and inserting in lieu thereof "handicapped children".

20 USC 612.

(4) The second sentence of section 3 of such Act is repealed. Section 7 of such Act is amended to read as follows:

Repeal.
20 USC 613.
20 USC 617.

"SEC. 7. There are authorized to be appropriated for carrying out this Act $11,500,000 for the fiscal year ending June 30, 1964; $14,500,000 for the fiscal year ending June 30, 1965; and $19,500,000 for the fiscal year ending June 30, 1966."

(5) The amendments made by this subsection shall apply in the case of fiscal years beginning after June 30, 1963, except that deaf children shall not be included as "handicapped children" for purposes of such amendments for the fiscal year ending June 30, 1964.

(b) Effective for fiscal years beginning after June 30, 1964, the first section of such Act is amended by adding at the end thereof the following new sentence: "The Commissioner is also authorized to

77 STAT. 295.

make grants to public or other nonprofit institutions of higher learning to assist them in establishing and maintaining scholarships, with
such stipends as may be determined by the Commissioner, for training
personnel preparing to engage in employment as teachers of the
deaf."

75 Stat. 576.

(c) (1) The first sentence of subsection (a) of section 6 of the Act
of September 22, 1961 (Public Law 87–276, 20 U.S.C. 676) is
amended by inserting immediately before the period at the end
thereof the following: ", and $1,500,000 for the fiscal year ending
June 30, 1964".

(2) Subsection (b) of such section 6 is amended by striking out
"1963" and inserting in lieu thereof "1964".

RESEARCH AND DEMONSTRATION PROJECTS IN EDUCATION OF
HANDICAPPED CHILDREN

SEC. 302. (a) There is authorized to be appropriated for the fiscal
year ending June 30, 1964, and each of the next two fiscal years, the
sum of $2,000,000 to enable the Commissioner of Education to make
grants to States, State or local educational agencies, public and nonprofit private institutions of higher learning, and other public or
nonprofit private educational or research agencies and organizations
for research or demonstration projects relating to education for
mentally retarded, hard of hearing, deaf, speech impaired, visually
handicapped, seriously emotionally disturbed, crippled, or other
health impaired children who by reason thereof require special education (hereinafter in this section referred to as "handicapped children"). Such grants shall be made in installments, in advance or by
way of reimbursement, and on such conditions as the Commissioner
of Education may determine.

(b) The Commissioner of Education is authorized to appoint such
special or technical advisory committees as he may deem necessary to
advise him on matters of general policy relating to particular fields of
education of handicapped children or relating to special services
necessary thereto or special problems involved therein.

(c) The Commissioner of Education shall also from time to time
appoint panels of experts who are competent to evaluate various types
of research or demonstration projects under this section, and shall
secure the advice and recommendations of such a panel before making
any such grant in the field in which such experts are competent.

(d) Members of any committee or panel appointed under this section who are not regular full-time employees of the United States
shall, while serving on the business of such committee or panel, be
entitled to receive compensation at rates fixed by the Secretary of
Health, Education, and Welfare, but not exceeding $75 per day, in-
cluding travel time; and, while so serving away from their homes or
regular place of business, they may be allowed travel expenses, including per diem in lieu of subsistence, as authorized by section 5 of

60 Stat. 810.

the Administrative Expenses Act of 1946 (5 U.S.C. 73b–2) for
persons in the Government service employed intermittently.

(e) The Commissioner of Education is authorized to delegate any
of his functions under this section, except the promulgation of regulations, to any officer or employee of the Office of Education.

TITLE IV—GENERAL

DEFINITIONS

SEC. 401. For purposes of this Act—

(a) The term "State" includes Puerto Rico, Guam, American Samoa, the Virgin Islands, and the District of Columbia.

(b) The term "facility for the mentally retarded" means a facility specially designed for the diagnosis, treatment, education, training, or custodial care of the mentally retarded, including facilities for training specialists and sheltered workshops for the mentally retarded, but only if such workshops are part of facilities which provide or will provide comprehensive services for the mentally retarded.

(c) The term "community mental health center" means a facility providing services for the prevention or diagnosis of mental illness, or care and treatment of mentally ill patients, or rehabilitation of such persons, which services are provided principally for persons residing in a particular community or communities in or near which the facility is situated.

(d) The terms "nonprofit facility for the mentally retarded", "nonprofit community mental health center", and "nonprofit private institution of higher learning" mean, respectively, a facility for the mentally retarded, a community mental health center, and an institution of higher learning which is owned and operated by one or more nonprofit corporations or associations no part of the net earnings of which inures, or may lawfully inure, to the benefit of any private shareholder or individual; and the term "nonprofit private agency or organization" means an agency or organization which is such a corporation or association or which is owned and operated by one or more of such corporations or associations.

(e) The term "construction" includes construction of new buildings, expansion, remodeling, and alteration of existing buildings, and initial equipment of any such buildings (including medical transportation facilities); including architect's fees, but excluding the cost of off-site improvements and the cost of the acquisition of land.

(f) The term "cost of construction" means the amount found by the Secretary to be necessary for the construction of a project.

(g) The term "title", when used with reference to a site for a project, means a fee simple, or such other estate or interest (including a leasehold on which the rental does not exceed 4 per centum of the value of the land) as the Secretary finds sufficient to assure for a period of not less than fifty years undisturbed use and possession for the purposes of construction and operation of the project.

(h) The term "Federal share" with respect to any project means—

(1) if the State plan under which application for such project is filed contains, as of the date of approval of the project application, standards approved by the Secretary pursuant to section 402 the amount determined in accordance with such standards by the State agency designated under such plan; or

(2) if the State plan does not contain such standards, the amount (not less than 33⅓ per centum and not more than either 66⅔ per centum or the State's Federal percentage, whichever is the lower) established by such State agency for all projects in the State: *Provided*, That prior to the approval of the first such project in the State during any fiscal year such State agency shall give to the Secretary written notification of the Federal share established under this paragraph for such projects in such State to be approved by the Secretary during such fiscal year, and the Federal share for such projects in such State approved during such fiscal year shall not be changed after such approval.

199

(i) The Federal percentage for any State shall be 100 per centum less that percentage which bears the same ratio to 50 per centum as the per capita income of such State bears to the per capita income of the United States, except that the Federal percentage for Puerto Rico, Guam, American Samoa, and the Virgin Islands shall be 66⅔ per centum.

(j) (1) The Federal percentages shall be promulgated by the Secretary between July 1 and August 31 of each even-numbered year, on the basis of the average of the per capita incomes of the States and of the United States for the three most recent consecutive years for which satisfactory data are available from the Department of Commerce. Such promulgation shall be conclusive for each of the two fiscal years in the period beginning July 1 next succeeding such promulgation; except that the Secretary shall promulgate such percentages as soon as possible after the enactment of this Act, which promulgation shall be conclusive for the fiscal year ending June 30, 1965.

(2) The term "United States" means (but only for purposes of this subsection and subsection (i)) the fifty States and the District of Columbia.

(k) The term "Secretary" means the Secretary of Health, Education, and Welfare.

STATE STANDARDS FOR VARIABLE FEDERAL SHARE

SEC. 402. The State plan approved under part C of title I or title II may include standards for determination of the Federal share of the cost of projects approved in the State under such part or title, as the case may be. Such standards shall provide equitably (and, to the extent practicable, on the basis of objective criteria) for variations between projects or classes of projects on the basis of the economic status of areas and other relevant factors. No such standards shall provide for a Federal share of more than 66⅔ per centum or less than 33⅓ per centum of the cost of construction of any project. The Secretary shall approve any such standards and any modifications thereof which comply with the provisions of this section.

PAYMENTS FOR CONSTRUCTION

SEC. 403. (a) Upon certification to the Secretary by the State agency, designated as provided in section 134 in the case of a facility for the mentally retarded, or section 204 in the case of a community mental health center, based upon inspection by it, that work has been performed upon a project, or purchases have been made, in accordance with the approved plans and specifications, and that payment of an installment is due to the applicant, such installment shall be paid to the State, from the applicable allotment of such State, except that (1) if the State is not authorized by law to make payments to the applicant, the payment shall be made directly to the applicant, (2) if the Secretary, after investigation or otherwise, has reason to believe that any act (or failure to act) has occurred requiring action pursuant to section 136 or section 206, as the case may be, payment may, after he has given the State agency so designated notice of opportunity for hearing pursuant to such section, be withheld, in whole or in part, pending corrective action or action based on such hearing, and (3) the total of payments under this subsection with respect to such project may not exceed an amount equal to the Federal share of the cost of construction of such project.

200

(b) In case an amendment to an approved application is approved as provided in section 135 or 205 or the estimated cost of a project is revised upward, any additional payment with respect thereto may be made from the applicable allotment of the State for the fiscal year in which such amendment or revision is approved.

JUDICIAL REVIEW

SEC. 404. If the Secretary refuses to approve any application for a project submitted under section 135 or 205, the State agency through which such application was submitted, or if any State is dissatisfied with his action under section 134(b) or 204(b) or section 136 or 206, such State, may appeal to the United States court of appeals for the circuit in which such State is located, by filing a petition with such court within sixty days after such action. A copy of the petition shall be forthwith transmitted by the clerk of the court to the Secretary, or any officer designated by him for that purpose. The Secretary thereupon shall file in the court the record of the proceedings on which he based his action, as provided in section 2112 of title 28, United States Code. Upon the filing of such petition, 72 Stat. 941. the court shall have jurisdiction to affirm the action of the Secretary or to set it aside, in whole or in part, temporarily or permanently, but until the filing of the record, the Secretary may modify or set aside his order. The findings of the Secretary as to the facts, if supported by substantial evidence, shall be conclusive, but the court, for good cause shown, may remand the case to the Secretary to take further evidence, and the Secretary may thereupon make new or modified findings of fact and may modify his previous action, and shall file in the court the record of the further proceedings. Such new or modified findings of fact shall likewise be conclusive if supported by substantial evidence. The judgment of the court affirming or setting aside, in whole or in part, any action of the Secretary shall be final, subject to review by the Supreme Court of the United States upon certiorari or certification as provided in section 1254 of title 28, United States Code. The commencement of proceedings under 62 Stat. 928. this section shall not, unless so specifically ordered by the court, operate as a stay of the Secretary's action.

RECOVERY

SEC. 405. If any facility or center with respect to which funds have been paid under section 403 shall, at any time within twenty years after the completion of construction—

(1) be sold or transferred to any person, agency, or organization (A) which is not qualified to file an application under section 135 or 205, or (B) which is not approved as a transferee by the State agency designated pursuant to section 134 (in the case of a facility for the mentally retarded) or section 204 (in case of a community mental health center), or its successor; or

(2) cease to be a public or other nonprofit facility for the mentally retarded or community mental health center, as the case may be, unless the Secretary determines, in accordance with regulations, that there is good cause for releasing the applicant or other owner from the obligation to continue such facility as a public or other nonprofit facility for the mentally retarded or such center as a community mental health center,

the United States shall be entitled to recover from either the transferor or the transferee (or, in the case of a facility or center which has ceased to be public or other nonprofit facility for the mentally retarded or community mental health center, from the owners thereof) an amount bearing the same ratio to the then value (as determined by the agreement of the parties or by action brought in the district court of the United States for the district in which the center is situated) of so much of such facility or center as constituted an approved project or projects, as the amount of the Federal participation bore to the cost of the construction of such project or projects. Such right of recovery shall not constitute a lien upon such facility or center prior to judgment.

STATE CONTROL OF OPERATIONS

SEC. 406. Except as otherwise specifically provided, nothing in this Act shall be construed as conferring on any Federal officer or employee the right to exercise any supervision or control over the administration, personnel, maintenance, or operation of any facility for the mentally retarded or community mental health center with respect to which any funds have been or may be expended under this Act.

CONFORMING AMENDMENT

60 Stat. 1048.
42 USC 291k.

SEC. 407. (a) The first sentence of section 633(b) of the Public Health Service Act is amended by striking out "eight" and inserting in lieu thereof "twelve". The second sentence thereof is amended to read: "Six of the twelve appointed members shall be persons who are outstanding in fields pertaining to medical facility and health activities, and three of these six shall be authorities in matters relating to the operation of hospitals or other medical facilities, one of them shall be an authority in matters relating to the mentally retarded and one of them shall be an authority in matters relating to mental health, and the other six members shall be appointed to represent the consumers of services provided by such facilities and shall be persons familiar with the need for such services in urban or rural areas."

(b) The terms of office of the additional members of the Federal Hospital Council authorized by the amendment made by subsection (a) who first take office after enactment of this Act shall expire, as designated by the Secretary at the time of appointment, one at the end of the first year, one at the end of the second year, one at the end of the third year, and one at the end of the fourth year after the date of appointment.

Approved October 31, 1963, 10:07 a.m.

LEGISLATIVE HISTORY:

HOUSE REPORTS: No. 694 (Comm. on Interstate & Foreign Commerce),
               No. 862 (Comm. of Conference).
SENATE REPORT: No. 180 (Comm. on Labor & Public Welfare).
CONGRESSIONAL RECORD, Vol. 109 (1963):
    May 27: Considered and passed Senate.
    Sept. 10: Considered and passed House, amended.
    Oct. 21: Conference report agreed to in House and Senate.

President Lyndon B. Johnson signs the
Community Mental Health Centers Construction
Amendments of 1965

President Jimmy Carter signs the Mental Health Systems Act of 1980. L to r: Senator Edward Kennedy, Mrs. Rosalynn Carter, President Carter, Secretary of Health and Human Services Patricia Harris, and Representative Henry Waxman

MENTAL HEALTH SYSTEMS ACT

Public Law 96–398
96th Congress

An Act

Oct. 7, 1980
[S. 1177]

To improve the provision of mental health services and otherwise promote mental health throughout the United States, and for other purposes.

Be it enacted by the Senate and House of Representatives of the United States of America in Congress assembled,

Mental Health
Systems Act.
42 USC 9401
note.

SHORT TITLE AND TABLE OF CONTENTS

SECTION 1. This Act may be cited as the "Mental Health Systems Act".

TABLE OF CONTENTS

FINDINGS

SEC. 2. The Congress finds—   42 USC 9401.
    (1) despite the significant progress that has been made in
making community mental health services available and in
improving residential mental health facilities since the original
community mental health centers legislation was enacted in
1963, unserved and underserved populations remain and there
are certain groups in the population, such as chronically mentally ill individuals, children and youth, elderly individuals,
racial and ethnic minorities, women, poor persons, and persons
in rural areas, which often lack access to adequate private and
public mental health services and support services;
    (2) the process of transferring or diverting chronically men-
tally ill individuals from unwarranted or inappropriate institu-

tionalized settings to their home communities has frequently not been accompanied by a process of providing those individuals with the mental health and support services they need in community-based settings;

(3) the shift in emphasis from institutional care to community-based care has not always been accompanied by a process of affording training, retraining, and job placement for employees affected by institutional closure and conversion;

(4) the delivery of mental health and support services is typically uncoordinated within and among local, State, and Federal entities;

(5) mentally ill persons are often inadequately served by (A) programs of the Department of Health and Human Services such as medicare, medicaid, supplemental security income, and social services, and (B) programs of the Department of Housing and Urban Development, the Department of Labor, and other Federal agencies;

(6) health care systems often lack general health care personnel with adequate mental health care training and often lack mental health care personnel and consequently many individuals with some level of mental disorder do not receive appropriate mental health care;

(7) present knowledge of methods to prevent mental illness through discovery and elimination of its causes and through early detection and treatment is too limited;

(8) a comprehensive and coordinated array of appropriate private and public mental health and support services for all people in need within specific geographic areas, based upon a cooperative local-State-Federal partnership, remains the most effective and humane way to provide a majority of mentally ill individuals with mental health care and needed support; and

(9) because of the rising demand for mental health services and the wide disparity in the distribution of psychiatrists, clinical psychologists, social workers, and psychiatric nurses, there is a shortage in the medical specialty of psychiatry and there are also shortages among the other health personnel who provide mental health services.

TITLE I—GENERAL PROVISIONS

PART A—DEFINITIONS

DEFINITION OF COMMUNITY MENTAL HEALTH CENTER

42 USC 9411.

SEC. 101. (a) For purposes of this Act, the term "community mental health center" means a legal entity (1) through which comprehensive mental health services are provided—

(A) principally to individuals residing in a mental health service area, with special attention to those who are chronically mentally ill,

(B) within the limits of its capacity, to any individual residing or employed in such area regardless of ability to pay for such services, current or past health condition, or any other factor, and

(C) in the manner prescribed by subsection (b),

and (2) which is organized in the manner prescribed by subsections (c) and (d).

(b)(1) The comprehensive mental health services which shall be provided through a community mental health center are as follows:

(A) Beginning on the date the community mental health center is established for purposes of section 201, the services provided through the center shall include—

(i) inpatient services, emergency services, and outpatient services;

(ii) assistance to courts and other public agencies in screening residents of the center's mental health service area who are being considered for referral to a State mental health facility for inpatient treatment to determine if they should be so referred and provision, where appropriate, of treatment for such persons through the center as an alternative to inpatient treatment at such a facility;

(iii) provision of followup care for residents of its mental health service area who have been discharged from inpatient treatment at a mental health facility;

(iv) consultation and education services which—

(I) are for a wide range of individuals and entities involved with mental health services, including health professionals, schools, courts, State and local law enforcement and correctional agencies, members of the clergy, public welfare agencies, health services delivery agencies, and other appropriate entities; and

(II) include a wide range of activities (other than the provision of direct clinical services) designed to develop effective mental health programs in the center's mental health service area, promote the coordination of the provision of mental health services among various entities serving the center's mental health service area, increase the awareness of the residents of the center's mental health service area of the nature of mental health problems and the types of mental health services available, and promote the prevention and control of rape and the proper treatment of the victims of rape; and

(v) the services described in subparagraph (B) or, in lieu of such services, the center shall have a plan approved by the Secretary under which the center will, during the three-year period beginning on such establishment date, assume in increments the provision of the services described in subparagraph (B) and will upon the expiration of such three-year period provide all the services described in subparagraph (B).

(B) After the expiration of such three-year period, a community mental health center shall provide, in addition to the services required by subparagraph (A), services which include—

(i) day care and other partial hospitalization services;

(ii) a program of specialized services for the mental health of children, including a full range of diagnostic, treatment, liaison, and followup services (as prescribed by the Secretary);

(iii) a program of specialized services for the mental health of the elderly, including a full range of diagnostic, treatment, liaison, and followup services (as prescribed by the Secretary);

(iv) a program of transitional half-way house services for mentally ill individuals who are residents of its mental health service area and who have been discharged from

209

inpatient treatment in a mental health facility or would without such services require inpatient treatment in such a facility; and

(v) provision of each of the following service programs (other than a service program for which there is not sufficient need (as determined by the Secretary) in the center's mental health service area, or the need for which in the center's mental health service area the Secretary determines is currently being met):

(I) A program for the prevention and treatment of alcoholism and alcohol abuse and for the rehabilitation of alcohol abusers and alcoholics.

(II) A program for the prevention and treatment of drug addiction and abuse and for the rehabilitation of drug addicts, drug abusers, and other persons with drug dependency problems.

Service coordination.

(2) The provision of comprehensive mental health services through a center shall be coordinated with the provision of services by other health and social service agencies (including public mental health facilities) in or serving residents of the center's mental health service area to ensure that persons receiving services through the center have access to all such health and social services as they may require. The center's services (A) may be provided at the center or satellite centers through the staff of the center or through appropriate arrangements with health professionals and others in the center's mental health service area, or, with the approval of the Secretary, in the case of inpatient services, emergency services, partial hospitalization, transitional half-way house services, and certain specialized services, through appropriate arrangements with health professionals and others serving the residents of the mental health service area, (B) shall be available and accessible to the residents of the area promptly, as appropriate, and in a manner which preserves human dignity and assures continuity and high quality care and which overcomes geographic, cultural, linguistic, and economic barriers to the receipt of services, and (C) when medically necessary, shall be available and accessible twenty-four hours a day and seven days a week.

Professional supervision.

(3)(A) The mental health care of every patient of a center shall be under the supervision of a member of the professional staff of the center. The center shall provide for having a member of its professional staff available to furnish necessary mental health care in case of an emergency.

Supervising physician.

(B) Any medical services provided by a center shall be under the supervision of a physician unless otherwise permitted by State law. Whenever possible, the supervising physician shall be a psychiatrist.

Governing body.

(c)(1) Except as provided in paragraph (2) or (3), a community mental health center shall have a governing body which (A) is composed of individuals who reside in the center's mental health service area and who, as a group, represent the residents of that area taking into consideration their employment, age, sex, and place of residence, and other demographic characteristics of the area, and (B) is required to meet at least once a month, to establish general policies for the center (including a schedule of hours during which services will be provided), to approve the center's annual budget, and to approve the selection of a director for the center. At least one-half of the members of such body shall be individuals who are not providers of health care.

210

(2)(A) Except as provided in subparagraph (B), in the case of a community mental health center which is operated by a governmental agency or a hospital, such center may, in lieu of meeting the requirements of paragraph (1), appoint a committee which advises it with respect to the operations of the center and which is composed of individuals who reside in the center's mental health service area, who are representative of the residents of the area as to employment, age, sex, place of residence, and other demographic characteristics, and at least one-half of whom are not providers of health care. A center to which this subparagraph applies shall submit to such a committee for its review any application for a grant under section 201.

(B) Subparagraph (A) does not apply with respect to a community mental health center which on the date of the enactment of this Act had a governing body which met the requirements of paragraph (1).

(3) Paragraphs (1) and (2) do not apply to a community mental health center which is operated by a primary care center, community health center, or migrant center and which meets the applicable requirements of part D of title III of the Public Health Service Act.

(4) For purposes of paragraphs (1) and (2), the term "provider of health care" has the same meaning as is prescribed for that term by section 1531(3) of the Public Health Service Act.

(d) A center shall, in accordance with regulations prescribed by the Secretary, have (1) an ongoing quality assurance program (including multidisciplinary utilization and peer review systems) respecting the center's services, (2) an integrated medical records system (including a drug use profile) which, in accordance with applicable Federal and State laws respecting confidentiality, is designed to provide access to all past and current information regarding the health status of each patient and to maintain safeguards to preserve confidentiality and to protect the rights of the patient, (3) a multidisciplinary professional advisory board, which is composed of members of the center's professional staff, to advise the governing board or the advisory committee in establishing policies governing medical and other services provided by such staff on behalf of the center, and (4) an identifiable administrative unit which shall be responsible for providing the consultation and education services described in subsection (b)(1)(A)(iv). The Secretary may waive the requirements of clause (4) with respect to any center if he determines that because of the size of such center or because of other relevant factors the establishment of the administrative unit described in such clause is not warranted.

OTHER DEFINITIONS

SEC. 102. For purposes of this Act:

(1) The term "Secretary" means the Secretary of Health and Human Services.

(2) The term "State" includes (in addition to the fifty States) the District of Columbia, the Commonwealth of Puerto Rico, the Virgin Islands, Guam, American Samoa, the Trust Territory of the Pacific Islands, and the Northern Mariana Islands.

(3) The term "State mental health authority" means the agency of a State designated under section 105 to be responsible for the mental health programs of the State.

(4) The term "mental health service area" means an area established under section 106.

(5) The term "nonprofit", as applied to any entity, means an entity which is owned and operated by one or more corporations

or associations no part of the net earnings of which inures or may lawfully inure to the benefit of any private shareholder or person.

(6) The term "priority population group" means an identifiable population group in a mental health service area which is unserved or underserved by mental health programs in such area as determined under a health systems plan or a State health plan in effect under section 1513 or 1524 of the Public Health Service Act.

42 USC 300l-2, 300m-3.

(7) The term "Governor" means the chief executive officer of a State.

PART B—STATE ADMINISTRATIVE RESPONSIBILITIES

STATE MENTAL HEALTH AUTHORITY

42 USC 9421.

SEC. 105. Each State shall designate an agency of the State to be responsible for the mental health programs of the State.

MENTAL HEALTH SERVICE AREAS

Redesignation.
42 USC 9422.

SEC. 106. (a) Each catchment area of a community mental health center designated under the Community Mental Health Centers Act is redesignated as a mental health service area.

Boundaries.

(b) A mental health service area in a State shall, except to the extent permitted under regulations of the Secretary, have boundaries which conform to or are within the boundaries of a health service area established under title XV of the Public Health Service Act and, to the extent practicable, conform to boundaries of one or more school districts or political or other subdivisions in the State.

42 USC 300k-1.

Boundary review; revision.

(c)(1) The State mental health authority of a State shall review the boundaries of any mental health service area in the State which does not meet the requirements of subsection (b) and shall make such revisions in the boundaries of the area as may be necessary to meet such requirements.

(2) The State mental health authority of a State may review the boundaries of any mental health service area in the State and may revise the boundary of any such area to—

(A) ensure that the size of such area is such that the services to be provided in the area are available and accessible to the residents of the area promptly, as appropriate, and

(B) ensure that the boundary of such area eliminates, to the extent possible, barriers to access to the services provided in the area, including barriers resulting from an area's physical characteristics, its residential patterns, its economic and social groupings, and its available transportation.

Notice; hearing.

(3) In conducting a review of a boundary under paragraph (1) or (2) a State mental health authority shall provide notice of its review and shall provide a reasonable opportunity for a hearing on its review and any proposed boundary revision.

ALLOTMENTS TO STATES TO IMPROVE THE ADMINISTRATION OF STATE MENTAL HEALTH PROGRAMS

42 USC 9423.

SEC. 107. (a) For the purpose of assisting State mental health authorities to improve the administration of State mental health programs and to carry out their activities under this Act relating to—

(1) planning and program design,

(2) data collection,
(3) data analysis,
(4) research,
(5) evaluation,
(6) setting and enforcing regulatory and other standards,
(7) reporting to the Secretary, and
(8) establishing, expanding, or operating mental health patients' rights protection programs,

the Secretary shall, for each fiscal year and in accordance with regulations, allot to the States the sums appropriated for such year under subsection (c) on the basis of the population and the financial need of the respective States. The populations of the States shall be determined on the basis of the latest figures for the populations of the States available from the Department of Commerce. Population determination.

(b) No allotment may be made to a State under subsection (a) unless the State has submitted to the Secretary an application for the allotment containing such information as the Secretary may require. Allotment application.

(c) There are authorized to be appropriated for allotments under subsection (a), $15,000,000 for the fiscal year ending September 30, 1982, $15,000,000 for the fiscal year ending September 30, 1983, and $15,000,000 for the fiscal year ending September 30, 1984. Appropriation authorization.

(d) Effective September 30, 1981, section 314(g) of the Public Health Service Act is repealed. Repeal.
42 USC 246.

TITLE II—GRANT PROGRAMS
GRANTS FOR COMMUNITY MENTAL HEALTH CENTERS

SEC. 201. (a)(1) The Secretary may make grants to any public or nonprofit private community mental health center to assist it in meeting its costs of operation (other than costs related to construction). 42 USC 9431.

(2) No application for a grant under paragraph (1) for a community mental health center which has not received a grant for its operation under the Community Mental Health Centers Act may be approved unless the application is accompanied by assurances, satisfactory to the Secretary, that the grant applied for and the State, local, and other funds and the fees, premiums, and third-party reimbursements which the applicant may reasonably be expected to collect in the year for which the grant would be made are sufficient to meet the projected costs of operation for that year.

(3) Grants under paragraph (1) may only be made for a grantee's costs of operation during the first eight years after its establishment. In the case of a community mental health center which received a grant under section 220 of the Community Mental Health Centers Act (as in effect before the date of enactment of the Community Mental Health Centers Amendments of 1975) or section 203(a) of such Act (as in effect after such date), such center shall, for purposes of grants under paragraph (1), be considered as having been in operation since its establishment for a number of years equal to the sum of the number of grants it received under such sections and the number of grants it has received under paragraph (1). Time limitation.

79 Stat. 428, 84 Stat. 56.
42 USC 2689 note.
42 USC 2689b.

(b) Each grant under subsection (a) to a community mental health center shall be made for the costs of its operation for the one-year period beginning on the first day of the month in which such grant is made, except that if at the end of such period a center has not obligated all the funds received by it under a grant, the center may use the unobligated funds under the grant in the succeeding year for the same purposes for which such grant was made but only if the center is eligible to receive a grant under subsection (a) for such succeeding year. Unobligated funds.

Grant
computation.
(c)(1) The amount of a grant for any year made under subsection (a) shall be the lesser of the amounts computed under subparagraph (A) or (B) as follows:

(A) An amount equal to the amount by which the grantee's projected costs of operation for that year exceed the total of State, local, and other funds and of the fees, premiums, and third-party reimbursements which the grantee may reasonably be expected to collect in that year.

(B)(i) Except as provided in clause (ii), an amount equal to the following percentages of the grantee's projected costs of operation: 80 percent of such costs for the first year of its operation, 65 percent of such costs for the second year of its operation, 50 percent of such costs for the third year of its operation, 35 percent of such costs for the fourth year of its operation, 30 percent of such costs for the fifth and sixth years of its operation, and 25 percent of such costs for the seventh and eighth years of its operation.

Designated
urban or rural
poverty area.
(ii) In the case of a grantee providing services for persons in an area designated by the Secretary as an urban or rural poverty area, an amount equal to the following percentages of the grantee's projected costs of operation: 90 percent of such costs for the first two years of its operation, 80 percent of such costs for the third year of its operation, 70 percent of such costs for the fourth year of its operation, 60 percent of such costs for the fifth year of its operation, 50 percent of such costs for the sixth year of its operation, 40 percent of such costs for the seventh year of its operation, and 30 percent of such costs for the eighth year of its operation.

Unobilgated
funds.
(2) The amount of a grant prescribed by paragraph (1) for a community mental health center for any year shall be reduced by the amount of unobligated funds from the preceding year which the center is authorized, under subsection (b)(1), to use in the year for which the grant is to be made.

Costs exceeded
by funds, grant
adjustment.
(3) If in a fiscal year the sum of—

(A) the total of State, local, and other funds, and of the fees, premiums, and third-party reimbursements collected in that year, and

(B) the amount of the grant received under subsection (a) by a center,

exceeds its actual costs of operation for that year, and if the center is eligible to receive a grant under subsection (a) in the succeeding year, an adjustment in the amount of that grant shall be made in such a manner that the center may retain such an amount (not to exceed 50 per centum of the amount by which such sum exceeded such costs) as the center can demonstrate to the satisfaction of the Secretary will be used to enable the center (i) to expand and improve its services, (ii) to increase the number of persons which it is able to serve, (iii) to modernize its facilities, (iv) to improve the administration of its service programs, and (v) to establish a financial reserve for the purpose of offsetting the decrease in the percentage of Federal participation in program operations in future years.

Operational
costs,
appropriation
authorization.
(d)(1) For initial grants under subsection (a) there are authorized to be appropriated $30,000,000 for the fiscal year ending September 30, 1982, $35,000,000 for the fiscal year ending September 30, 1983, and $40,000,000 for the fiscal year ending September 30, 1984.

(2) There are authorized to be appropriated for the fiscal year ending September 30, 1982, and for each of the next nine fiscal years such sums as may be necessary to make grants, for the number of years prescribed by subsection (a)(3), to community mental health centers which received an initial grant for operations under the Community Mental Health Centers Act or this Act for a fiscal year beginning before October 1, 1984.

42 USC 2689.

(3) Of the total amount appropriated under paragraphs (1) and (2) for any fiscal year, the Secretary may not obligate more than 5 percent for grants under subsection (a) to community mental health centers which are operated by hospitals and which have advisory committees as prescribed by section 101(c)(2).

Restriction.

GRANTS FOR SERVICES FOR CHRONICALLY MENTALLY ILL INDIVIDUALS

SEC. 202. (a)(1) The Secretary may make grants to any State mental health authority, community mental health center, or other public or nonprofit private entity for projects for the provision of mental health and related support services for chronically mentally ill individuals. No grant may be made under this subsection for a project unless the project provides for at least the following:

42 USC 9432.

Service requirements.

(A) The identification of the chronically mentally ill individuals residing in the area to be served by the project.

(B) Assistance to such individuals in gaining access to essential mental health services, medical and dental care and rehabilitation services, and employment, housing, and other support services designed to enable chronically mentally ill individuals to function outside of inpatient institutions to the maximum extent of their capabilities.

(C) Assuring the availability, for each such chronically mentally ill individual who needs both mental health and related support services, of an individual to assume responsibility for seeing to it that the individual receives any such service that the individual needs.

(D) Coordinating the provision of mental health and related support services to such individuals with the provision of other services to them.

(2) A grant under this subsection for a project in a mental health service area served by a community mental health center may be made only to the community mental health center or to the State mental health authority of the State in which the area is located, except that, if the Secretary finds that because of exceptional circumstances in the mental health service area the chronically mentally ill individuals in the area would be otherwise underserved, a grant may be made to any other public or private nonprofit entity.

Recipients; restriction, exception.

(3) In considering applications for grants under this subsection, the Secretary shall give special consideration to applications for projects designed to supplement and strengthen existing community support services.

Applications, special consideration.

(b) The Secretary may make grants to any State mental health authority to—

Grants, purposes.

(1) improve the skills of personnel providing services to chronically mentally ill individuals by providing or arranging for the provision of inservice training, other training, or retraining for such personnel; or

(2) coordinate the operations of State agencies or intrastate regional agencies responsible for mental health and related support services for chronically mentally ill individuals, and coordinate the provision of mental health and support services for chronically mentally ill individuals with the provision of services to such individuals under titles IV, V, XVI, XVIII, XIX, and XX of the Social Security Act and under the Rehabilitation Act of 1973, the United States Housing Act, the Comprehensive Employment and Training Act, the Developmental Disabilities

42 USC 601, 701, 1381, 1395, 1396, 1397.
29 USC 701 note.
42 USC 1437 note.
29 USC 801 note.

42 USC 6001
note, 42 USC
3001 note.
Limitation.

Grant
computation.

Assistance and Bill of Rights Act, the Older Americans Act, and other Federal and State statutes.

(c)(1) No entity may receive more than eight grants under this section.

(2) The amount of any grant under subsection (a) or (b) shall be determined by the Secretary, except that the amount of—

(A) the first and second grant may not exceed 90 percent of the costs (as determined by the Secretary) of the project for which the grant is made;

(B) the third grant may not exceed 80 percent of such costs;

(C) the fourth grant may not exceed 70 percent of such costs;

(D) the fifth grant may not exceed 60 percent of such costs;

(E) the sixth grant may not exceed 50 percent of such costs;

(F) the seventh grant may not exceed 40 percent of such costs; and

(G) the eighth grant may not exceed 30 percent of such costs.

Costs exceeded
by funds, grant
adjustment.

(3) If in a fiscal year the sum of—

(A) the total of State, local, and other funds, and of the fees, premiums, and third-party reimbursements collected in that year, and

(B) the amount of the grant received under subsection (a) by an entity,

exceeds its actual costs of operation for that year and if the entity is eligible to receive a grant under subsection (a) in the succeeding year, an adjustment in the amount of that grant shall be made in such a manner that the entity may retain such an amount (not to exceed 50 per centum of the amount by which such sum exceeded such costs) as the entity can demonstrate to the satisfaction of the Secretary will be used to enable the entity (i) to expand and improve its services, (ii) to increase the number of persons which it is able to serve, (iii) to modernize its facilities, (iv) to improve the administration of its service programs, and (v) to establish a financial reserve for the purpose of offsetting the decrease in the percentage of Federal participation in program operations in future years.

(d)(1) Except as provided in paragraph (3), no grant may be made to an entity under subsection (a) or (b) unless the entity meets the requirements of paragraph (2).

Governing body.

(2)(A) Except as provided in subparagraph (B), an applicant for a grant under subsection (a) to provide the services described in that subsection shall have a governing body which (i) is composed of individuals who reside in the entity's mental health service area and who, as a group, represent the residents of that area taking into consideration their employment, age, sex, and place of residence, and other demographic characteristics of the area, and (ii) is required to meet at least once a month, to establish general policies for the entity (including a schedule of hours during which services will be provided), to approve the entity's annual budget, and to approve the selection of a director for the entity. At least one-half of the members of such body shall be individuals who are not providers of health care.

Advisory
committee.

(B) An applicant which is a hospital, a State agency, or other public or nonprofit private entity which does not have as its primary purpose the provision of mental health services under grants under subsection (a) may appoint a committee which advises it with respect to the operations of the entity which are funded with a grant under subsection (a) or (b) and which is composed of individuals who reside in the entity's mental health service area, who are representative of the residents of the area as to employment, age, sex, place of residence, and other demographic characteristics, and at least one-half of whom are not providers of health care.

(3) Paragraph (1) does not apply with respect to an entity which is a primary care center, community health center, or migrant health center and which meets the applicable requirements of part D of title III of the Public Health Service Act.

42 USC 255.

(4) For purposes of paragraph (2), the term "provider of health care" has the same meaning as is prescribed for that term by section 1531(3) of the Public Health Service Act.

"Provider of health care." 42 USC 300n.

(e) For grants under subsections (a) and (b) there are authorized to be appropriated $45,000,000 for the fiscal year ending September 30, 1982, $50,000,000 for the fiscal year ending September 30, 1983, and $60,000,000 for the fiscal year ending September 30, 1984.

Appropriation authorization.

GRANTS FOR SERVICES FOR SEVERELY MENTALLY DISTURBED CHILDREN AND ADOLESCENTS

SEC. 203. (a) The Secretary may make grants to any State mental health authority, community mental health center, or other public or nonprofit private entity for the provision of mental health and related support services for severely mentally disturbed children and adolescents and for members of their families. The services which may be provided under a grant under this subsection shall include at least one of the following:

42 USC 9433.

Service requirements.

(1) The identification and assessment of the needs of severely mentally disturbed children and adolescents and the provision of needed mental health and related support services which are not provided by existing programs.

(2) Assuring the availability of appropriate personnel to be responsible for providing, or arranging for the provision of, the needed mental health and related support services for such children and adolescents.

(3) The provision of auxiliary mental health services under the Education for all Handicapped Children Act of 1975 to such children and adolescents who are handicapped.

20 USC 1401 note.

(4) The establishment of cooperative arrangements with juvenile justice authorities, educational authorities, and other authorities and agencies that come in contact with such children and adolescents to ensure referral of such children and adolescents for appropriate mental health and related support services.

A grant made under this subsection for a project in a mental health service area served by a community mental health center may be made only to the community mental health center or to the State mental health authority of the State in which the area is located, except that, if the Secretary finds that because of exceptional circumstances in the mental health service area the severely mentally disturbed children and adolescents in the area would otherwise be underserved, a grant may be made to any other public or private nonprofit entity.

Recipients; restriction, exception.

(b) The Secretary may make grants to any public entity for projects to coordinate the provision of mental health and related support services to severely mentally disturbed children and adolescents with the activities of community agencies and State agencies and with the provision of services available to such children and adolescents under titles IV, V, XVI, XIX, and XX of the Social Security Act and under the Education for All Handicapped Children Act of 1975, the Developmental Disabilities Assistance and Bill of Rights Act, the Rehabilitation Act of 1973, and other Federal and State statutes.

Grants, purposes.

42 USC 601, 701, 1381, 1396, 1397. 20 USC 1401 note. 42 USC 6001 note. 29 USC 701 note.

Limitation.

Grant
computation.

(c)(1) No entity may receive more than eight grants under this section.

(2) The amount of any grant under subsection (a) or (b) shall be determined by the Secretary, except that the amount of—

(A) the first and second grant may not exceed 90 percent of the costs (as determined by the Secretary) of the project for which the grant is made;

(B) the third grant may not exceed 80 percent oɪ such costs;

(C) the fourth grant may not exceed 70 percent of such costs;

(D) the fifth grant may not exceed 60 percent of such costs;

(E) the sixth grant may not exceed 50 percent of such costs;

(F) the seventh grant may not exceed 40 percent of such costs; and

(G) the eighth grant may not exceed 30 percent of such costs.

Costs exceeded
by funds, grant
adjustment.

(3) If in a fiscal year the sum of—

(A) the total of State, local, and other funds, and of the fees, premiums, and third-party reimbursements collected in that year, and

(B) the amount of the grant received under subsection (a) by an entity,

exceeds its actual costs of operation for that year and if the entity is eligible to receive a grant under subsection (a) in the succeeding year, an adjustment in the amount of that grant shall be made in such a manner that the entity may retain such an amount (not to exceed 50 per centum of the amount by which such sum exceeded such costs) as the entity can demonstrate to the satisfaction of the Secretary will be used to enable the entity (i) to expand and improve its services, (ii) to increase the number of persons which it is able to serve, (iii) to modernize its facilities, (iv) to improve the administration of its service programs, and (v) to establish a financial reserve for the purpose of offsetting the decrease in the percentage of Federal participation in program operations in future years.

(d)(1) Except as provided in paragraph (3), no grant may be made to an entity under subsection (a) or (b) unless the entity meets the requirements of paragraph (2).

Governing body.

(2)(A) Except as provided in subparagraph (B), an applicant for a grant under subsection (a) to provide the services described in that subsection shall have a governing body which (i) is composed of individuals who reside in the entity's mental health service area and who, as a group, represent the residents of that area taking into consideration their employment, age, sex, and place of residence, and other demographic characteristics of the area, and (ii) is required to meet at least once a month, to establish general policies for the entity (including a schedule of hours during which services will be provided), to approve the entity's annual budget, and to approve the selection of a director for the entity. At least one-half of the members of such body shall be individuals who are not providers of health care.

Advisory
committee.

(B) An applicant which is a hospital, a State agency, or other public or nonprofit private entity which does not have as its primary purpose the provision of mental health services under grants under subsection (a) may appoint a committee which advises it with respect to the operations of the entity which are funded with a grant under subsection (a) or (b) and which is composed of individuals who reside in the entity's mental health service area, who are representative of the residents of the area as to employment, age, sex, place of residence, and other demographic characteristics, and at least one-half of whom are not providers of health care.

218

(3) Paragraph (1) does not apply with respect to an entity which is a primary care center, community health center, or migrant health center and which meets the applicable requirements of part D of title III of the Public Health Service Act.

42 USC 255.

(4) For purposes of paragraph (2), the term "provider of health care" has the same meaning as is prescribed for that term by section 1531(3) of the Public Health Service Act.

"Provider of health care." 42 USC 300n.

(e) For grants under subsections (a) and (b) there are authorized to be appropriated $10,000,000 for the fiscal year ending September 30, 1982, $12,000,000 for the fiscal year ending September 30, 1983, and $15,000,000 for the fiscal year ending September 30, 1984.

Appropriation authorization.

GRANTS FOR MENTAL HEALTH SERVICES FOR ELDERLY INDIVIDUALS AND OTHER PRIORITY POPULATIONS

SEC. 204. (a)(1) The Secretary may make grants to any public or nonprofit private entity for projects for services for elderly individuals. Each such project shall include at least the following:

42 USC 9434.

Service requirements.

(A) The location of elderly individuals in the mental health service area or areas served by the entity who are in need of mental health services.

(B) The provision or arrangement for the provision of medical differential diagnoses of elderly individuals in such area or areas to distinguish between their need for mental health services and other medical care.

(C) The specification of the mental health needs of elderly individuals in such area or areas and the mental health and support services required to meet such needs.

(D) The provision of—

(i) the mental health and support services specified under subparagraph (C) in the communities in such area or areas, or

(ii) such services for elderly individuals in nursing homes and intermediate care facilities in such area or areas and training of the employees of such homes and facilities in the provision of such services.

(2) The Secretary may make grants to any public or nonprofit private entity in a mental health service area in which, as determined by the Secretary, the services described in paragraph (1) are being provided to enable the entity to—

Grants, purposes.

(A) assure the availability of appropriate personnel to be responsible for the provision of or for arranging for the provision of such services to elderly individuals; or

(B) coordinate the provision of such services to elderly individuals with (i) the area agency on aging (as defined in the Older Americans Act) and other community agencies providing mental health and related support services for elderly individuals, and (ii) with the provision of services available to elderly individuals under titles XVI, XVIII, XIX, and XX of the Social Security Act and under the Older Americans Act, the Comprehensive Alcohol Abuse and Alcoholism Prevention, Treatment, and Rehabilitation Act of 1970, the Drug Abuse Prevention, Treatment, and Rehabilitation Act, the United States Housing Act, the Domestic Volunteer Service Act of 1973, and other Federal and State statutes.

42 USC 1381, 1395, 1396, 1397. 42 USC 3001 note. 42 USC 4541 note. 21 USC 1101 note, 42 USC 1437 note.

(3)(A) No entity may receive more than eight grants under paragraph (1) or (2).

42 USC 4951 note.

(B) The amount of any grant under paragraph (1) or (2) shall be determined by the Secretary, except that the amount of—

Limitation. Grant computation.

(i) the first and second grant may not exceed 90 percent of the costs (as determined by the Secretary) of the project for which the grant is made;

    (ii) the third grant may not exceed 80 percent of such costs;

    (iii) the fourth grant may not exceed 70 percent of such costs;

    (iv) the fifth grant may not exceed 60 percent of such costs;

    (v) the sixth grant may not exceed 50 percent of such costs;

    (vi) the seventh grant may not exceed 40 percent of such costs; and

    (vii) the eighth grant may not exceed 30 percent of such costs.

Costs exceeded by funds, grant adjustment.

(C) If in a fiscal year the sum of—

    (i) the total of State, local, and other funds, and of the fees, premiums, and third-party reimbursements collected in that year, and

    (ii) the amount of the grant received under paragraph (1) by an entity,

exceeds its actual costs of operation for that year and if the entity is eligible to receive a grant under paragraph (1) in the succeeding year, an adjustment in the amount of that grant shall be made in such a manner that the entity may retain such an amount (not to exceed 50 per centum of the amount by which such sum exceeded such costs) as the entity can demonstrate to the satisfaction of the Secretary will be used to enable the entity (I) to expand and improve its services, (II) to increase the number of persons which it is able to serve, (III) to modernize its facilities, (IV) to improve the administration of its service programs, and (V) to establish a financial reserve for the purpose of offsetting the decrease in the percentage of Federal participation in program operations in future years.

Recipients; restriction, exception.

(D) A grant made under paragraph (1) for a project in a mental health service area served by a community mental health center may be made only to the community mental health center or to the State mental health authority of the State in which the area is located, except that, if the Secretary finds that because of exceptional circumstances in the mental health service area the elderly individuals in the area would otherwise be underserved, a grant may be made to any other public or private nonprofit entity.

(E)(i) Except as provided in clause (iii), no grant may be made to an entity under paragraph (1) or (2) unless the entity meets the requirements of clause (ii).

Governing body.

(ii)(I) Except as provided in subclause (I), an applicant for a grant under paragraph (1) to provide the services described in that paragraph shall have a governing body which is composed of individuals who reside in the entity's mental health service area and who, as a group, represent the residents of that area taking into consideration their employment, age, sex, and place of residence, and other demographic characteristics of the area, and which is required to meet at least once a month, to establish general policies for the entity (including a schedule of hours during which services will be provided), to approve the entity's annual budget, and to approve the selection of a director for the entity. At least one-half of the members of such body shall be individuals who are not providers of health care.

Advisory committee.

(II) An applicant which is a hospital, a State agency, or other public or nonprofit private entity which does not have as its primary purpose the provision of mental health services under grants under paragraph (1) may appoint a committee which advises it with respect to the operations of the entity which are funded with a grant under paragraph (1) or (2) and which is composed of individuals who reside in the entity's mental health service area, who are representative of the residents of the area as to employment, age, sex, place of residence, and other demographic characteristics, and at least one-half of whom are not providers of health care.

(iii) Clause (i) does not apply with respect to an entity which is a primary care center, community health center, or migrant health center and which meets the applicable requirements of part D of title III of the Public Health Service Act.

42 USC 255.

(iv) For purposes of clause (ii), the term "provider of health care" has the same meaning as is prescribed for that term by section 1531(3) of the Public Health Service Act.

"Provider of health care."
42 USC 300n.

(b)(1) The Secretary may make grants to any public or nonprofit private entity for any project for mental health services which—

(A) is designed to serve principally one or more priority population groups in a mental health service area, and

(B) is available to all residents of the area.

(2) A grant made under paragraph (1) for a project in a mental health service area served by a community mental health center may be made only to the community mental health center or to the State mental health authority of the State in which the area is located and only if the Secretary finds that because of exceptional circumstances in the mental health service area priority populations in the area would be otherwise underserved.

Recipients, restriction.

(3)(A) Not more than four grants may be made under paragraph (1) to the same entity for mental health services for the same priority population group or groups, except that, if the entity is a community mental health center or other entity in a mental health service area served by a community mental health center, the number of grants which it may receive for the same population group or groups may not exceed two.

Limitation.

(B) In any fiscal year not more than two grants may be made under paragraph (1) for projects in one mental health service area and the total number of grants that may be made for projects in such an area under paragraph (1) may not exceed eight.

(C) The amount of any grant under paragraph (1) shall be determined by the Secretary, except that the amount of—

Grant computation.

(i) the first such grant may not exceed 90 percent of the costs of the project (as determined by the Secretary) for which the grant is made,

(ii) the second such grant may not exceed 80 percent of such costs,

(iii) the third such grant may not exceed 70 percent of such costs, and

(iv) the fourth such grant may not exceed 60 percent of such costs.

(D) If in a fiscal year the sum of—

Costs exceeded by funds, grant adjustment.

(i) the total of State, local, and other funds, and of the fees, premiums, and third-party reimbursements collected in that year, and

(ii) the amount of the grant received under paragraph (1) by an entity,

exceeds its actual costs of operation for that year and if the entity is eligible to receive a grant under paragraph (1) in the succeeding year, an adjustment in the amount of that grant shall be made in such a manner that the entity may retain such an amount (not to exceed 50 per centum of the amount by which such sum exceeded such costs) as the entity can demonstrate to the satisfaction of the Secretary will be used to enable the entity (I) to expand and improve its services, (II) to

221

increase the number of persons which it is able to serve, (III) to modernize its facilities, (IV) to improve the administration of its service programs, and (V) to establish a financial reserve for the purpose of offsetting the decrease in the percentage of Federal participation in program operations in future years.

(4) For purposes of this subsection, if a grant could be made under subsection (a) or section 202 or 203 for a project designed primarily to serve a particular population group, such population group shall not be included in the priority population groups for which grants are authorized under this subsection.

Criteria.

(c) An application for a grant under subsection (b) may be approved only if—

(1) the application contains satisfactory assurances that the project for which the application is made will lead to increased or more appropriate mental health services for a priority population group or to the development of mental health services for such a group;

(2) the application contains satisfactory assurances that members of the priority population group or groups to be served by the project will be afforded reasonable opportunity to comment on performance under the project; and

(3) the applicant (A) will during the first three years that it receives a grant under subsection (b) provide outpatient mental health services and any two of the following mental health services determined to be of the greatest need for the priority population to be served by the applicant: inpatient, screening, followup, consultation and education, and emergency services, and (B) unless the applicant is a community mental health center or a State mental health authority receiving a grant under subsection (b) as authorized by paragraph (2) of that subsection, has a plan satisfactory to the Secretary for the provision of all the mental health services described in clause (A) upon the expiration of the first three years that it receives a grant under subsection (b).

The Secretary may not approve an application of an entity which has received a grant for three years under subsection (b) unless the applicant is providing all the mental health services described in paragraph (3)(A).

(d)(1) Except as provided in paragraph (3), no grant may be made to an entity under subsection (b) unless the entity meets the requirements of paragraph (2).

Governing body.

(2)(A) Except as provided in subparagraph (B), an applicant for a grant under subsection (b) to provide the services described in that subsection shall have a governing body which (i) is composed of individuals who reside in the entity's mental health service area and who, as a group, represent the residents of that area taking into consideration their employment, age, sex, and place of residence, and other demographic characteristics of the area, and (ii) is required to meet at least once a month, to establish general policies for the entity (including a schedule of hours during which services will be provided), to approve the entity's annual budget, and to approve the selection of a director for the entity. At least one-half of the members of such body shall be individuals who are not providers of health care.

Advisory committee.

(B) An applicant which is a hospital, a State agency, or other public or nonprofit private entity which does not have as its primary purpose the provision of mental health services under grants under subsection (b) may appoint a committee which advises it with respect to the operations of the entity which are funded with a grant under subsection (b) and which is composed of individuals who reside in the entity's mental health service area, who are representative of the residents of the area as to employment, age, sex, place of residence, and other demographic characteristics, and at least one-half of whom are not providers of health care.

(3) Paragraph (1) does not apply with respect to an entity which is a primary care center, community health center, or migrant health center and which meets the applicable requirements of part D of title III of the Public Health Service Act. 42 USC 255.

(4) For purposes of paragraph (2), the term "provider of health care" has the same meaning as is prescribed for that term by section 1531(3) of the Public Health Service Act. "Provider of health care." 42 USC 300n.

(e) For grants under this section there are authorized to be appropriated $30,000,000 for the fiscal year ending September 30, 1982, $35,000,000 for the fiscal year ending September 30, 1983, and $40,000,000 for the fiscal year ending September 30, 1984. Not less than 40 percent of the amount appropriated under this subsection for any fiscal year shall be obligated by the Secretary for grants under subsection (a). Appropriation authorization.

GRANTS FOR NON-REVENUE-PRODUCING SERVICES

SEC. 205. (a)(1) The Secretary may make grants to any public or nonprofit private community mental health center to assist in meeting the costs (as determined by the Secretary by regulation) of— Service requirements. 42 USC 9435.

(A) providing the consultation and education services described in clause (iv) of section 101(b)(1)(A),

(B) providing the followup services described in clause (iii) of such section,

(C) administering the mental health service programs of the center,

(D) providing individuals who will be responsible for assuring that individuals in need of both mental health services and support services receive each of the services that they need, and

(E) any other non-revenue-producing service which the Secretary determines is appropriate for a community mental health center to provide.

(2) To be eligible for a grant under paragraph (1) a community mental health center must— Eligibility.

(A) have received a grant under section 203(a) of the Community Mental Health Centers Act, under section 220 of such Act as in effect before July 29, 1975, or under section 201 of this Act; and 42 USC 2689b. 79 Stat. 428, 84 Stat. 56.

(B) because of the limitations on the period for which a center may receive such a grant or on the number of such grants the center may receive, be no longer eligible to receive such a grant.

(b) An application for a grant under subsection (a) shall contain assurances satisfactory to the Secretary that the applicant will, during the period which it receives a grant under subsection (a), provide, at a minimum— Assurances.

(1) the comprehensive mental health services described in clauses (i) through (iv) of section 101(b)(1)(A), and

(2) any service described in section 101(b)(1)(B) which the center was providing in the last year it received a grant under the Community Mental Health Centers Act or this Act for its operations. 42 USC 2689 note.

Such an application shall also include information regarding the extent to which and manner in which the applicant has served chronically mentally ill individuals in prior years (if such service has been provided) and proposes to serve chronically mentally ill individuals during the fiscal year for which the grant is sought.

(c)(1) No community mental health center may receive more than five grants under subsection (a).

(2) The amount of a grant under subsection (a) shall be determined by the Secretary, except that no grant may exceed the product of $1.25 and the population of the mental health service area of the community mental health center receiving the grant. The population of a mental health service area shall be determined on the basis of the latest figures for the populations of the States available from the Department of Commerce.

(d) For grants under subsection (a) there are authorized to be appropriated $30,000,000 for the fiscal year ending September 30, 1982, $35,000,000 for the fiscal year ending September 30, 1983, and $40,000,000 for the fiscal year ending September 30, 1984.

GRANTS FOR MENTAL HEALTH SERVICES IN HEALTH CARE CENTERS

SEC. 206. (a)(1) For the purpose of assisting health care centers to participate appropriately in the provision of mental health services to their patients, the Secretary may make grants to—

(A) any public or nonprofit private entity which provides mental health services that include at least twenty-four-hour emergency services, outpatient services, and consultation and education services (as described in section 101(b)(1)(A)(iv)) and has in effect an agreement of affiliation, described in paragraph (2), with an entity which is a health care center; or

(B) any public or nonprofit private health care center which has in effect an agreement of affiliation, described in paragraph (2), with an entity described in subparagraph (A).

(2) An agreement of affiliation referred to in paragraph (1) is an agreement between a mental health services entity described in paragraph (1)(A) and a health care center which agreement—

(A) describes the geographical area the residents of which will be served by the mental health services to be provided under the agreement;

(B) provides for the employment of at least one mental health professional to serve as a liaison between the parties to the agreement and includes a description of the qualifications to be required of that person and of any other professional mental health personnel to be employed under the agreement;

(C) provides satisfactory assurances that the mental health services entity will make mental health services available to patients of the center referred to it by the liaison or other mental health professionals; and

(D) includes transportation arrangements and other arrangements for effecting referral from the center to the mental health · services entity of patients needing the services of such entity.

(b) Any grant under subsection (a) may be made for a project for any one or more of the following:

(1) The costs of the liaison or other mental health professionals providing services in the health care center in accordance with an agreement of affiliation.

(2) Mental health services provided by other personnel of the center which the mental health services entity determines can be appropriately provided by such personnel.

(3) Consultation and inservice training on mental health provided to personnel of the health care center by the mental health services entity.

(4) Establishing liaison between the center and other providers of mental health services or support services.

(c)(1) No entity may receive more than eight grants under subsection (a). Limitation.

(2) The amount of any grant under subsection (a) shall be determined by the Secretary, except that the amount of— Grant computation.

(A) the first and second grant may not exceed 90 percent of the costs (as determined by the Secretary) of the project for which the grant is made;

(B) the third grant may not exceed 80 percent of such costs;

(C) the fourth grant may not exceed 70 percent of such costs;

(D) the fifth grant may not exceed 60 percent of such costs;

(E) the sixth grant may not exceed 50 percent of such costs;

(F) the seventh grant may not exceed 40 percent of such costs; and

(G) the eighth grant may not exceed 30 percent of such costs.

(3) If in a fiscal year the sum of— Costs exceeded by funds, grant adjustment.

(A) the total of State, local, and other funds, and of the fees, premiums, and third-party reimbursements collected in that year, and

(B) the amount of the grant received under subsection (a) by a center or other entity,

exceeds its actual costs of operation for that year and if the center or entity is eligible to receive a grant under subsection (a) in the succeeding year, an adjustment in the amount of that grant shall be made in such a manner that the center or entity may retain such an amount (not to exceed 50 per centum of the amount by which such sum exceeded such costs) as the center or entity can demonstrate to the satisfaction of the Secretary will be used to enable the center or entity (i) to expand and improve its services, (ii) to increase the number of persons which it is able to serve, (iii) to modernize its facilities, (iv) to improve the administration of its service programs, and (v) to establish a financial reserve for the purpose of offsetting the decrease in the percentage of Federal participation in program operations in future years.

(d) For grants under subsection (a) there are authorized to be appropriated $15,000,000 for the fiscal year ending September 30, 1982, $17,500,000 for the fiscal year ending September 30, 1983, and $20,000,000 for the fiscal year ending September 30, 1984. Appropriation authorization.

(e) For purposes of this section, the term "health care center" includes an outpatient facility operated in connection with a hospital, a primary care center, a community health center, a migrant health center, a clinic of the Indian Health Service, a skilled nursing home, an intermediate care facility, and an outpatient health care facility of a medical group practice, a public health department, or a health maintenance organization.

GRANTS AND CONTRACTS FOR INNOVATIVE PROJECTS

SEC. 207. (a) The Secretary may make grants to any public or nonprofit private entity for— 42 USC 9437.

(1) projects for the training and retraining of employees adversely affected by changes in the delivery of mental health

225

services and for providing such employees assistance in securing employment;

(2) projects for the innovative use of personnel in the management and delivery of mental health services; and

(3) any other innovative project of national significance respecting mental health services and mental health services personnel.

The Secretary may enter into contracts for the projects described in this subsection with any private entity which is engaged solely in the provision of mental health services.

Limitation.

(b)(1) The total number of grants and contracts which an entity may receive under subsection (a) may not exceed five.

Amount, determination.

(2) The amount of any grant or contract under subsection (a) shall be determined by the Secretary.

Application

(c) No contract may be entered into under subsection (a) unless an application therefor has been submitted to and approved by the Secretary. The application shall be submitted in such form and manner and shall contain such information as the Secretary may prescribe.

(d) Of the total amount appropriated for any fiscal year under sections 201 through 206, 5 percent is available to the Secretary in such fiscal year for grants and contracts under subsection (a). Of the funds obligated in any fiscal year by the Secretary for such grants and contracts, not less than 50 percent shall be obligated for approvable projects described in subsection (a)(1).

GRANTS FOR THE PREVENTION OF MENTAL ILLNESS AND THE PROMOTION OF MENTAL HEALTH

42 USC 9438.

Sec. 208. (a) The Secretary may make grants to any public or nonprofit private entity for projects for the prevention of mental illness and the promotion of mental health or to demonstrate the effectiveness of intervention techniques and mental health promotion activities in the—

(1) maintenance and improvement of the mental health of individuals and groups of individuals particularly susceptible to mental illness,

(2) prevention of the onset of mental illness in such individuals and groups,

(3) prevention of the deterioration of the mental health of such individuals and groups,

(4) education of the general public regarding mental health problems and mental illness, the prevention of mental health problems and mental illness, and the promotion of mental health, and

(5) provision of screening, consultation, referral, and education in public school systems and in places of employment to detect and prevent early mental health problems and to promote mental health.

(b) Projects supported by grants under subsection (a) shall be consistent with national goals and priorities regarding the prevention of mental illness and promotion of mental health determined by the Director of the National Institute of Mental Health under section 455(d)(1) of the Public Health Service Act.

42 USC 289k-l.
Application requirements.

(c) An application for a grant under subsection (a) shall—

(1) define the techniques and mental health promotion activities to be funded by the grant;

226

(2) define the individuals or groups of individuals to be served by such techniques and activities; and

(3) provide for the evaluation of the effectiveness of such techniques and activities and describe the methodology to be used in making such evaluation.

(d) No entity may receive more than eight grants under subsection (a). The amount of a grant under subsection (a) shall be determined by the Secretary.

Limitation.
Amount, determination.

(e) For the purpose of grants under subsection (a) there are authorized to be appropriated $6,000,000 for the fiscal year ending September 30, 1982, $7,000,000 for the fiscal year ending September 30, 1983, and $8,000,000 for the fiscal year ending September 30, 1984.

Appropriation authorization.

TITLE III—GENERAL PROVISIONS RESPECTING GRANT PROGRAMS

PART A—STATE MENTAL HEALTH SERVICE PROGRAMS

STATE MENTAL HEALTH SERVICES PROGRAMS

SEC. 301. The State mental health authority of and any entity in a State is not eligible to receive a grant or contract under title II or this title for any fiscal year unless such State has in effect a State mental health services program which—

42 USC 9451.

(1) has been prepared by the State mental health authority in consultation with the Statewide Health Coordinating Council of the State, and

(2) is consistent with the provisions relating to mental health services of the State health plan prepared in accordance with section 1524(c)(2) of the Public Health Service Act.

42 USC 300m-3.

CONTENTS OF PROGRAMS

SEC. 302. A State mental health services program shall be submitted in such form and manner as the Secretary prescribes. The program shall consist of an administrative part and a services part as follows.

42 USC 9452.

(1) The administrative part shall—

Administrative part.

(A) provide that the State mental health authority will assume responsibility for administration of the program;

(B) provide for the designation of a State advisory council to consult with the State mental health authority in administering the program, which council shall include—

State advisory council.

(i) representatives of nongovernmental organizations or groups, and of State agencies, concerned with the planning, operation, or use of facilities for the provision of mental health services, and

(ii) representatives of consumers and providers of such services who are familiar with the need for such services,

and the nonprovider members of which shall constitute at least one-half of the membership of the council;

(C) provide that the State mental health authority will make such reports in such form and containing such information as the Secretary may from time to time reasonably require, and will keep such records and afford such access thereto as the Secretary may find necessary to assure the correctness and verification of such reports;

Reports; records, access.

(D) provide that any statistics or other data included in the program or on which the program is based will conform to such criteria, standards, and other requirements relating to their form, method of collection, content, or other aspects as the Secretary may prescribe;

(E) provide that the State mental health authority will from time to time, but not less often than annually, review the program and submit to the Secretary appropriate modifications thereof which it considers necessary;

(F) include provisions, meeting such requirements as the Office of Personnel Management may prescribe, relating to the establishment and maintenance of personnel standards on a merit basis; and

(G) include a statement of the arrangements made pursuant to section 801.

(2) The services part shall—

(A) identify the mental health service areas within the State;

(B) identify the need in each mental health service area of the State for mental health and related support services after consideration of—

(i) the demographic, economic, cultural, and social characteristics of the population of the area, and

(ii) the special mental health services needs in the area of chronically mentally ill individuals, emotionally disturbed children and adolescents, elderly individuals, and other priority population groups;

(C) identify and evaluate the public and private mental health facilities, the mental health personnel, and the mental health services available in each mental health service area, and determine the additional facilities, personnel, and services necessary to meet the mental health needs of each area;

(D) identify the methods used (i) to determine the mental health needs of each mental health service area, and (ii) to evaluate the facilities, personnel, and services of each mental health service area;

(E) provide the information described in subparagraphs (B) through (D) for mental health services and related support service needs which relate to more than one mental health service area;

(F) list the mental health service needs of each mental health service area in the order of priority that such needs should be addressed through the use of existing Federal, State, and local resources;

(G) identify measures which need to be taken to alleviate geographic, cultural, linguistic, and economic barriers with respect to the delivery of mental health services in the mental health service areas;

(H) identify the legal rights of persons in the State who are mentally ill or otherwise mentally handicapped and describe any measure which needs to be taken to protect such rights;

(I) describe the actions which need to be taken by the State and entities in communities of the State to coordinate the provision of mental health and related support services in the State;

(J) describe, in specific terms, the actions the State mental health authority will take—

(i) to continue the provision of appropriate services which have been provided by local entities in the State with financial assistance under the Community Mental Health Centers Act and this Act and for which Federal financial assistance is no longer available;

42 USC 2689 note.

(ii) to promote the development of comprehensive mental health services in each mental health service area where such services are currently unavailable;

(iii) to ensure substantially that, within a five-year period after the program is in effect in the State (or within such longer period as the Secretary, upon request of the State mental health authority, permits)—

(I) residents of public inpatient mental health facilities who have been inappropriately placed in such facilities are discharged, and, to the extent appropriate, are placed in the least-restrictive settings and provided mental health and related support services appropriate to such persons' level of functioning;

Inappropriate placement, discharge; least-restrictive setting.

(II) persons who need to be placed in inpatient mental health facilities are placed in the least-restrictive settings and provided mental health and related support services appropriate to such persons' level of functioning; and

(III) persons who are discharged from, or are in need of placement in, inpatient mental health facilities are informed of available community-based facilities and programs providing mental health and related support services, and provided access to a sufficient number of adequately staffed and adequately funded community-based facilities and programs providing mental health and related support services; and

Facilities and programs, information and access.

(iv) to assist the courts and other public agencies, and appropriate private agencies, in screening persons being considered for inpatient care in mental health facilities in the State in order to determine if such care is medically or psychologically indicated;

Screening.

(K) include a description of the services made available for mentally ill individuals in the State under titles IV, V, XVI, XVIII, XIX, and XX of the Social Security Act and under the Education for All Handicapped Children Act of 1975, the Older Americans Act, the Developmental Disabilities Assistance and Bill of Rights Act, the Comprehensive Alcohol Abuse and Alcoholism Prevention, Treatment, and Rehabilitation Act of 1970, the Drug Abuse Prevention, Treatment, and Rehabilitation Act, and other relevant Federal statutes;

Service description.

42 USC 601, 701, 1381, 1395, 1396, 1397.
20 USC 1401 note.
42 USC 3001 note.
42 USC 6001 note.
42 USC 4541 note.
21 USC 1101 note.

(L) describe the steps being taken in the State to coordinate the provision of services under this Act with the provision of services under the Acts referred to in subparagraph (K); and

Service coordination.

(M) contain or be accompanied by such additional information or assurances and meet such other requirements as the Secretary prescribes in order to achieve the purposes of this Act.

MENTAL HEALTH PROVISIONS OF STATE HEALTH PLANS

42 USC 300m-2.

SEC. 303. Section 1523(a)(1)(B) of the Public Health Service Act is amended by inserting after "the statewide health needs of the State" the following: ", including the need for mental health services in the State,".

PART B—APPLICATIONS AND RELATED PROVISIONS

STATE ADMINISTRATION

42 USC 9461.

SEC. 305. (a) The Secretary may enter into an agreement with any qualified State mental health authority of a State under which the authority will be the exclusive agent for the State and entities within the State for purposes of the financial assistance programs authorized by title II (other than the programs authorized by sections 207 and 208).

Qualified State mental health authority.

(b) For purposes of subsection (a), a qualified State mental health authority is an authority which meets the following requirements:

(1) A State mental health authority shall demonstrate to the satisfaction of the Secretary (A) that it is effectively implementing its State mental health services program prepared pursuant to section 301, and (B) that it, or another agency of the State, is making a good faith effort to establish and implement procedures for carrying out the requirements of paragraph (2).

Chronically mentally ill individuals, discharge monitoring.

(2)(A) For the purpose of eliminating the overconcentration of chronically mentally ill individuals in any community or group of communities in a State, the State mental health authority of the State shall monitor the discharge and diversion of such individuals into communities by inpatient mental health facilities.

Service program.

(B) A State mental health authority shall administer a program of services for chronically mentally ill individuals in the State who have been discharged or diverted from inpatient mental health facilities. Such program shall include at least the following:

Discharge, notification.

(i) The timely notification by the inpatient mental health facilities in the State to the appropriate community mental health centers or other entities of the discharge of and the location of the residence of each chronically mentally ill individual who has given an informed consent to such notification.

Prerelease consultation.

(ii) Before a chronically mentally ill individual is discharged from an inpatient mental health facility into a community, a prerelease consultation between the facility and the appropriate community mental health center or other entity respecting the individual if the individual has given an informed consent to such consultation. Such consultation shall take place without delaying the discharge of such individual from the mental health facility. Such consultation shall include a preliminary evaluation of the physical, mental, social, and monetary needs of the individual to be discharged, and an identification of the services and programs for which such individual is eligible.

Treatment and services plan.

(iii) Development by each inpatient mental health facility of a written treatment and services plan for each chronically mentally ill individual who is to be discharged or who is diverted by the facility and who has given an informed consent to the development of such plan. The plan shall be developed in consultation with a case manager in the community mental health center or other appropriate entity in the mental health service area in which such individual will or does reside. Such plan shall—

(I) to the maximum extent feasible, be developed with the participation of the individual discharged or diverted and the family of such individual;

(II) include appropriate living arrangements suited to the needs of the individual, and, if the individual resides or is to reside in a residence in which there are at least three other chronically mentally ill individuals with whom the individual is not related by blood or marriage and which charges the individual for residing in the residence, assure that the residence meets the requirements prescribed under subparagraph (C) or meets the comparable requirements established under section 1616(e) of the Social Security Act.

42 USC 1382e.

(III) describe appropriate mental health services and other needed services, such as medical and dental services, rehabilitation services, vocational training and placement, social services, and living skills training; and

(IV) identify specific programs and services for which the individual is eligible, including income support.

There shall be a periodic reevaluation of the plan at least every one hundred and twenty days.

Periodic reevaluation.

(iv) In the case of a chronically mentally ill individual for whom a plan has been developed under clause (iii), designation of a case manager to be responsible for the implementation of the plan and the coordination of services under the plan.

(v) The establishment and enforcement of minimum standards for the provision of followup care for the chronically mentally ill by community mental health centers and other appropriate entities.

Compliance with the informed consent requirements of the program shall be determined in accordance with the law of the State in which the program is in effect.

(C) A State mental health authority shall develop a program for regulating, in accordance with guidelines established by the Secretary, residences in which there are at least four chronically mentally ill individuals who are not related by blood or marriage, which charge such individuals for residing in the residence, and which do not meet the comparable requirements established under section 1616(e) of the Social Security Act. Such program shall include the following:

(i) Minimum standards for approval of a residence, including a standard which requires a mechanism to be available to the residents who are chronically mentally ill to provide referral to and assistance in reaching appropriate medical, dental, mental health, and other services not available at a residence, compliance with appropriate life safety, fire, and sanitation codes, and access for visitation during reasonable hours without prior notice by appropriate mental health and social service staff.

Residence approval, minimum standards.

(ii) Procedures for the evaluation, inspection, and monitoring of the compliance of the residence with the requirements of the program.

(iii) Remedies for noncompliance with such requirements.

"Educational or informational services.

(D) A State mental health authority shall provide educational or informational services to educate the population of the State regarding the problems of chronically mentally ill individuals, the need for community involvement in programs designed to resolve the problems of chronically mentally ill individuals outside institutional settings, and the resources available or needed to help such programs succeed.

(E) A State mental health authority shall improve the skills of personnel involved in providing services for chronically mentally ill individuals through inservice training, retraining, or other training of such personnel.

Biennial report to Secretary.

(F) A State mental health authority shall provide satisfactory assurances to the Secretary that it will submit a biennial report to the Secretary regarding its efforts and progress under this paragraph, including the manner in which the needs of chronically mentally ill individuals in each mental health service area in the State are being met within the community and the State's progress in implementing mechanisms to ensure that, as chronically mentally ill individuals are discharged from mental health facilities, increased State mental health funds are available for community-based care.

"Agreement application.

(c) No agreement may be entered into under subsection (a) with a State mental health authority unless the authority has submitted an application to the Secretary in such form and manner as the Secretary shall prescribe. The Secretary shall publish a notice in the Federal Register identifying the States which have made an application for an agreement under subsection (a) and, in considering an application, the Secretary shall provide a reasonable opportunity for submission of comments on the application.

Notice, publication in Federal Register.

Grants to States.

(d) The Secretary may make grants to States which have entered into agreements under subsection (a) for purposes of assisting the States in meeting the costs of carrying out the agreements. For grants authorized by this subsection there are authorized to be appropriated $3,000,000 for the fiscal year ending September 30, 1982, $4,000,000 for the fiscal year ending September 30, 1983, and $5,000,000 for the fiscal year ending September 30, 1984.

Appropriation authorization.

PROCESSING OF APPLICATIONS BY STATE MENTAL HEALTH AUTHORITIES

42 USC 9462.
Ante, p. 1571.

SEC. 306. (a) Each applicant for a grant under title II (other than an applicant for a grant under section 207 or 208) shall submit its application to the State mental health authority for its State in accordance with such requirements as the authority may prescribe.

(b)(1) If a State mental health authority has entered into an agreement under section 305, the authority shall carry out the following:

Hearing.

(A) The authority shall consider the applications submitted to it in accordance with subsection (a), and, in the course of such consideration, shall provide the applicants and other interested persons with a reasonable opportunity for a hearing before the authority on the applications. The authority shall also provide a reasonable opportunity for a hearing on applications the authority proposes to submit for itself to the Secretary.

(B) The authority may modify any application submitted to it and may return an application to an applicant.

(C) The authority shall (i) rank all the applications which the authority proposes to transmit to the Secretary in the order in which the authority determines the applications should be funded when approved by the Secretary, and (ii) in accordance with the agreement entered into under section 305, transmit such applications to the Secretary.

If the State mental health authority modifies or returns an application, the State mental health authority shall provide the applicant involved with a statement of the reasons for the modification or return.

(2) If a State mental health authority has not entered into an agreement under section 305, the authority shall carry out the following:

(A) The authority shall consider the applications submitted to it in accordance with subsection (a), and, in the course of such consideration, shall provide the applicants and other interested persons with a reasonable opportunity for a hearing before the authority on the applications. The authority shall also provide a reasonable opportunity for a hearing on applications the authority proposes to submit for itself to the Secretary.

Hearing.

(B) For each category of grants under title II for which an application was submitted to or proposed by the authority, the authority shall (i) rank all the applications for such category of grants in the order in which the authority determines the applications should be funded when approved by the Secretary, and (ii) in accordance with regulations issued by the Secretary, transmit such applications to the Secretary.

(c)(1) An applicant may appeal to the Secretary a decision of a State mental health authority under subsection (b)(1) to return to the applicant its application or to modify its application. In reviewing the decision of the authority, the Secretary shall provide the authority and the applicant involved a reasonable opportunity for a hearing on the appeal of the decision of the authority. If the Secretary finds that the decision of the authority was arbitrary or capricious, the Secretary—

(A) shall, if the decision of the authority was to return the application, return the application to the authority for ranking, and

(B) shall, if the decision of the authority was to modify the application, provide the authority an opportunity to change its rank of the application, and the Secretary may consider the application without regard to the modifications.

(2) An applicant may appeal to the Secretary a decision of a State mental health authority under subsection (b)(2) ranking the application. In reviewing the decision of the authority, the Secretary shall provide the authority and the applicant involved a reasonable opportunity for a hearing on the appeal of the decision of the authority. If the Secretary finds that, on the basis of the record established in the hearing provided under the preceding sentence, there is substantial evidence that the activity proposed in the application involved would better carry out the purposes of the section under which it would be funded than other applications under that section given a higher rank, the Secretary may consider the application without regard to the rank given the application by the State mental health authority.

(3) A decision of the Secretary under paragraph (1) or (2) is not subject to judicial review.

(d) If a State mental health authority fails to carry out, in accordance with an agreement entered into under section 305 or with regulations issued by the Secretary, its responsibilities under subsection (b) with respect to applications submitted to it, the applicants

233

under such applications shall be provided an opportunity to submit their applications directly to the Secretary.

APPLICATIONS

42 USC 9463.
Ante, pp. 1585,
1571.

SEC. 307. (a) No grant may be made under this title or title II unless an application therefor is submitted to and approved by the Secretary. The application shall be in such form, submitted in such manner, and contain such information, as the Secretary may require.

Ante, pp. 1573,
1575, 1577.

(b) An application for a grant under section 201, 202, 203, or 204 must, in addition to the application requirements prescribed in the section under which the grant is to be made, contain or be accompanied by—

Financial plan and budget.

(1) a financial plan and budget covering the year for which the grant is sought (and such additional period as the Secretary may require) showing the sources of funding for the project and allocating the funds available for the project among the various types of services to be provided or assisted or the various types of activities to be conducted or assisted and among the various population groups to which the project is directed;

(2) a statement of the objectives of the project;

(3) with respect to health services which are to be provided, assurances satisfactory to the Secretary that—

Fees, schedule.

(A) the applicant (i) has prepared a schedule of fees or payments for the provision of its services designed to cover its reasonable costs of operation and a corresponding schedule of discounts to be applied to the payment of such fees or payments which discounts are adjusted on the basis of the patient's ability to pay; (ii) has made and will continue to make every reasonable effort (I) to secure from patients payment for services in accordance with such approved schedules, and (II) to collect reimbursement for health services to persons described in subparagraph (B) on the basis of the full amount of fees and payments for such services without application of any discount, and (iii) has submitted to the Secretary such reports as the Secretary may require to determine compliance with this subparagraph; and

(B) the applicant has made or will make and will continue to make every reasonable effort to collect appropriate reimbursement for its costs in providing services to persons who are entitled to insurance benefits under title XVIII of the Social Security Act, to medical assistance under a State plan approved under title XIX of such Act, or to assistance for medical expenses under any other public assistance program or private health insurance program; and

42 USC 1395.
42 USC 1396.

(C) the applicant will adopt and enforce a policy (i) under which fees for the provision of mental health services through the applicant will be paid to the applicant, and (ii) which prohibits health professionals who provide such services to patients through the applicant from providing such services to such patients except through the applicant.

(4) in the case of a project which will serve a population which includes a substantial proportion of individuals of limited English-speaking ability, assurances satisfactory to the Secretary that the applicant has (A) developed a plan and made arrangements responsive to the needs of such population for providing services to the extent practicable in the language and cultural context most appropriate to such individuals, and (B) identified

234

an individual on its staff who is fluent in both that language and English and whose responsibilities shall include providing guidance to such individuals and to appropriate staff members with respect to cultural sensitivity and bridging linguistic and cultural differences;

(5) assurances that the applicant has in effect a system, satisfactory to the Secretary, to assure that an employee of the applicant who reports to any officer or employee of the Department of Health and Human Services or appropriate State authority any failure on the part of the applicant to comply with an applicable requirement of this Act or regulation of the Secretary or requirement of State law will not on account of such report be discharged or discriminated against with respect to the employee's compensation or the terms, conditions, or privileges of the employee's employment; .

Requirement or regulation, noncompliance.

(6) satisfactory assurances that each facility to be used in the provision of mental health or support services to be supported by the grant applied for meets the requirements of applicable fire and safety codes imposed by State law;

(7) information on the organization and operation of the applicant;

(8) satisfactory assurances that the applicant will submit such reports, at such times and containing such information, as the Secretary may request and maintain such records as the Secretary may find necessary for purposes of this Act, and afford the Secretary and the Comptroller General of the United States such access to such records and other documents as may be necessary for an effective audit of the project;

Records and other documents, accessability.

(9) satisfactory assurances that funds made available under this Act will be used to supplement and, to the extent practical, increase the level of non-Federal funds that would, in the absence of those Federal funds, be made available for the purpose for which the funds under this Act are made available, and will in no event supplant such non-Federal funds;

Non-Federal funds, increase.

(10) satisfactory assurances that measures have been taken by the applicant to consult with members of the group or groups to be served, members of the public, and affected organizations and agencies during the development of the application, and to give reasonable opportunities to members of such groups, members of the public, and interested organizations and agencies to comment on the application;

(11) assurances that the applicant has made satisfactory efforts to coordinate the services to be provided with other mental health and support services in the same area;

(12) in the case of a grant under section 201 or 202, information regarding the extent to which and manner in which the applicant has served chronically mentally ill individuals in prior years (if such service has been provided) and proposes to serve chronically mentally ill individuals during the fiscal year for which the grant is sought;

(13) statistics and other information requested by the Secretary necessary to evaluate the compliance of the application with the requirements of this section;

(14) satisfactory assurance that the project is consistent with the State mental health services program; and

(15) such other information and material and such other assurances as the Secretary may prescribe.

235

Ante, pp. 1571,
1573, 1575, 1577.
(c) If an entity has received a grant under section 201, 202, 203, 204, or 206, the entity is not eligible to apply for a grant under another of such sections unless it continues to provide the service it provided under the grant it received or the Secretary determines that the service is not needed.

(d) If a grant is made for any fiscal year under section 202, 203, or 204(a) for a project in a mental health service area, no more than one grant may be made for such fiscal year for a project in such mental health service area under any one of the other such sections.

INDIAN TRIBES AND ORGANIZATIONS

42 USC 9464.
Ante, pp. 1585,
1571.
SEC. 308. (a) Except as provided in this section, the requirements of this title and title II shall apply with respect to any application of an Indian tribe, intertribal organization, or urban Indian organization made for a grant under title II.

(b)(1) Any Indian tribe or intertribal organization may apply directly to the Secretary for a grant under title II for the provision of mental health services if such services will be available within or will specifically serve—

(A) a federally recognized Indian reservation,

(B) any land area in Oklahoma that is held in trust by the United States for Indians or that is a restricted Indian-owned land area,

43 USC 1602.
(C) a native village in Alaska (as defined in section 3(c) of the Alaska Native Claims Settlement Act), or

25 USC 1601
note.
(D) an Indian community the members of which are recognized as eligible for services under the Indian Health Care Improvement Act.

(2) An application of an Indian tribe or intertribal organization authorized by paragraph (1)—

(A) shall also be submitted by the applicant to the Indian Health Service and may not be approved by the Secretary unless the Indian Health Service certifies that the application is consistent with the Tribal Specific Health Plan of the tribe or tribes to be served by the grant,

(B) shall not be subject to consideration by a State mental health authority,

(C) may be made without regard to the State mental health services program in effect in the State in which the tribe or organization is located, and

(D) may be considered, approved, and funded by the Secretary without regard to the mental health service area or areas in which the services under the grant will be provided.

(c) If the application of any Indian tribe, intertribal organization, or urban Indian organization for a grant under title II requests that the Indian Health Service or any entity of the Service provide the mental health services under the grant to members of such tribe or organization—

(1) the application shall not be subject to consideration by a State mental health authority, and

(2) if the application is approved, payments under the grant shall be made to the Indian Health Service or entity of the Service as requested in the application.

(d) For purposes of this section—

"Indian tribe."
25 USC 450f
note.
(1) the term "Indian tribe" has the same meaning as is given that term by the Indian Self-Determination Act, and

236

(2) the term "urban Indian organization" has the same meaning as is given that term by the Indian Health Care Improvement Act.

"Urban Indian organization."

PROCEDURES

SEC. 309. In considering any application for a grant or contract under this title or title II, the Secretary shall provide a reasonable opportunity for the submission of comments on the application. If the Secretary does not approve an application, the Secretary shall provide the applicant and the State mental health authority of the State in which the applicant is located to the Secretary with a statement of the reasons of the Secretary for not approving the application.

42 USC 9465.
Ante, pp. 1585, 1571.

PART C—PERFORMANCE

PERFORMANCE CONTRACTS

SEC. 315. No payment may be made under any grant or contract made or entered into under title II or this title unless the Secretary has entered into a contract with the entity to which the grant has been made or with which the contract has been entered into specifying the following with respect to the performance of the activities for which the grant or contract was made or entered into:

42 USC 9471.

(1) A schedule for the performance of such activities.

(2) The standards by which the performance of such activities by the entity will be monitored and evaluated, the incentives which will be provided the entity to meet such standards, and the role of the Secretary and of consumers and representatives of communities affected by such activities in such monitoring and evaluation.

(3) The methods and format which will be used in collecting and transmitting data to the Secretary respecting the performance of such activities.

(4) An expeditious and impartial method for the resolution of disputes between the entity and the Secretary respecting the performance of such activities.

(5) Such other matters which the Secretary includes in the contract to carry out the purposes of the section under which the grant or contract was made or entered into.

PERFORMANCE STANDARDS

SEC. 316. (a) The Secretary shall prescribe standard measures of performance designed to test the quality and extent of performance by the recipients of grants and contracts under title II and this title and the extent to which such performance has helped to achieve the national or other objectives for which the grants or contracts were made or entered into.

42 USC 9472.

(b) In determining whether or not to approve an application for a grant or contract under title II or this title, the Secretary shall consider the performance by the applicant under any prior grant or contract under title II or this title as measured under subsection (a).

Ante, pp. 1571, 1585.

EVALUATION AND MONITORING

SEC. 317. (a) With the approval of the Secretary, any recipient of a grant or contract under title II or this title may use a portion of that grant or contract for evaluation of the project or activity involved.

42 USC 9473.

237

Ante, pp. 1571, 1585.

(b) Not more than 1 per centum of the total amount appropriated under title II and this title for any fiscal year shall be used by the Secretary, or through contracts with State mental health authorities or other entities, to monitor activities of the recipients of grants and contracts under title II or this title to determine if the requirements of this Act applicable to the receipt of such grants or contracts are being met.

PART D—ENFORCEMENT

ENFORCEMENT

42 USC 9481.

Proposed payments, stoppage order.

SEC. 321. (a) If the Secretary determines that there has been a substantial and persistent failure—

(1) by a State mental health authority to implement its State mental health services program in accordance with the requirements of part A of this title, the Secretary may issue a proposed order to stop payments under title II and this title to any entity in the State, including the State mental health authority, until the Secretary is satisfied that such failure has been or will be corrected, or

(2) by any entity in a State which is receiving funds under a grant or contract under title II or this title to comply with the requirements of this title (other than the requirements of part A), the Secretary may issue a proposed order to stop payments under such grant or contract until the Secretary is satisfied that such failure has been or will be corrected.

The Secretary shall notify each entity affected by an order issued under this subsection of the effect of the order.

Hearing.

(b) If the Secretary issues an order under subsection (a), the Secretary shall provide a reasonable opportunity for an informal hearing for the entities affected by the order. Such a hearing shall be held in the State in which such entities are located. If after such a hearing the Secretary reaffirms the determination on which the order was based, the Secretary may discontinue payments as specified in the proposed order or as revised by the Secretary after the hearing.

PART E—MISCELLANEOUS

NATIONAL INSTITUTE OF MENTAL HEALTH PREVENTION UNIT

42 USC 289k-1.

Administrative unit, designation.

SEC. 325. Section 455 of the Public Health Service Act is amended by adding at the end thereof the following new subsection:

"(d) The Director shall designate an administrative unit in the Institute to—

"(1) design national goals and establish national priorities for—

"(A) the prevention of mental illness, and

"(B) the promotion of mental health,

"(2) encourage and assist local entities and State agencies to achieve the goals and priorities described in paragraph (1), and

"(3) develop and coordinate Federal prevention policies and programs and to assure increased focus on the prevention of mental illness and the promotion of mental health.".

TECHNICAL ASSISTANCE

SEC. 326. Such portion as the Secretary may determine, but not more than 2 percent, of the total amount appropriated under title II for any fiscal year is available to the Secretary to provide technical assistance, including short-term training, to any State mental health authority or other entity which is or has been a recipient of a grant under title II or this title to assist it in developing, or in better administering, the mental health services program or programs for which it is responsible.

42 USC 9491.

INDIRECT PROVISION OF SERVICES

SEC. 327. Except as provided in section 101(b)(2), any mental health service which an entity is responsible for providing in a mental health service area under a grant or contract under title II may be provided by it directly at its primary or satellite facilities or through arrangements with other entities or health professionals and others in, or serving residents of, the same mental health service area.

42 USC 9492.

COOPERATIVE AGREEMENTS

SEC. 328. In lieu of providing funds under a grant under title II or this title, the Secretary may provide such funds under a cooperative agreement, and all requirements which would apply with respect to such a grant shall apply to the cooperative agreement.

42 USC 9493.

TITLE IV—ASSOCIATE DIRECTOR FOR MINORITY CONCERNS

ASSOCIATE DIRECTOR FOR MINORITY CONCERNS

SEC. 401. (a) Section 455 of the Public Health Service Act (as amended by section 325 of this Act) is amended by adding at the end thereof the following new subsection:

42 USC 289k-1.

"(e)(1) The Director of the National Institute of Mental Health shall designate an Associate Director for Minority Concerns.

Designation.

"(2) The Secretary, acting through the Associate Director for Minority Concerns, shall—

Functions.

"(A) develop and coordinate prevention, treatment, research, and administrative policies and programs to assure increased emphasis on the mental health needs of minority populations.

"(B) support programs and projects relating to the delivery of mental health services to minority populations, including demonstration programs and projects;

"(C) develop a plan to increase the representation of minority populations in mental health service delivery and manpower programs;

"(D) support programs of basic and applied social and behavioral research on the mental health problems of minority populations;

"(E) study the effects of discrimination on institutions and individuals, including majority institutions and individuals;

"(F) develop systems to assist minority populations in adapting to, and coping with, the effects of discrimination;

"(G) support and develop research, demonstration, and training programs designed to eliminate institutional discrimination; and

"(H) provide increased emphasis on the concerns of minority populations in training programs, service delivery programs, and research endeavors of the Institute.".

Effective date.
42 USC 289k-1
note.

(b) The amendment made by subsection (a) shall take effect on the date of the enactment of this Act or October 1, 1980, whichever occurs later.

TITLE V—MENTAL HEALTH RIGHTS AND ADVOCACY

BILL OF RIGHTS

State laws,
review and
revision.
42 USC 9501.

SEC. 501. It is the sense of the Congress that each State should review and revise, if necessary, its laws to ensure that mental health patients receive the protection and services they require; and in making such review and revision should take into account the recommendations of the President's Commission on Mental Health and the following:

(1) A person admitted to a program or facility for the purpose of receiving mental health services should be accorded the following:

Appropriate
treatment and
related services.

(A) The right to appropriate treatment and related services in a setting and under conditions that—

(i) are the most supportive of such person's personal liberty; and

(ii) restrict such liberty only to the extent necessary consistent with such person's treatment needs, applicable requirements of law, and applicable judicial orders.

Individualized
written
treatment or
service plan.

(B) The right to an individualized, written, treatment or service plan (such plan to be developed promptly after admission of such person), the right to treatment based on such plan, the right to periodic review and reassessment of treatment and related service needs, and the right to appropriate revision of such plan, including any revision necessary to provide a description of mental health services that may be needed after such person is discharged from such program or facility.

Service
planning,
participation.

(C) The right to ongoing participation, in a manner appropriate to such person's capabilities, in the planning of mental health services to be provided such person (including the right to participate in the development and periodic revision of the plan described in subparagraph (B)), and, in connection with such participation, the right to be provided with a reasonable explanation, in terms and language appropriate to such person's condition and ability to understand, of—

(i) such person's general mental condition and, if such program or facility has provided a physical examination, such person's general physical condition;

(ii) the objectives of treatment;

(iii) the nature and significant possible adverse effects of recommended treatments;

(iv) the reasons why a particular treatment is considered appropriate;

240

(v) the reasons why access to certain visitors may not be appropriate; and

(vi) any appropriate and available alternative treatments, services, and types of providers of mental health services.

(D) The right not to receive a mode or course of treatment, established pursuant to the treatment plan, in the absence of such person's informed, voluntary, written consent to such mode or course of treatment, except treatment—

(i) during an emergency situation if such treatment is pursuant to or documented contemporaneously by the written order of a responsible mental health professional; or

(ii) as permitted under applicable law in the case of a person committed by a court to a treatment program or facility.

(E) The right not to participate in experimentation in the absence of such person's informed, voluntary, written consent, the right to appropriate protections in connection with such participation, including the right to a reasonable explanation of the procedure to be followed, the benefits to be expected, the relative advantages of alternative treatments, and the potential discomforts and risks, and the right and opportunity to revoke such consent. *Experimentation, right of nonparticipation.*

(F) The right to freedom from restraint or seclusion, other than as a mode or course of treatment or restraint or seclusion during an emergency situation if such restraint or seclusion is pursuant to or documented contemporaneously by the written order of a responsible mental health professional. *Freedom from restraint or seclusion.*

(G) The right to a humane treatment environment that affords reasonable protection from harm and appropriate privacy to such person with regard to personal needs. *Humane treatment.*

(H) The right to confidentiality of such person's records.

(I) The right to access, upon request, to such person's mental health care records, except such person may be refused access to— *Records, right of access.*

(i) information in such records provided by a third party under assurance that such information shall remain confidential; and

(ii) specific material in such records if the health professional responsible for the mental health services concerned has made a determination in writing that such access would be detrimental to such person's health, except that such material may be made available to a similarly licensed health professional selected by such person and such health professional may, in the exercise of professional judgment, provide such person with access to any or all parts of such material or otherwise disclose the information contained in such material to such person.

(J) The right, in the case of a person admitted on a residential or inpatient care basis, to converse with others privately, to have convenient and reasonable access to the telephone and mails, and to see visitors during regularly scheduled hours, except that, if a mental health professional treating such person determines that denial of access to a particular visitor is necessary for treatment purposes, such

241

mental health professional may, for a specific, limited, and reasonable period of time, deny such access if such mental health professional has ordered such denial in writing and such order has been incorporated in the treatment plan for such person. An order denying such access should include the reasons for such denial.

(K) The right to be informed promptly at the time of admission and periodically thereafter, in language and terms appropriate to such person's condition and ability to understand, of the rights described in this section.

(L) The right to assert grievances with respect to infringement of the rights described in this section, including the right to have such grievances considered in a fair, timely, and impartial grievance procedure provided for or by the program or facility.

(M) Notwithstanding subparagraph (J), the right of access to (including the opportunities and facilities for private communication with) any available—

(i) rights protection service within the program or facility;

(ii) rights protection service within the State mental health system designed to be available to such person; and

(iii) qualified advocate;

for the purpose of receiving assistance to understand, exercise, and protect the rights described in this section and in other provisions of law.

(N) The right to exercise the rights described in this section without reprisal, including reprisal in the form of denial of any appropriate, available treatment.

(O) The right to referral as appropriate to other providers of mental health services upon discharge.

(2)(A) The rights described in this section should be in addition to and not in derogation of any other statutory or constitutional rights.

(B) The rights to confidentiality of and access to records as provided in subparagraphs (H) and (I) of paragraph (1) should remain applicable to records pertaining to a person after such person's discharge from a program or facility.

(3)(A) No otherwise eligible person should be denied admission to a program or facility for mental health services as a reprisal for the exercise of the rights described in this section.

(B) Nothing in this section should—

(i) obligate an individual mental health or health professional to administer treatment contrary to such professional's clinical judgment;

(ii) prevent any program or facility from discharging any person for whom the provision of appropriate treatment, consistent with the clinical judgment of the mental health professional primarily responsible for such person's treatment, is or has become impossible as a result of such person's refusal to consent to such treatment;

(iii) require a program or facility to admit any person who, while admitted on prior occasions to such program or facility, has repeatedly frustrated the purposes of such admissions by withholding consent to proposed treatment; or

(iv) obligate a program or facility to provide treatment services to any person who is admitted to such program or facility solely for diagnostic or evaluative purposes.

(C) In order to assist a person admitted to a program or facility in the exercise or protection of such person's rights, such person's attorney or legal representatives should have reasonable access to—

Records and information, accessability.

    (i) such person;

    (ii) the areas of the program or facility where such person has received treatment, resided, or had access; and

    (iii) pursuant to the written authorization of such person, the records and information pertaining to such person's diagnosis, treatment, and related services described in paragraph (1)(I).

(D) Each program and facility should post a notice listing and describing, in language and terms appropriate to the ability of the persons to whom such notice is addressed to understand, the rights described in this section of all persons admitted to such program or facility. Each such notice should conform to the format and content for such notices, and should be posted in all appropriate locations.

Notice.

(4)(A) In the case of a person adjudicated by a court of competent jurisdiction as being incompetent to exercise the right to consent to treatment or experimentation described in subparagraph (D) or (E) of paragraph (1), or the right to confidentiality or access to records described in subparagraph (H) or (I) of such paragraph, or to provide authorization as described in paragraph (3)(C)(iii), such right may be exercised or such authorization may be provided by the individual appointed by such court as such person's guardian or representative for the purpose of exercising such right or such authorization.

incompetent persons.

(B) In the case of a person who lacks capacity to exercise the right to consent to treatment or experimentation under subparagraph (D) or (E) of paragraph (1), or the right to confidentiality of or access to records described in subparagraph (H) or (I) of such paragraph, or to provide authorization as described in paragraph (3)(C)(iii), because such person has not attained an age considered sufficiently advanced under State law to permit the exercise of such right or such authorization to be legally binding, such right may be exercised or such authorization may be provided on behalf of such person by a parent or legal guardian of such person.

Incapacitated persons.

(C) Notwithstanding subparagraphs (A) and (B), in the case of a person admitted to a program or facility for the purpose of receiving mental health services, no individual employed by or receiving any remuneration from such program or facility should act as such person's guardian or representative.

GRANTS FOR PROTECTION AND ADVOCACY PROGRAMS

SEC. 502. (a)(1) The Secretary may make grants to any public or nonprofit private entity for projects to protect and advocate the rights of mentally ill individuals if the entity—

Public or nonprofit private entity, eligibility. 42 USC 9502.

    (A) has the authority and ability to pursue legal, administrative, and other appropriate remedies to ensure the protection of the rights of mentally ill individuals, and

    (B) is independent of any entity which provides treatment or services to mentally ill individuals.

(2) A grant under paragraph (1) for the first fiscal year for which funds are appropriated under subsection (d) may be made only to an entity of the government of a State designated by the Governor of the State or a public or nonprofit private entity in a State recommended by the Governor of the State. A grant under paragraph (1) for a succeeding fiscal year may be made to any public or nonprofit private entity, except that in considering an application of an entity which is not an entity of State government designated by the Governor or

Hearing.

which has not been recommended by the Governor of a State, the Secretary shall notify the Governor of the State in which such entity is located of the application and shall provide the Governor and other interested persons a reasonable opportunity for a hearing on the application.

Training and technical assistance.

(b) The Secretary may make grants to any public or nonprofit private entity for the provision of training and technical assistance for entities carrying out projects to protect and advocate the rights of mentally ill individuals.

(c) No grant may be made under subsection (a) or (b) unless an application therefor is submitted to and approved by the Secretary. The application shall be submitted in such form and manner, and shall contain such information, as the Secretary may prescribe.

Appropriation authorization.

(d) For grants under subsections (a) and (b), there are authorized to be appropriated $10,000,000 for the fiscal year ending September 30, 1982, $12,500,000 for the fiscal year ending September 30, 1983, and $15,000,000 for the fiscal year ending September 30, 1984. Not more than 10 percent and not less than 5 percent of the amount appropriated under this subsection for any fiscal year shall be obligated for grants under subsection (b).

TITLE VI—RAPE PREVENTION AND CONTROL

RAPE PREVENTION AND CONTROL

42 USC 9511.

SEC. 601. (a) The Secretary, acting through the National Center for the Prevention and Control of Rape (hereafter in this section referred to as the "Center"), may, directly or by grant, carry out the

Study and investigation.

(1) A continuing study of rape, including a study and investigation of—

(A) the effectiveness of existing Federal, State, and local laws dealing with rape;

(B) the relationship, if any, between traditional legal and social attitudes toward sexual roles, the act of rape, and the formulation of laws dealing with rape;

(C) the treatment of the victims of rape by law enforcement agencies, hospitals or other medical institutions, prosecutors, and the courts;

(D) the causes of rape, identifying to the degree possible—

(i) social conditions which encourage sexual attacks, and

(ii) the motives of offenders, and

(E) the impact of rape on the victim and family of the victim;

(F) sexual assaults in correctional institutions;

(G) the estimated actual incidence of forcible rape as compared to the reported incidence of forcible rape and the reasons for any difference between the two; and

(H) the effectiveness of existing private and local and State government educational, counseling, and other programs designed to prevent and control rape.

Summaries, publication.

Report to Congress.

(2) The compilation, analysis, and publication of summaries of the continuing study conducted under paragraph (1) and the research and demonstration projects conducted under paragraph (5). The Secretary shall submit not later than March 30, 1983, to the Congress a summary of such study and projects together with a review of their effectiveness and recommendations where appropriate.

244

(3) The development and maintenance of an information clearinghouse with regard to—

(A) the prevention and control of rape;

(B) the treatment and counseling of the victims of rape and their families; and

(C) the rehabilitation of offenders.

Information clearinghouse.

(4) The compilation and publication of training materials for personnel who are engaged or intend to engage in programs designed to prevent and control rape.

Training materials.

(5) Assistance to community mental health centers and other qualified public and nonprofit private entities in conducting research and demonstration projects concerning the prevention and control of rape, including projects (A) for the planning, development, implementation, and evaluation of alternative methods used in the prevention and control of rape, the treatment and counseling of the victims of rape and their families, and the rehabilitation of offenders; (B) for the application of such alternative methods; and (C) for the promotion of community awareness of the specific locations in which, and the specific social and other conditions under which sexual attacks are most likely to occur.

(6) Assistance to community mental health centers in meeting the costs of providing consultation and education services respecting rape.

Costs, assistance.

(b) The Secretary shall appoint an advisory committee to advise, consult with, and make recommendations to the Secretary on the implementation of subsection (a). The recommendations of the committee shall be submitted directly to the Secretary without review or revision by any person without the consent of the committee. The Secretary shall appoint to such committee persons who are particularly qualified to assist in carrying out the functions of the committee. A majority of the members of the committee shall be women. Members of the advisory committee shall receive compensation at rates, not to exceed the daily equivalent of the annual rate in effect for grade GS-18 of the General Schedule, for each day (including traveltime) they are engaged in the performance of their duties as members of the advisory committee and, while so serving away from their homes or regular places of business, each member shall be allowed travel expenses, including per diem in lieu of subsistence, in the same manner as authorized by section 5703 of title 5, United States Code, for persons in Government service employed intermittently.

Advisory committee, appointment.

Membership.

Compensation.

45 FR 69201.

(c) No grant may be made under subsection (a) unless an application therefor is submitted to and approved by the Secretary. The application shall be submitted in such form and manner and contain such information as the Secretary may prescribe.

(d) For the purpose of carrying out subsection (a), there are authorized to be appropriated $6,000,000 for the fiscal year ending September 30, 1981, $1,500,000 for the fiscal year ending September 30, 1982, $1,500,000 for the fiscal year ending September 30, 1983.

Appropriation authorization.

(e) For purposes of subsection (a), the term "rape" includes statutory and attempted rape and any other criminal sexual assault (whether homosexual or heterosexual) which involves force or the threat of force.

"Rape."

(f) Part D of the Community Mental Health Centers Act is repealed.

Repeal.
42 USC 2689q.

245

GRANTS FOR SERVICES FOR RAPE VICTIMS

42 USC 9512.

SEC. 602. (a) The Secretary may make grants to any public or nonprofit private entity to assist in meeting the cost of—

(1) providing counseling and followup counseling for rape victims and the immediate family of rape victims;

(2) providing assistance in securing mental health, social, medical, and legal services for rape victims; and

(3) demonstration projects to develop and implement methods of preventing rape and assisting rape victims.

(b)(1) No grant may be made under subsection (a) unless an application therefor is submitted to and approved by the Secretary. The application shall be submitted in such form and manner and contain such assurances as the Secretary may require that the applicant will comply with the requirements of subsection (e) and such other information as the Secretary may prescribe.

Amount, limitation.

(2) The amount of any grant under this section shall be determined by the Secretary, except that the amount may not exceed 90 per centum of the cost of the project (as determined by the Secretary) with respect to which the grant is made.

(c)(1) In carrying out this section, the Secretary shall coordinate with other activities related to rape carried out by the Secretary and the heads of other Federal departments and agencies.

Grant review panel, establishment.

(2) The Secretary shall establish a grant review panel to make recommendations to the Secretary with respect to the approval of applications for grants under subsection (a). The Secretary shall appoint individuals to the panel who are or have been engaged in the provision of services to rape victims.

Appropriation authorization.

(d)(1) There are authorized to be appropriated for grants under subsection (a) $6,000,000 for the fiscal year ending September 30, 1981, $9,000,000 for the fiscal year ending September 30, 1982, $12,000,000 for the fiscal year ending September 30, 1983, and $12,000,000 for the fiscal year ending September 30, 1984.

Funding limits.

(2) The Secretary may in a fiscal year obligate not more than 7.5 percent of the funds appropriated for that fiscal year under paragraph (1) to provide, upon request, technical assistance in the development and submission of applications for a grant under subsection (a). Such assistance shall be provided only to those entities which the Secretary determines do not possess the resources or expertise necessary to develop and submit such an application.

Information disclosure.

(e) No officer or employee of the Federal Government or of any recipient of a grant under subsection (a) may use or disclose any personally identifiable information obtained, in carrying out an activity assisted by such grant, by the recipient (or an officer or employee of the recipient) from a rape victim or a rape victim's immediate family unless such use or disclosure is necessary to carry out the activity or is made with the consent of the person who supplied the information. Such information shall be immune from legal process and may not, without the consent of the person furnishing the information, be admitted as evidence or otherwise used in any civil or criminal action or other judicial or administrative proceeding.

246

TITLE VII—EXTENSION OF COMMUNITY MENTAL HEALTH CENTERS ACT

ONE-YEAR EXTENSION OF COMMUNITY MENTAL HEALTH CENTERS ACT

SEC. 701. (a) Subsection (d) of section 202 of the Community Mental Health Centers Act (42 U.S.C. 2689a(d)) (relating to grants for planning) is amended by striking out "for the fiscal year ending September 30, 1980" and inserting in lieu thereof "each for the fiscal year ending September 30, 1980, and the next fiscal year".

(b) Subsection (d) of section 203 of such Act (relating to grants for initial operation) is amended—

(1) in paragraph (1), by (A) striking out "and" after "1979,", and (B) inserting before the period a comma and the following: "and $37,000,000 for the fiscal year ending September 30, 1981"; and

42 USC 2689b.

(2) effective October 1, 1981, by striking out "(1)" and paragraph (2).

(c) Subsection (c) of section 204 of such Act (42 U.S.C. 2689c(c)) (relating to grants for consultation and education services) is amended (1) by striking out "and" after "1979,", and (2) by inserting before the period a comma and the following: "and $15,000,000 for the fiscal year ending September 30, 1981".

(d)(1) Section 213 of such Act (42 U.S.C. 2689h) (relating to financial distress grants) is amended (1) by striking out "and" after "1978,", and (B) by inserting after "1979," the following: "and $20,000,000 for the fiscal year ending September 30, 1981,".

(2) Section 212(c) of such Act (42 U.S.C. 2689g(c)) of such Act is amended by striking out "five" and inserting in lieu thereof "six".

(e) Section 206(e)(2)(B) of such Act (42 U.S.C. 2689e(e)(2)(B)) is amended by striking out "the fiscal year ending September 30, 1979, and during the fiscal year ending September 30, 1980" and inserting in lieu thereof "the fiscal years ending September 30, 1979, September 30, 1980, and September 30, 1981".

TITLE VIII—MISCELLANEOUS

EMPLOYEE PROTECTION

SEC. 801. (a)(1) Each State mental health authority shall have in effect equitable arrangements to protect the interests of employees affected adversely by actions taken by the State mental health authority to emphasize outpatient mental health services. Such arrangements shall include arrangements designed to preserve employee rights and benefits and to provide training and retraining of employees, where necessary, for work in mental health or other fields and arrangements under which maximum effort will be made to place employees in employment. The arrangements required by this paragraph shall be established by a State mental health authority in accordance with regulations issued by the Secretary with the concurrence of the Secretary of Labor.

42 USC 9521.

(2) The Secretary shall issue the regulations referred to in paragraph (1) not later than six months after the date of the enactment of this Act.

Regulations.

(b) Whenever the Secretary, after reasonable notice and opportunity for a hearing to the State mental health authority involved, finds (after consultation with the Secretary of Labor) that there is a failure to comply substantially with the requirements of subsection (a), the Secretary may, until the Secretary is satisfied that there will no

Noncompliance.

Ante, pp. 1570, 1588.
Report to congressional committees.

Contents.

longer be any such failure, discontinue payments to the State mental health authority under sections 107 and 305.

(c) Not later than March 1, 1983, and March 1, 1984, the Secretary of Health and Human Services shall submit to the Committee on Labor and Human Resources of the Senate and the Committee on Interstate and Foreign Commerce of the House of Representatives a report on actions taken under subsection (a). The report shall include the comments of the Secretary of Labor on such actions and shall include—

(1) a statement of the number, by State, of public inpatient mental health facilities which have been closed or partially closed since the date of the enactment of this Act,

(2) a statement of the number, by State, of public employees who were adversely affected by such closings,

(3) a summary, by State, of the arrangements made under subsection (a) for such employees and the cost of carrying out such arrangements,

(4) a description of agency procedures, resources, and personnel used to implement subsections (a) and (b), and

Ante, p. 1583.
(5) a description of the training and retraining projects funded under section 207.

REPORT ON SHELTER AND BASIC LIVING NEEDS OF CHRONICALLY MENTALLY ILL INDIVIDUALS

Report to congressional committees.
42 USC 9522.

SEC. 802. (a) The Secretary of Health and Human Services and the Secretary of Housing and Urban Development shall jointly submit a report to the Committees on Labor and Human Resources and Banking, Housing, and Urban Affairs of the Senate, and the Committees on Interstate and Foreign Commerce and Banking, Finance, and Urban Affairs of the House of Representatives, relating to Federal efforts to respond to the shelter and basic living needs of chronically mentally ill individuals.

Contents.

(b) The report required by subsection (a) shall include—

(1) an analysis of the extent to which chronically mentally ill individuals remain inappropriately housed in institutional facilities or have otherwise inadequate or inappropriate housing arrangements;

(2) an analysis of available permanent noninstitutional housing arrangements for the chronically mentally ill;

(3) an evaluation of ongoing permanent and demonstration programs, funded in whole or in part by Federal funds, which are designed to provide noninstitutional shelter and basic living services for the chronically mentally ill, including—

(A) a description of each program;

(B) the total number of individuals estimated to be eligible to participate in each program, the number of individuals served by each program, and an estimate of the total population each program expects to serve; and

(C) an assessment of the effectiveness of each program in the provision of shelter and basic living services;

(4) recommendations of measures to encourage States to coordinate and link the provisions in State health plans which relate to mental health and, in particular, the shelter and basic living needs of chronically mentally ill individuals, with local and State housing plans;

(5) recommendations for Federal legislation relating to the provision of permanent residential noninstitutional housing

arrangements and basic living services for chronically mentally ill individuals, including an estimate of the cost of such recommendations; and

(6) any other recommendations for Federal initiatives which, in the judgment of the Secretary of Health and Human Services and the Secretary of Housing and Urban Development, will lead to improved shelter and basic living services for chronically mentally ill individuals.

(c) The report required by subsection (a) shall be submitted to the committees referred to in subsection (a) no later than January 1, 1981.

OBLIGATED SERVICE FOR MENTAL HEALTH TRAINEESHIPS

SEC. 803. (a) Section 303 of the Public Health Service Act is amended by adding at the end thereof the following new subsection:

"(d)(1) Any individual who has received a clinical traineeship, in psychology, psychiatry, nursing, or social work, under subsection (a)(1) that was not of a limited duration or experimental nature (as determined by the Secretary) is obligated to serve, in service determined by the Secretary to be appropriate in the light of the individual's training and experience, at the rate of one year for each year (or academic year, whichever the Secretary determines to be appropriate) of the traineeship.

"(2) The service required under paragraph (1) shall be performed—

"(A) for a public inpatient mental institution providing inpatient care or any entity receiving a grant under the Mental Health Systems Act,

"(B) in a health manpower shortage area (as determined under subpart II of part D of this title), or

"(C) in any other area or for any other entity designated by the Secretary,

and shall begin within such period after the termination of the traineeship as the Secretary may determine. In developing criteria for determining for which institutions or entities or in which areas, referred to in the preceding sentence, individuals must perform service under paragraph (1), the Secretary shall give preference to institutions, entities, or areas which in his judgment have the greatest need for personnel to perform that service. The Secretary may permit service for or in other institutions, entities, or areas if the Secretary determines that the request for such service is supported by good cause.

"(3) Any individual who fails to perform the service required under this subsection within the period prescribed by the Secretary is obligated to repay to the United States an amount equal to three times the cost of the traineeship (including stipends and allowances) plus interest at the maximum legal rate at the time of payment of the traineeship, multiplied, in any case in which the service so required has been performed in part, by the percentage which the length of the service not so performed is of the length of the service so required to be performed.

"(4)(A) In the case of any individual any part of whose obligation to perform service under this subsection exists at the same time as any part of the individual's obligation to perform service under section 752 or 753 (because of receipt of a scholarship under subpart IV of part C of title VII) or the individual's obligation to perform service under section 472 (because of receipt of a National Research Service

42 USC 242a.

Ante, p. 1564.

42 USC 254d.

Repayment to U.S.

42 USC 294u, 294v.
42 USC 294t.
42 USC 289l-1.

249

Award), or both, the same service may not be used to any extent to meet more than one of those obligations.

"(B) In any case to which subparagraph (A) is applicable and in which one of the obligations is to perform service under section 752 or 753, the obligation to perform service under that section must be met (by performance of the required service or payment of damages) before the obligation to perform service under this subsection or under section 472.

"(C) In any case to which subparagraph (A) is applicable, if any part of the obligation to perform service under section 472 exists at the same time as any part of the obligation to perform service under this subsection, the manner and time of meeting each obligation shall be prescribed by the Secretary.

"(5) In disseminating application forms to individuals desiring traineeships, the Secretary shall include with such forms a fair summary of the liabilities under this subsection of an individual who receives a traineeship.".

(b) The amendment made by subsection (a) applies in the case of any academic year (of any traineeship awarded under section 303(a)(1) of the Public Health Service Act) beginning after the date of the enactment of this Act if the award for such academic year is made after such date.

42 USC 294u, 294v.

42 USC 289l-1

42 USC 242a note.

42 USC 242a.

CONFORMING AMENDMENTS

SEC. 804. (a) The second sentence of section 455(a) of the Public Health Service Act (42 U.S.C. 289k-1(a)) (relating to the National Institute of Mental Health) is amended—

(1) by striking out "and" after "sections 301 and 303 of this Act" and inserting in lieu thereof a comma; and

(2) by inserting ", and the Mental Health Systems Act" after "Mental Retardation Facilities and Community Mental Health Centers Construction Act of 1963 (other than part C of title II)".

(b) Section 507 of the Public Health Service Act (42 U.S.C. 225a) (relating to grants to Federal institutions) is amended—

(1) by striking out "and" after "drug dependence,"; and

(2) by inserting ", and appropriations under title VI of the Mental Health Systems Act" before "shall also be available".

(c) Section 513 of the Public Health Service Act (42 U.S.C. 229b) (relating to evaluation of programs) is amended by inserting "the Mental Health Systems Act," after "Community Mental Health Centers Act,".

(d) Section 1513(e)(1)(A)(i) of the Public Health Service Act (42 U.S.C. 300l-2(e)(1)(A)) (relating to functions of health systems agencies) is amended by inserting "the Mental Health Systems Act," after "Community Mental Health Centers Act,".

Ante, p. 1564.

42 USC 2661 note.

Ante, p. 1602.

42 USC 2681 note.

42 USC 300l-2.

SPECIAL PAY FOR PUBLIC HEALTH SERVICE PHYSICIANS AND DENTISTS

SEC. 805. Section 208(a) of the Public Health Service Act (42 U.S.C. 210(a)) is amended (1) by inserting "(1)" after "(a)", and (2) by adding at the end the following:

"(2) Commissioned medical and dental officers in the Regular and Reserve Corps shall while on active duty be paid special pay in the same amounts as, and under the same terms and conditions which apply to, the special pay now or hereafter paid to commissioned medical and dental officers of the Armed Forces under chapter 5 of title 37, United States Code.".

37 USC 301.

CONTRACT AUTHORITY

SEC. 806. The authority of the Secretary to enter into contracts   42 USC 9523.
under this Act shall be effective for any fiscal year only to such extent
or in such amounts as are provided in advance by appropriation Acts.

TITLE IX—MECHANIZED CLAIMS PROCESSING AND INFORMATION RETRIEVAL SYSTEMS

MECHANIZED CLAIMS PROCESSING AND INFORMATION RETRIEVAL SYSTEMS

SEC. 901. Section 1903 of the Social Security Act is amended by   42 USC 1396b.
adding at the end thereof the following new subsection:

"(r)(1)(A) In order to receive payments under paragraphs (2) and (7)
of subsection (a) without being subject to per centum reductions set
forth in subparagraph (C) of this paragraph, a State must provide
that mechanized claims processing and information retrieval systems
of the type described in subsection (a)(3)(B) and detailed in an advance
planning document approved by the Secretary are operational on or
before the deadline established under subparagraph (B).

"(B) The deadline for operation of such systems for a State is the
earlier of (i) September 30, 1982, or (ii) the last day of the sixth month
following the date specified for operation of such systems in the
State's most recently approved advance planning document submitted before the date of the enactment of this subsection.

"(C) If a State fails to meet the deadline established under subparagraph (B), the per centums specified in paragraphs (2) and (7) of
subsection (a) with respect to that State shall each be reduced by 5
percentage points for the first two quarters beginning on or after
such deadline, and shall be further reduced by an additional 5
percentage points after each period consisting of two quarters during
which the Secretary determines the State fails to meet the requirements of subparagraph (A); except that—

"(i) neither such per centum may be reduced by more than 25
percentage points by reason of this paragraph; and

"(ii) no reduction shall be made under this paragraph for any
quarter following the quarter during which such State meets the
requirements of subparagraph (A).

"(2)(A) In order to receive payments under paragraphs (2) and (7) of
subsection (a) without being subject to the per centum reductions set
forth in subparagraph (C) of this paragraph, a State must have its
mechanized claims processing and information retrieval systems, of
the type required to be operational under paragraph (1), initially
approved by the Secretary in accordance with paragraph (5)(A) on or
before the deadline established under subparagraph (B).

"(B) The deadline for approval of such systems for a State is the last
day of the fourth quarter that begins after the date on which the
Secretary determines that such systems became operational as
required under paragraph (1).

"(C) If a State fails to meet the deadline established under subparagraph (B), the per centums specified in paragraphs (2) and (7) of
subsection (a) with respect to that State shall each be reduced by 5
percentage points for the first two quarters beginning after such
deadline, and shall be further reduced by an additional 5 percentage
points at the end of each period consisting of two quarters during
which the State fails to meet the requirements of subparagraph (A);
except that—

251

"(i) neither such per centum may be reduced by more than 25 percentage points by reason of this paragraph, and

"(ii) no reduction shall be made under this paragraph for any quarter following the quarter during which such State's systems are approved by the Secretary as provided in subparagraph (A).

"(D) Any State's systems which are approved by the Secretary for purposes of subsection (a)(3)(B) on or before the date of the enactment of this subsection shall be deemed to be initially approved for purposes of this subsection.

"(3)(A) When a State's systems are initially approved, the 75 per centum Federal matching provided in subsection (a)(3)(B) shall become effective with respect to such systems, retroactive to the first quarter beginning after the date on which such systems became operational as required under paragraph (1), except as provided in subparagraph (B).

Percentum reductions.

"(B) In the case of any State which was subject to a per centum reduction under paragraph (2), the per centum specified in subsection (a)(3)(B) shall be reduced by 5 percentage points for the first two quarters beginning after the deadline established under paragraph (2)(B), and shall be further reduced by an additional 5 percentage points at the end of each period consisting of two quarters beginning after such deadline and before the date on which such systems are initially approved, except that no reduction shall be made under this paragraph for any quarter following the quarter during which the State's systems are initially approved by the Secretary.

Approved systems, review.

"(4)(A) The Secretary shall review all approved systems not less often than once each fiscal year, and shall reapprove or disapprove any such systems. Systems which fail to meet the current performance standards, system requirements, and any other conditions for approval developed by the Secretary under paragraph (6) shall be disapproved. Any State having systems which are so disapproved shall be subject to a per centum reduction under subparagraph (B). The Secretary shall make the determination of reapproval or disapproval and so notify the States not later than the end of the first quarter following the review period.

"(B) If the Secretary disapproves a State's systems under subparagraph (A), the Secretary shall, with respect to such State for quarters beginning after the determination of disapproval and before the first quarter beginning after such systems are reapproved, reduce the per centum specified in subsection (a)(3)(B) to a per centum of not less than 50 per centum and not more than 70 per centum as the Secretary determines to be appropriate and commensurate with the nature of noncompliance by such State; except that such per centum may not be reduced by more than 10 percentage points in any 4-quarter period by reason of this subparagraph. No State shall be subject to a per centum reduction under this paragraph (i) before the fifth quarter beginning after such State's systems were initially approved, or (ii) on the basis of a review conducted before October 1, 1981.

Waiver.

"(C) The Secretary may retroactively waive a per centum reduction imposed under subparagraph (B), if the Secretary determines that the State's systems meet all current performance standards and other requirements for reapproval and that such action would improve the administration of the State's plan under this title, except that no such waiver may extend beyond the four quarters immediately prior to the quarter in which the State's systems are reapproved.

"(5)(A) In order to be initially approved by the Secretary, mechanized claims processing and information retrieval systems must be of the type described in subsection (a)(3)(B) and must meet the following requirements:

"(i) The systems must be capable of developing provider, physician, and patient profiles which are sufficient to provide specific information as to the use of covered types of services and items, including prescribed drugs.

"(ii) The State must provide that information on probable fraud or abuse which is obtained from, or developed by, the systems, is made available to the State's medicaid fraud control unit (if any) certified under subsection (q) of this section.

"(iii) The systems must meet all performance standards and other requirements for initial approval developed by the Secretary under paragraph (6).

"(B) In order to be reapproved by the Secretary, mechanized claims processing and information retrieval systems must meet the requirements of subparagraphs (A)(i) and (A)(ii) and performance standards and other requirements for reapproval developed by the Secretary under paragraph (6).

"(6) The Secretary, with respect to State systems, shall— *Functions.*

"(A) develop performance standards, system requirements, *Performance standards, development.* and other conditions for approval for use in initially approving such State systems, and shall further develop written approval procedures for conducting reviews for initial approval, including specific criteria for assessing systems in operation to insure that all such performance standards and other requirements are met;

"(B) by not later than October 1, 1980, develop an initial set of performance standards, system requirements, and other conditions for reapproval for use in reapproving or disapproving State systems, and shall further develop written reapproval procedures for conducting reviews for reapproval, including specific criteria for reassessing systems operations over a period of at least six months during each fiscal year to insure that all such performance standards and other requirements are met on a continuous basis;

"(C) provide that reviews for reapproval, conducted before *Systems performance data base, development.* October 1, 1981, shall be for the purpose of developing a systems performance data base and assisting States to improve their systems, and that no per centum reduction shall be made under paragraph (4) on the basis of such a review;

"(D) insure that review procedures, performance standards, and other requirements developed under subparagraph (B) are sufficiently flexible to allow for differing administrative needs among the States, and that such procedures, standards, and requirements are of a nature which will permit their use by the States for self-evaluation;

"(E) notify all States of proposed procedures, standards, and other requirements at least one quarter prior to the fiscal year in which such procedures, standards, and other requirements will be used for conducting reviews for reapproval;

"(F) periodically update the systems performance standards, system requirements, review criteria, objectives, regulations, and guides as the Secretary shall from time to time deem appropriate;

"(G) provide technical assistance to States in the development *Technical assistance to States.* and improvement of the systems so as to continually improve the capacity of such systems to effectively detect cases of fraud or abuse;

253

42 USC 1395.
Coding system,
development.

"(H) for the purpose of insuring compatibility between the State systems and the systems utilized in the administration of title XVIII—

"(i) develop a uniform identification coding system (to the extent feasible) for providers, other persons receiving payments under the State plans (approved under this title) or under title XVIII, and beneficiaries of medical services under such plans or title;

Liaison between
States, carriers
and intermed-
iaries.

"(ii) provide liaison between States and carriers and intermediaries having agreements under title XVIII to facilitate timely exchange of appropriate data; and

"(iii) improve the exchange of data between the States and the Secretary with respect to providers and other persons who have been terminated, suspended, or otherwise sanctioned under a State plan (approved under this title) or under title XVIII;

Reasonable
costs,
definitions.

"(I) develop and disseminate clear definitions of those types of reasonable costs relating to State systems which are reimbursable under the provisions of subsection (a)(3) of this section; and

Report to
Congress.

"(J) report on or before October 1, 1981, to the Congress on the extent to which States have developed and operated effective mechanized claims processing and information retrieval systems.

Waiver.

"(7)(A) The Secretary shall waive the provisions of this subsection with respect to initial operation and approval of mechanized claims processing and information retrieval systems with respect to any State which—

"(i) had a 1976 population (as reported by the Bureau of the Census) of less than 1,000,000 and which made total expenditures (including Federal reimbursement) for which Federal financial participation is authorized under this title of less than $100,000,000 in fiscal year 1976 (as reported by such State for such year), or

"(ii) is a Commonwealth, or territory or possession, of the United States,

if such State reasonably demonstrates, and the Secretary does not formally disagree, that the application of such provisions would not significantly improve the efficiency of the administration of such State's plan under this title.

Timetable.

"(B) If the Secretary determines that the application of the provisions described in subparagraph (A) to a State would significantly improve the efficiency of the administration of the State's plan under this title, the Secretary may withdraw the State's waiver under subparagraph (A) and, in such case, the Secretary shall impose a timetable for such State with respect to compliance with the provisions of this subsection and the imposition of per centum reductions. Such timetable shall be comparable to the timetable established under this subsection as to the amount of time allowed such State to comply and the timing of per centum reductions.

"(8)(A) The per centum reductions provided for under this subsection shall not apply to a State for any quarter with respect to which the Secretary determines that such State is unable to comply with the relevant requirements of this subsection—

"(i) for good cause (but such a waiver may not be for a period in excess of 2 quarters), or

"(ii) due to circumstances beyond the control of such State.

Report to
Congress.

"(B) If the Secretary determines under subparagraph (A) that such a reduction will not apply to a State, the Secretary shall report to the

Congress on the basis for each such determination and on the modification of all time limitations and deadlines as described in subparagraph (C).

"(C) For purposes of determining all time limitations and deadlines imposed under this subsection, any time period during which a State was found under subparagraph (A)(ii) to be unable to comply with requirements of this subsection due to circumstances beyond its control shall not be taken into account, and the Secretary shall modify all such time limitations and deadlines with respect to such State accordingly.".

Time limitations and deadlines, modification.

Approved October 7, 1980.

*U.S. GOVERNMENT PRINTING OFFICE: 1980-0-341-166/6149

LEGISLATIVE HISTORY:

HOUSE REPORTS: No. 96-977 accompanying H.R. 7299 (Comm. on Interstate and Foreign Commerce) and No. 96-1367 (Comm. of Conference).
SENATE REPORTS: No. 96-712 (Comm. on Labor and Human Resources) and No. 96-980 (Comm. of Conference).
CONGRESSIONAL RECORD, Vol. 126 (1980):
    July 24, considered and passed Senate.
    Aug. 22, H.R. 7299 considered and passed House; passage vacated and S. 1177, amended, passed in lieu.
    Sept. 24, Senate agreed to conference report.
    Sept. 30, House agreed to conference report.

WEEKLY COMPILATION OF PRESIDENTIAL DOCUMENTS, Vol. 16, No. 41:
    Oct. 7, Presidential statement.

CHAPTER NOTES

Chapter 2

2-1. Interest groups represented on the Joint Commission of Mental Illness and Health were: American Academy of Neurology, Academy of Pediatrics, American Association for the Advancement of Science, American Association on Mental Deficiency, American Association of Psychiatric Clinics for Children, American College of Chest Physicians, American Hospital Association, American Legion, American Medical Association, American Nurses Association and the National League for Nursing (Coordinated Council of), American Occupational Therapy Association, American Orthopsychiatric Association, American Personnel and Guidance Association, American Psychiatric Association, American Psychoanalytic Association, American Psychological Association, American Public Health Association, American Public Welfare Association, Association for Physical and Mental Rehabilitation, Association of State and Territorial Health Officers, Association of American Medical Colleges, Catholic Hospital Association, Central Inspection Board, Children's Bureau, Department of Health, Education and Welfare, Council of State Governments, Department of Defense, National Association for Mental Health, National Association of Social Workers, National Committee Against Mental Illness, National Education Association, National Institute of Mental Health, National Medical Association, National Rehabilitation Association, Office of Vocational Rehabilitation, Department of Justice, Veterans Administration.

Chapter 3

3-1. All the figures for the following calculations were drawn from the Bureau of the Budget's report, "BOB Analysis of Proposed National Action Program for Mental Health," 3 December 1962. BOB obtained these figures from the Biometry Division of NIMH under Dr. Morton Kramer and the Division of Manpower Training under Dr. Eli Rubenstein.

Federal subsidies would cover up to 50 percent of staffing costs (37 percent of operating costs) for each center on a declining basis for two or three years. Consequently, the federal government would pay 20 percent of the estimated $530 million operating cost for centers in 1970 and 30 percent of the total cost of $725 million for building and operating them.

The arguments in support of this position were as follows. The Department of Health, Education, and Welfare (HEW) had stopped far short of the recommendations of the joint commission that the federal government bear two-thirds of the costs of all mental health community clinics (and seven-eighths of the increase for mental health care over the 1960 level). Instead, it proposed that the federal government bear 60 percent of the cost of building the mental health centers and also share in the *initial staffing* costs of a center. The partial HEW subsidy for staffing costs was designed to help communities get comprehensive centers started, but to stop short of a permanent subsidy.

The arguments against the position were: HEW visualized a major federal commitment to support the *construction* and, temporarily, the operation of community mental health facilities. The grants for staffing purposes, however, would contrast with the existing situation whereby HEW subsidized mental health care only through limited demonstration and research projects. It would also be inconsistent with the existing pattern in general hospitals (including mental hospitals) whereby Hill-Burton construction grants, but no federal operating subsidies, were provided.

Yet, even though a permanent subsidy might be eschewed, it was questionable whether communities would undertake to operate centers if there was no federal subsidy after the second or third year. Could the pattern of the fifteen- or twenty-fold increase in community mental health services between 1949 and 1961—with only $5 million of federal grants per year—be repeated on a large scale?

HEW and the president's interagency committee proposed the obligation of $330 million between 1965 and 1969 to build 500 mental health centers (in addition to $150 million for mental retardation facility construction). By 1970 the construction rate would be 150 mental health centers per year ($117 million) *plus* perhaps $50 million of mental retardation facilities.

Training outlays would increase from $55 million in 1963 to $190 million in 1970, representing an increase from 46 percent to 66 percent in the proportion of federal funds to total training outlays. This would include Department of Labor outlays under the manpower development and training program to increase the employment of ancillary personnel from 100,000 to 180,000 by 1970.

HEW's Estimates of CMHCs' Need for Mental Health Personnel

Specialty	1950	1960	1970	1980
		(In thousands)		
Psychiatrist	5.5	13.0	23.5	36.0
Clinical psychologist	3.5	9.0	20.6	40.0
Psychiatric social worker	3.0	7.2	16.5	35.0
Psychiatric nurse	10.0	15.0	25.9	52.0
Total	22.0	44.2	86.5	163.0

The arguments for this position were: HEW estimated that, at a minimum, necessary employment in the four core specialties would be as shown in the Table above.

HEW had considered the feasibility of making available this personnel. On the crucial question of the shortage of psychiatrists, it was pointed out that the ratio of physicians per 100,000 population had increased from 3.2 in 1949 to 7.1 in 1960; both HEW and the interagency committee believed that even without a special effort the upward trend would continue. The increase in the number of psychiatrists was being accelerated by NIMH through the retraining of 475 general practitioners a year. NIMH proposed to increase this number from 750 to 1,500 per year.

The arguments against this position were as follows. Attaining the HEW estimates would be exceedingly difficult. The number of psychiatrists would have to increase 80 percent by 1970, although the number of active physicians in the country would increase less than 20 percent. If all specialties continued to increase at current rates, there would be more specialists than general practitioners by 1980; the trends toward specialization would then have to level off.

The number of social workers for psychiatric service in competition with public assistance, child welfare and juvenile delinquency programs would have to rise 2.3 times between 1960 and 1970 to more than double their own employment. The capacity of the schools of social work was, however, not adequate to meet these needs. The employment of psychiatric nurses would have to rise 73 percent by 1970, about three times the likely increase in the total supply of professional nurses.

The shortage of psychiatrists was particularly crucial, because the ratio of active physicians per 1,000 population could be increased very little by 1980, even with the proposed doctor training bill. If the proportion of psychiatrists was to be doubled at the same time that medical research was expanding rapidly, this would mean a reduction in the ratio of general practitioners and other specialists available to provide service to people with no mental illnesses. BOB projected the number of physicians per 100,000 population as shown in the following Table.

The critical issue that could determine whether there would be a new national program, rather than a continuation of demonstration efforts, was personnel. The BOB's Michael March maintained that there would not be sufficient psychiatric personnel for a sustained national effort. Other BOB staff, especially Atwell, disagreed but their arguments were not cogent enough to defeat March's position. March argued that more training funds for health professions should not be shifted to psychiatry. The issue remained unresolved in the Bureau of the Budget.

3-2. Felix had detailed one of his key people, Bertram Brown, to the President's Panel on Mental Retardation. Brown provided staff work to the panel and, at the same time, served as the NIMH liaison to the Kennedy White House. At the request of Meyer Feldman in the fall of 1962, Brown and Michael March of the Bureau of the Budget consolidated the recommendations of the panel on retardation and the efforts of the president's

BOB Projections of Number of Available Physicians per 100,000 Population

Type of Physician	1949	1960	1970	1980 (with training bill)
All active physicians	128.4	125.9	125.4	127.3
Psychiatrists	3.2	7.1	11.2	13.7

interagency committee on mental health (Interview 1972i.). Intensive budgetary and legislative review of both efforts ensued, resulting in the president's separate mental retardation and mental health legislative packages.

3-3. Warren proposed the elimination of doctors' salaries in exchange for the provision of salaries for the support of paramedical personnel (nurses, therapists, social workers and others) and/or provision for demonstration programs including salaries for the same (Warren 1963).

3-4. There were a few deviations in the Senate committee report from the House report (House Report 1965, Senate Report 1965).

1. The House had not gone into the matter of leadership of the centers. The Senate committee (after referring to psychologists, psychiatric social workers, and psychiatric nurses) said: "Specifically, overall leadership of the health center program may be carried out by any one of the major mental health professions."

2. The Senate committee did not see the financial role of the federal government as declining. It deleted the House statement: "No further Federal funds will thereafter be available for the costs of the staffing covered by the prior grants, and the financing of these costs will thereafter be the responsibility of the states and localities involved." The Senate committee seems to have prepared for the contingency of permanent subsidy. The Senate authorized staffing grants to continue through 1972. The House had cut them off in 1969.

3. Both the House and Senate bills declared that staffing grants could be made only if the services to be provided were described in the state plan. The Senate, however, deleted the House comment: "The Committee envisions appropriate regulations under this provision which will assure that recommendations of the state mental health authority will be given due weight by both the local community and by the Federal Government in its review of each project application." Yolles did not want the control of the operating costs to shift to the states by means of the regulations. The state authorities were left with the Senate statement: "State authorities responsible for mental health planning under Title III of the Public Health Service Act can contribute important program perspectives and play a highly significant coordinating role."

4. The Senate report added language calling for the coordination of mental health center programs, not duplication of school guidance and

counseling programs under the Elementary and Secondary Education Act of 1965, or housing, antipoverty and welfare programs.
5. The Senate increased the total money by $51 million.

Chapter 4

4-1. The extent of a CMHC's program area (the "community" of a CMHC) was defined in demographic terms as one containing a population of 75,000 to 200,000 within specific geopolitical boundaries. This service area, for which the 1963 law holds the CMHC responsible, may be several counties of a rural state, an entire small city, a few contiguous suburbs in a metropolitan area, or one or two neighborhoods in a densely populated inner city. These population catchment areas not only would reflect the demographic and geographic diversity of the nation, but also the variations in age, race, language and culture, and socioeconomic status. CMHC responsiveness to the unique needs of its service area population was identified as one goal of the governing board, or advisory committee, of each CMHC; moreover, a needs-assessment phase was required as part of the funding process.

The "center" of a CMHC was to be a network, linked through an administrative core, for the delivery of mental health services and the coordination of mental health services with other health and human services in a given local area. A typical CMHC would be a network of services offered in locations such as state mental and community general hospitals, free-standing clinics, church basements, school classrooms and residential care homes. The effort to reach patients in all parts of the service area meant that CMHC service staff might work in several different locations in one day or during a week. The network's administrative core, which would receive and disburse the federal grant money, would be a nonprofit corporation set up to deliver and assure delivery of a continuum of mental health services.

In practice, a CMHC is an affiliation of two or more community agencies (for example, a social agency and a general hospital), which jointly assure provision of the continuum of essential services. Most CMHCs deliver services directly, using their own staffs, and also have formal or informal understandings with other entities to provide services. These affiliation agreements specify the terms of cooperation for services' provision. For example, a CMHC formed by social welfare agencies may affiliate with a general hospital which agrees to provide inpatient hospitalization space, a specific number of beds for CMHC patients, in exchange for financial assistance and/or for reimbursements for the costs of hospitalization. In some well-developed urban areas as many as eighteen different agencies have organized to form a CMHC. By way of contrast, some rural-area CMHCs have had to develop the five essential services and their linkages where few or none existed before. For example, the eastern Montana CMHC has a vast, sixteen-county service area. Prior to its establishment there were no psychiatrists or psychologists in private practice, no psychiatric hospitals, mental health clinics, psychiatric social workers or psychiatric nurses in that area of the state. Now emergency cases are seen within four hours because the CMHC has service facilities in two cities as well as mobile service teams.

4-2. The point is also made in the opening essay of *The Enduring Asylum* that, in the history of madness and government in the U.S., "while putative ameliorations are often received with great enthusiasm, there is a danger in accepting them without a critical assessment of the resources necessary to sustain them. Complex, multidimensional, recalcitrant social problems such as mental illness require complex, multifaceted solutions." This book assesses the processes and outcomes of the deinstitutionalization of the Massachusetts Worcester State Hospital, one of the oldest and most influential of mental asylums. It shows how those institutions have endured despite their failings because they remain the only places that provide custody, control and treatment (in that order) of society's most disadvantaged and disturbed individuals (Morrissey et al. 1980).

4-3. The first set of amendments had been passed in 1967 when Congress extended the authorizations for construction and initial staffing grants, and amended the definition of the term "construction" so as to permit the acquisition of existing buildings for use by CMHCs. These 1970 amendments also reflected the policy of a changed, Republican administration in that, for the first time, funds to preserve the initial investment were to be provided at the expense of developing new programs in areas without federal grants; 420 programs had been funded by this time, although only 245 were operational. The amendments entitled these CMHCs to grants over an eight-year, rather than a fifty-one-month, period, which had been stipulated in the 1965 amendments. In addition, a new program of initiation grants was added for the purpose of assessing local needs for mental health services, designing programs and developing services.

4-4. This outline history (Table) was prepared for NIMH administrative use in 1980 by Samuel Buker, deputy director of the Division of Mental Health Service Programs.

4-5. "Patient-care episodes" are defined as the number of residents in inpatient facilities at the beginning of the year (or the number of persons on the rolls of non-inpatient facilities) plus the total admissions to these facilities during the year (that is, new admissions, readmissions, and returns from long-term leave). This index, therefore, provides a duplicated count of persons and is not equal to a true annual prevalence rate or the annual prevalence rate for treated mental disorder, which would require unduplicated person counts.

Chapter 5

5-1. The special population task panels of the PCMH included: Asian/Pacific Americans, Black Americans, Americans of European Ethnic Origin, Hispanic Americans, American Indians and Alaska Natives, Physically Handicapped Americans, Women, Elderly, Rural Mental Health, Migrant and Seasonal Farmworkers, and the Special Working Group on the Mental Health Problems of Vietnam Era Veterans.

Comprehensive Community Mental Health Programs—1964-1980

Fiscal Year	Public Law	Major Legislation Significance	Obligations (in $M) In Year	Obligations (in $M) Cumulative	Number of CMHCs-Cumulative Funded	Number of CMHCs-Cumulative Operational	Number of CMHCs-Cumulative Tot. Term.	% U.S. Population Covered	No. of Patients Treated
1964	88-164	CMHC Act—construction only	$ 0	$ 0	0	0	0	0	0
1965	89-105	Staffing support (51 mos.) CMHC Amendment	0	0	0	0	0	0	(unk)
1966			55	55	130	104	0	7	156,000 (est)
1969	90-574	Alcohol and Addiction support—CMHC Amendments	75	294	376	175	0	11	318,500
1970	91-211	Staffing extended to 8 years; CMHC poverty rates introduced; Part F MH Children added	72	365	420	245	0	27	497,350
1975	94-63 enacted	Title III, Health Revenue Sharing and Health Services Act	223	1,228	603	507	0	41	1,618,746
1976	94-63	From 5 to 12 req. services operations fund base, CMHC. From 3 to 6 grant programs	251	1,478	650	547	30	43	1,877,676
1978	95-83	1 year renewal, CMHC. PCMH report	268	1,978	726	625	90	47	2,361,250
1979	95-622	CMHC 2-year renewal, with minor technical changes, anticipating major revision. Carter Message and S 1177-HR 4156 introduced.	310	2,288	763	701	167	50 (115M)	2,639,996
1980	96-32		290	2,578	796	740	203	52 (119M)	3,082,100
1981	96-398	Mental Health Systems Act	323	2,901	796	758	306	54	3,314,734
					Develop. 26	26			39,000

5-2. The national plan process examined programmatic and fiscal policies simultaneously. The process was carried out by staff of NIMH and the Health Care Financing Administration with assistance from many other agencies of HEW (later renamed Health and Human Services, or HHS) as well as other federal departments, and representatives of consumer, provider and assurer groups. Their efforts produced a comprehensive analysis of the number, location, needs and potentials of the population of the chronic mentally ill. The process also identified needed improvements in the financing, organization and delivery of community services. It culminated in the recommendation of a series of incremental program and financing reforms. Published in December 1980, just weeks before the Carter administration left office, *Toward a National Plan for the Chronically Mentally Ill* was "intended to stimulate further public dialogue on the subject" (Steering Committee 1981).

5-3. The remaining titles of the Carter administration's Mental Health Systems Act follow: The first placed special emphasis on the needs of the chronic mentally ill adult and severely disturbed child. Funds were available to states that would support mental health and related support services such as linkages with programs providing income maintenance, housing, patient rehabilitation, training, community living, day care and general medical care. The second title encouraged states to develop innovative programs for the prevention and early detection of mental disorders. The third title was designed to provide assistance to states to improve their financial administrative and data systems in order to improve accountability. Title IV was the main community mental health title. Title V was a pilot "program" for states to administer all the federal grants. Title VI emphasized payback by mental health professionals who received federal support for training to serve in underserved areas and facilities. This final title also required each state to develop a mental health plan that would identify mental health needs and services and address the protection of the human and civil rights of mental patients and the employment rights of institutional personnel affected by the shift from hospital to community care.

BIBLIOGRAPHY

Allegheny County 1974. "Where does public mental health hurt?" A therapeutic conversation. Consultant Panel Report to the Mental Health/Mental Retardation Program, G.C. Lowe, Jr., Administrator. Pittsburgh: Mimeographed.

American Psychiatric Association 1980. *Diagnostic and Statistical Manual of Mental Disorders, Third Edition.* Washington: American Psychiatric Association.

AMA 1962. News release from the American Medical Association, 1 March.

AMA 1963. Letter from F. J. L. Blasingame, M.D., to Honorable Kenneth A. Roberts, Chairman. 28 June.

Arnoff, F.N. 1975. Social consequences of policy toward mental illness. Science 188:1277-1281.

Atwell, R. 1964. Confidential memorandum to Philip Sirotkin. NIMH administrative files.

Bachrach, L.L. 1982. Young adult chronic patients: An analytical review of the literature. Hosp. & Comm. Psychiat. 33:189-197.

Baxter E. and Hopper K. 1981. *Private Lives/Public Spaces: Homeless Adults on the Streets of New York.* New York: Community Service Society.

Beer, S. 1976. Presidential Address, American Political Science Association annual meeting, 12 November.

Beers, C.W. 1925. *A Mind That Found Itself.* New York: Doubleday, Paget and Company.

Beigel, A., Sharfstein, S.S., and Wolfe, J.C. 1979. Toward increased psychiatric presence in Community Mental Health Centers. Hosp. & Comm. Psychiat. 30(11):763-67.

Beinecke, R.H. 1979. Title III of PL 94-63: The Community Mental Health Center Amendments of 1975. Unpublished.

The Blue Sheet 1963. 10 July, Washington: Drug Research Reports.

Bockoven, J.A. 1972. *Moral Treatment in Community Mental Health.* New York: Springer.

Bryant, T. 1979. Public Committee on Mental Health. Washington, D.C.

Caplan, R.B. 1969. *Psychiatry and the Community in Nineteenth Century America.* New York: Basic Books.

Celebrezze, A., Wirtz, W. and Gleason, A. 1962. Letter of transmittal to the President from the Office of the Secretary, DHEW, 4 November. NIMH administrative files.

Clarke, G.J. 1979. In defense of deinstitutionalization. Milbank Memorial Fund Quarterly/Health and Society 57 (Fall):461-479.

Cohen, W.J. 1963. Memorandum for Honorable Meyer Feldman. Subject: S. 1576—Conference Committee. 18 September.

Cohen, W.J. 1975. Letter to Henry A. Foley, 1 April.

Congressional Record 1963. 10 September.

Congressional Record 1965. 27 July.

Davis, V.T. 1963. Memorandum from the president of the National Association of State Mental Health Program Directors, 16 October.

Democratic Party 1960. Plank adopted at the quadrennial convention, Los Angeles, July 1960, and quoted by Senate President John E. Powers, Massachusetts, at Governor's Conference on Mental Health, Chicago, Illinois, 10 November 1961.

Deutsch, A. 1948. *The Shame of the States.* New York: Harcourt, Brace.

Drew, E.B. 1967. The health syndicate: Washington's noble conspirators. The Atlantic, December:75-82.

Ewalt, J.R. 1957. Digest of the first annual report, Joint Commission on Mental Illness and Health, year 1956. Cambridge, Mass.: Joint Commission.

Ewalt, J.R. 1958. Second annual report of the Joint Commission on Mental Illness and Health.

Ewalt, J.R. 1959. Third annual report of the Joint Commission on Mental Illness and Health.

Ewalt, J.R. 1979. The mental health movement, 1949-1979. Milbank Memorial Fund Quarterly/Health and Society 57 (Fall):507-515.

Faulkner, L.R. and Eaton, J.S., Jr. 1979. Administrative relationships between Community Mental Health Centers and academic psychiatry departments. Amer. J. Psychiat. 136:1040-44.

Fein, R. 1958. *The Economics of Mental Illness.* New York: Basic Books.

Felicetti, D.A. 1975. *Mental Health and Retardation Politics: The Mind Lobbies in Washington.* New York: Praeger.

Felix, R.H. 1962. Memorandum to Chief, Community Services Branch; Chief, Research Grants and Fellowship Branch; Chief, Training Branch, NIMH, 23 April. NIMH administrative files.

Felix, R.H. 1971. "The Challenges—Past, Present, and Future." Address at the Twenty-Fifth Anniversary of the National Mental Health Act, Washington Hilton Hotel, Washington, 28 June. Unpublished.

Fogarty, J.F. 1961. "Progress Toward Mental Health—A Joint Responsibility." Address to National Governors' Conference on Mental Health, Chicago, 10 November.

GAO 1977. *Returning the Mentally Disabled to the Community: Government Needs to Do More.* (H D) 76-152. Washington: U.S. Govt. Printing Office.

GAO 1980. *Jail Inmates' Mental Health Care Neglect: State and Federal Attention Needed.* (GGD) 81-5. Washington: U.S. Govt. Printing Office.

Goldman, H.H., Gattozzi, A.A. and Taube, C.A. 1981. Defining and counting the chronically mentally ill. Hosp. & Comm. Psychiat. 32(1):21-27.

Gorman, M. 1948. Oklahoma attacks its snake pits. The Reader's Digest 53 (September):139-160.

Gorman, M. 1963. How Mental Health Associations Can Rally Support for the President's Mental Health Program. Distributed as memorandum from

Philip E. Ryan, executive director of National Association for Mental Health, Inc., to executive directors, NAMH Divisions.

Grob, G.N. 1966. *The State and the Mentally Ill: A History of Worcester State Hospital in Massachusetts, 1830-1920.* Chapel Hill: University of North Carolina Press.

Grob, G.N. 1973. *Mental Institutions in America: Social policy to 1875.* New York: The Free Press.

Gruenberg, E.M. and Archer, J. 1979. Abandonment of responsibility for the seriously mentally ill. Milbank Memorial Fund Quarterly/Health and Society 57 (Fall):485-506.

Gurin, G., Veroff, J., and Feld, S. 1960. *Americans View Their Mental Health.* New York: Basic Books.

Harris, O. 1965.*Quoted in* Senator Hill accuses AMA of opposing mental health aid. New York Times, 20 February.

Hartley, W.B. 1980. Closing mental health's revolving door. Kiwanis Magazine, January.

Hearings 1955a. Subcommittee on Public Health, Committee on Interstate and Foreign Commerce, House of Representatives. 8, 9, 10 and 11 March.

Hearings 1955b. Subcommittee on Health and Education, Committee on Education and Labor, U.S. Senate.

Hearings 1963. Subcommittee of the Committee on Interstate and Foreign Commerce, House of Representatives. 26, 27 and 28 March.

Hearings 1965. Committee on Interstate and Foreign Commerce, House of Representatives. 2, 3, 4 and 5 March.

Hearings 1979a. Subcommittee on Health and Scientific Research, Committee on Labor and Human Resources, U.S. Senate, 24 May and 11 June.

Hearings 1979b. Subcommittee on Health and the Environment, Committee on Interstate and Foreign Commerce, House of Representatives. 14, 25 and 26 June. Serial No. 96-30.

Hearings 1980. Community Mental Health Centers Program—Oversight. House of Representatives. 5 February. Serial No. 96-101.

Hearings 1981. Subcommittee on Health and the Environment, Committee on Interstate and Foreign Commerce, House of Representatives. 5 and 6 April.

Hill, L. 1965. *Quoted in* Senator Hill accuses AMA of opposing mental health aid. New York Times, 20 February.

Hogarty, G.E., Goldberg, S.C., Schooler, N.R., and the Collaborative Study Group 1974. Drugs and sociotherapy in the aftercare of schizophrenic patients. Archives of General Psychiatry 31:609-618.

House Report 1965. No. 248, 89th Congress, 1st Session.

Interview 1972   a.   Robert Atwell, January.
              b.   Robert Barclay, June.
              c.   Dr. Walter Barton, March.
              d.   Dr. Francis Braceland, April.
              e.   Dr. Bertram S. Brown, March.
              f.   Wilbur Cohen, May and June.
              g.   Dr. Jack Ewalt, April.

    h.   Rashi Fein, January and April.
    i.   Dr. Robert Felix, February.
    j.   Mike Gorman, March.
    k.   Boisfeuillet Jones, April.
    l.   James Menger, June.
    m. Patrick Moynihan, June.
    n.   Dr. James Shannon, March.
    o.   Philip Sirotkin, April.
    p.   George Van Stadden, March and April.
    q.   Dr. Stanley Yolles, March.

Interview 1973. Ruth Knee, February.

Johnson, L.B. 1965a. The nation's problems of health. In *No. 755. Public Papers of the President, 1963-64, Vol. II.* Washington: U.S. Govt. Printing Office.

Johnson, L.B. 1965b. Health message to the 89th Congress. 7 January.

Johnson, L.B. 1966. Remarks at the Signing of the CMHC Act Amendments. 4 August 1965. *Public Papers of the President, 1965, Vol. II.* Washington: U.S. Govt. Printing Office.

Joint Commission on Mental Illness and Health 1961. *Action For Mental Health.* New York: Basic Books.

Jones, B. 1963. Message from Boisfeuillet Jones to Robert Felix typed by LKR.

Kennedy, E.M. 1979. Community mental health care: new services from old systems. Milbank Memorial Fund Quarterly/Health and Society 57 (Fall):480-484.

Klerman, G.L. 1977. Better but not well: Social and ethical issues in the deinstitutionalizations of the mentally ill. Schizophrenia Bulletin 3:617-631.

Lamb, R.H. 1979. The new asylums in the community, Archives of General Psychiatry 36:129-134.

Lipowski, Z.J. 1981. Holistic-medical foundations of American psychiatry: A bicentennial. Amer. J. Psychiat. 138:888-895.

McDonald, M.C. 1982. Yolles looks over the years, unhappy with the present. Psychiatric News, 21 May.

Memorandum 1963. Recent action by AMA house of delegates on Community Mental Health Center Bill (June 19, 1963 — Atlantic City). Prepared by the National Association of State Mental Health Program Directors.

Mental Health Association, 1980. Letter to Hon. Harrison A. Williams from Allan Moltzen (MHA), Clarence J. Martin (Assn. for Advancement of Psychology), Joseph J. Bevilacqua (Natl. Assn. State Mental Health Program Directors), James Evans (Natl. Assn. Social Workers), John Wolfe (Natl. Council CMHCs), and Paul Friedman (Mental Health Law Project). 30 January.

Morrissey, J.P., Goldman, H.H., Klerman, L.V. and Associates 1980. *The Enduring Asylum. Cycles of Institutional Reform at Worcester State Hospital.* New York: Grune & Stratton.

NAMH Council 1961. Suggested modifications by NAMH Council to NIMH position paper on Recommendations of the Joint Commission on Mental

Illness and Health to Special Assistant to the Secretary, Health and Medical Affairs, DHEW, 20 September 1961. NIMH administrative files.

NASMHPD 1963a. Doctors favor temporary operation support of centers. Information: National Association of State Mental Health Program Directors, 26 September.

NASMHPD 1963b. Memorandum to all state mental health directors. Information: National Association of State Mental Health Program Directors, 10 October.

New York Times 1979. Release of mentally ill spurring doubt. 18, 19, and 20 November.

NIMH Task Force 1962. Report on implementation of recommendations of the Joint Commission on Mental Illness and Health, 5 January. NIMH administrative files.

NIMH 1978. *Community Mental Health Centers: The Federal Investment.* DHEW Pub. No. ADM 78-677. Washington: U.S. Govt. Printing Office.

Notes 1963. Notes on a conversation between Robert Atwell and George Van Stadden regarding the Bureau of the Budget, 7 March.

Ozarin, L.D. and Sharfstein, S.S. 1978. The aftermath of deinstitutionalization: Problems and solutions. Psychiatric Quarterly 50:128-132.

PCMH 1978. Report to the President from the President's Commission on Mental Health. Washington: U.S. Govt. Printing Office.

Redick, R.W. 1974. *Patterns in Use of Nursing Homes by the Aged Mentally Ill.* Statistical Note 107. Rockville, MD: Division of Biometry and Epidemiology, NIMH.

Regier, D.A. 1978. Memorandum #41: Nursing home residents with mental disorders or senility, U.S. 1977. Rockville, MD: Division of Biometry and Epidemiology, NIMH.

Regier, D.A., Goldberg, I.D. and Taube, C.A. 1978. The de facto U.S. mental health services system. Archives of General Psychiatry 35:685-693.

Regier, D.A. and Taube, C.A. 1981. The delivery of mental health services. In *American Handbook of Psychiatry,* Vol. 7 (eds., S. Arieti and H.K.H. Brodie), pp. 715-733.

Reichenbach, L. 1977. *The Federal Community Mental Health Centers Program and the Policy of Deinstitutionalization.* Prepared for the National Institute of Mental Health under grant MH27738-02; principal investigator, L.E. Lynn, Jr. Unpublished.

Rothman, D.J. 1971. *The Discovery of the Asylum.* Boston: Little-Brown.

Ryan, P.E. 1963. Memorandum to Max Silverstein from Executive Director, The National Association for Mental Health, Inc., 4 September.

Schooler, N.R., Goldberg, S.C., Boothe, H., and Cole, J.O. 1967. One year after discharge: adjustment of schizophrenic patients. Amer. J. Psychiat. 123:8, 981-995.

Shannon, J.E. 1961. Memorandum on implementation of the final report of the Joint Commission on Mental Illness and Health. 10 October. NIMH administrative files.

Sharfstein, S.S. 1978. Will community mental health survive in the 1980s? Amer. J. Psychiat. 135:1363-1365.

Sharfstein, S.S. 1979. Community Mental Health Centers: returning to basics. Amer. J. Psychiat. 136:1077-1079.

Sharfstein, S.S. 1982. Medicaid cutbacks and block grants: Crisis or opportunity for community mental health? Amer. J. Psychiat. 139:466-470.

Sharfstein, S.S., Turner, J.E.C., and Clark, H.W. 1978. Financing issues in the delivery of services to the chronically mentally ill and disabled. In *The Chronic Mental Patient* (Ed., J. Talbot). Washington: American Psychiatric Association.

Shriver, E.K. 1974. Letter to Henry A. Foley, 3 January.

Steering Committee 1981. *Toward a National Plan for the Chronically Mentally Ill*. Report to the Secretary by the DHHS Steering Committee on the Chronically Mentally Ill, December 1980. (ADM) 81-1077. Washington: U.S. Govt. Printing Office.

Stein, L. and Test, M.A. 1980. Alternative to mental hospital treatment I. Conceptual model, treatment program, and clinical evaluation. Archives of General Psychiatry 37:392-397.

Taube, C.A., Regier, D.A. and Rosenfeld, A.H. 1978. Mental disorders in health, United States—1978 (chapter V). Hyattsville, MD: (PHS)78-1232.

Tuerk, I. 1965. Statement on H.R. 2985, March 5, 1965 for Hearings 1965 (op. cit.). Reproduced by the National Association of State Mental Health Program Directors.

Turner, J.E. and TenHoor, W.S. 1978. The NIMH Community Support Program: Pilot approach to a needed social reform. Schizophrenia Bulletin 4:319-348.

U.S. News and World Report 1979. Mental patients: A "forgotten minority" in U.S. 19 November: 49-52.

U.S. Senate Report 1965. No.366, Calender No.355, 89th Congress, 1st Session.

U.S. Senate 1976. Special Committee on Aging. Nursing home care in the United States: Failure in public policy. Supporting Paper #7, Pub. No. 67-4750. Washington: U.S. Govt. Printing Office.

Veroff, J., Douvan, E., and Kulka, R.A. 1981b. *The Inner American: A Self-Portrait from 1957 to 1976.* New York: Basic Books.

Veroff, J., Kulka, R.A. and Douvan, E. 1981a. *Mental Health in America: Patterns of Help-Seeking from 1957 to 1976.* New York: Basic Books.

Ward, D.F. 1965. *Quoted in* Senator Hill accuses AMA of opposing mental health aid. New York Times, 20 February.

Warren, S.L. 1963. Information memorandum for the President—urgent. From Stafford L. Warren, M.D., Special Assistant to the President for Mental Retardation, 2 October.

Weisbrod, B.A., Test, M.A., and Stein, L.I. 1980. Alternative to mental hospital treatment II, economic benefit-cost analysis. Archives of General Psychiatry 37:400-405.

White, G.E. 1982. *Earl Warren: A Public Life.* Oxford Univ. Press. Quoted by reviewer J.E. Clayton in the Washington Post Book World, 1 August.

Wilson, W. 1956. *Congressional Government.* New York: Meridian Edition.

Windle, C. and Scully, D. 1976. Community Mental Health Centers and the decreasing use of state mental hospitals. Comm. Mental Health Journal 12:239-43.

Witkin, M.J. 1980. *Trends in Patient Care Episodes in Mental Health Facilities, 1955-1977*. Statistical Note 154. Rockville, MD: Division of Biometry and Epidemiology, NIMH.

Yolles, S. 1962. "Yolles' Green Book," titled *A Proposal for a Comprehensive Mental Health Program to Implement the Findings of the Joint Commission on Mental Illness and Health, April.* NIMH administrative files.

Younger, J.A. 1963. Letter to Mr. Robert H. Klein, 4 October.

INDEXES

Name Index

Subject Index

Name Index

Subject Index

279